THE GODS OF THE GREEKS

THE GODS
OF THE GREEKS

C. KERÉNYI

THAMES AND HUDSON

*Professor Kerényi wrote this book for
and on the suggestion of Thames and Hudson
The German text has been rendered
into English by Norman Cameron*

First published in 1951
Reprinted in paperback 1979
Reprinted 1982

Library of Congress Catalog Card Number 79-66133

Printed and bound in Great Britain by Billings and Sons Limited

TO MY WIFE DILDIL

CONTENTS

vii

CONTENTS

CONTENTS

CONTENTS

ILLUSTRATIONS

PLATES

PLATES

PLATES

ILLUSTRATIONS IN THE TEXT

INTRODUCTION

THIS book owes its origin to the conviction, shared by the
publishers and the author, that the time has come to write a
Mythology of the Greeks for *adults*: that is to say, not only for
specialists concerned with classical studies, with the history of
religion, or with ethnology; still less for children, for whom in
the past the classical myths were either remodelled or, at least,
carefully selected so as to accord with the viewpoints of a
traditional education; but simply for adults whose primary
interest—which may entail an interest in any of the branches
of learning mentioned above—is in the study of human beings.
The contemporary form that this interest takes is, of course, an
interest in psychology. And, as a great exponent of modern
humanistic thought has admitted, it is precisely psychology that
"contains within itself an interest in myth, just as all creative
writing contains within itself an interest in psychology".

These words were spoken in 1936 by Thomas Mann in his
lecture on "Freud and the future". Whilst paying tribute to
the services rendered by the psychologist of the Unconscious,
of the deeper levels of the soul, the great writer did, in fact,
look beyond him into the future. He depicted with unsur-
passable clarity the spiritual situation in which the author of
this book, for his part, finds justification for his mythological
work. Psychology's thrusting back into the childhood of the
individual soul is, to quote his words,

> "at the same time a thrusting back into the childhood of
> mankind—into the primitive and the mythical. Freud
> himself recognised that all natural science, medicine and
> psychotherapy had been for him a life-long and tortuous
> return to his primary youthful passion for the history of
> man, for the origins of religion and morals. The associa-
> tion of the words 'psychology' and 'deeper levels' has also
> a chronological significance: the depths of the human soul

I

are also 'Primordial Times', that deep 'Well of Time' in which Myth has its home and from which the original norms and forms of life are derived. For Myth is the foundation of life; it is the timeless pattern, the religious formula to which life shapes itself, inasmuch as its characteristics are a reproduction of the Unconscious. There is no doubt about it, the moment when the story-teller acquires the mythical way of looking at things, the gift of seeing the typical features of characteristics and events"—

so, revealingly, states the author of *Joseph and his Brethren*—

"that moment marks a beginning in his life. It means a peculiar intensification of his artistic mood, a new serenity in his powers of perception and creation. This is usually reserved for the later years of life; for whereas in the life of mankind the mythical represents an early and primitive stage, in the life of the individual it represents a late and mature one."

This experience undergone fifteen years ago by a great writer may perhaps today be more widely shared, and not necessarily bound up with advanced years. It is to adults who have had this experience that the author seeks to present the mythology of the Greeks, as if he were presenting to them a Classical Writer, a poet entirely unconcerned with posterity and as uninhibited as Aristophanes. The author hopes to find readers whose understanding has been matured by the literature and the psychology of our time; readers who do not find it too difficult to adopt Thomas Mann's attitude towards the archaic massiveness and freedom, the monotony and desultory extravagance of that unsurpassably spontaneous documentation of human nature which is known as Greek Mythology; readers who can enjoy all this, and, indeed, can realise that the recognised classical writers require, to complement them, just such documentation as this, if they are to give a real picture of Greek antiquity. By "documentation" the author means historical documentation, and not psychological interpretation. If the

entire mythological legacy of the Greeks is freed from the super-
ficial psychology of previous presentations, and is revealed in
its original context as material *sui generis* and having its own
laws, then, as an inevitable result, this mythology will itself
have the same effect as the most direct psychology—the effect,
indeed, of an activity of the psyche externalised in images.

A similar direct externalisation of the psyche is to be found,
of course, in dreams. The degree of directness of the images
presented in dreams and in mythology is, to say the least, very
much the same. In this respect, dreams and mythology are
nearer to one another than dreams and poetry. For this reason
the author, in his *Introduction to a Science of Mythology* (London, 1951, p. 32), written in collaboration with Professor Jung,
considered himself justified in speaking of the "individual
mythology" of modern men and women as a synonym for
their psychology. With equal justification any great mythology
might—if one chose to ignore its artistic aspects—be styled a
"collective psychology". One must not, of course, altogether
disregard the fact that mythology is also fundamentally a
special, creative, and therefore also an artistic, activity of the
psyche. Nevertheless, it is a special sort of activity. It encroaches
on poetry, but nevertheless it is an activity of its own kind, to
be ranked with poetry, music, the plastic arts, philosophy and
the sciences. Nor should it be confused with gnosticism or
theology: from these it is distinguished—as it is distinguished
also from all kinds of theosophy, and even from the pagan
theologies—by its artistically creative character. The stuff of
mythology is composed of something that is greater than the
story-teller and than all human beings—"as they are now", said
Homer—but always as something visible, perceptible or, at
least, capable of being expressed in images, and never as the
Godhead *in abstracto*, or even as the Godhead *in concreto*, if the
latter is to be regarded as unimaginable. Mythology must
transcend the individual, and must exercise over human beings
a power that seizes hold of the soul and fills it with images;
but this is all that is required of it. These images are the stuff

of mythology, just as tones are the stuff of music: "such stuff as dreams are made on", to quote Shakespeare; an entirely human stuff, which presented itself to the man who gave it shape, to the myth⁄teller, as something objective, something pouring, as it were, from a super⁄individual source; and it also presents itself to the audience—despite the new shape that the narrator has given it, despite the new "variation"—not as the narrator's subjective creation, but again as something objective.

The same human stuff, however, at once changes its nature, if it is left as "dead matter", taken out of the medium in which it lived. In the same way a printed poem or a musical score is "dead matter"—something different from what it was in the soul of the person for whom it first resounded. It is not difficult to restore it to itself: one does this by translating it back into its original medium, into an outward and inward resonance. Similarly mythology, in order to be communicated in its true nature, must be translated back into its medium, the medium in which it still inwardly and outwardly "resounded"—that is to say, awoke echoes. The Greek word *mythologia* contains the sense not only of "stories" (*mythoi*), but also of "telling" (*legein*): a form of narration that originally was also echo⁄awakening, in that it awoke the awareness that the story personally concerned the narrator and the audience. If the fragments of Greek mythology that have been handed down to us are to be restored from "dead matter" to their live selves, they must be translated back into the medium of such narration and such participation by the audience.

This book is an experimental attempt to translate the mythology of the Greeks back, to some extent at least, into its original medium, into mythological *story⁄telling*. The experiment calls for an artificially constructed situation, an openly admitted fiction. This fictitious situation will be based on a typical discovery of a living mythology, a discovery which the author referred to in his book *Die antike Religion*, in which he used it to answer the question: "What is mythology?" This discovery was made by Sir George Grey. In 1845 this statesman was sent by the British Government to New Zealand, and shortly thereafter was appointed Governor-General. In 1855 appeared his *Polynesian Mythology and Traditional History of the New Zealand Race, as furnished by their Priests and Chiefs* (London, John Murray). Sir George Grey describes in his Foreword how he came to write this work. The experiences that led him to do so are so interesting that they might be recorded in the foreword to any account of a live mythology—or to any mythology that is presented as live material.

"When I arrived," states Sir George, "I found Her Majesty's native subjects engaged in hostilities with the Queen's troops, against whom they had up to that time contended with considerable success; so much discontent also prevailed generally amongst the native population, that where disturbances had not yet taken place, there was too much reason to apprehend they would soon break out, as they shortly afterwards did, in several parts of the Islands. I soon perceived that I could neither successfully govern, nor hope to conciliate, a numerous and turbulent people, with whose language, manners, customs, religion, and modes of thought I was quite unacquainted. In order to redress their grievances, and apply remedies, which would neither wound their feelings, nor militate against their prejudices, it was necessary that I should be able at all times, and in all places, patiently to listen to the tales of their wrongs or sufferings, and, even if I could not assist them, to give them a kind reply, couched in such terms as should leave no doubt on their minds that I clearly understood and felt for them, and was really disposed towards them. . . .

"Those reasons, and others of equal force, made me feel it to be my duty to make myself acquainted, with the least possible delay, with the language of the New Zealanders, as also with their manners, customs, and prejudices. But I soon found that this was a far more difficult matter than

I had first supposed. The language of the New Zealanders is a very difficult one to understand thoroughly: there was then no dictionary of it published (unless a vocabulary can be so called); there were no books published in the language, which would enable me to study its construc- tion; it varied altogether in form from any of the ancient or modern languages which I knew; and my thoughts and time were so occupied with the cares of the govern- ment of a country then pressed upon by many difficulties, and with a formidable rebellion raging in it, that I could find but very few hours to devote to the acquisition of an unwritten and difficult language. I, however, did my best, and cheerfully devoted all my spare moments to a task, the accomplishment of which was necessary to enable me to perform properly every duty to my country and to the people I was appointed to govern.

"Soon, however, a new and quite unexpected difficulty presented itself. On the side of the rebel party were engaged, either openly or covertly, some of the oldest, least civilised, and most influential chiefs in the Island. With them I had either personally, or by written communications, to discuss questions which involved peace or war, and on which the whole future of the Islands and of the native race depended, so that it was in the highest degree essential that I should fully and entirely comprehend their thoughts and intentions, and that they should not in any way misunderstand the nature of the engagements into which I entered with them. To my surprise, however, I found that these chiefs, either in their speeches to me, or in their letters, frequently quoted, in explanation of their views and intentions, fragments of ancient poems or proverbs, or made allusions which rested on an ancient system of mythology; and although it was clear that the most impor- tant parts of their communications were embodied in these figurative forms, the interpreters were quite at fault, they could then rarely (if ever) translate the poems or explain the allusions, and there was no publication in existence which threw any light upon these subjects, or which gave the meaning of the great mass of the words which the natives upon such occasions made use of; so that I was compelled to content myself with a short general statement of what some other native believed that the writer of the letter intended to convey as his meaning by the fragment of the poem he had quoted, or by the allusions he had made. I should add, that even the great majority of the young Christian natives were quite as much at fault on these subjects as were the European interpreters.

"Clearly, however, I could not, as Governor of the country, permit so close a veil to remain drawn between myself and the aged and influential chiefs, whom it was my duty to attach to British interests and to the British race, whose regard and confidence, as also that of their tribes, it was my desire to secure, and with whom it was necessary that I should hold the most unrestricted inter-course. Only one thing could, under such circumstances, be done, and that was to acquaint myself with the ancient language of the country, to collect its traditional poems and legends, to induce their priests to impart to me their mythology, and to study their proverbs. For more than eight years I devoted a great part of my available time to these pursuits. Indeed I worked at this duty in my spare moments in every part of the country I traversed, and during my many voyages from portion to portion of the Islands. I was also always accompanied by natives, and still at every possible interval pursued my inquiries into these subjects. . . ."

The reader is now requested to imagine that we are paying a visit, with intentions similar to those of Sir George Grey, to a Greek island. If he has studied the classics, the reader will remember having been in a similar situation to the Governor's: in order to understand the Greeks, he found it necessary to study not only their language, but also their mythology. On this occasion, however, he does not need to study Greek grammar, or to use dictionaries of mythology. He is in some⁄ what the same situation as the Comte de Marcellus, French minister to the Sublime Porte, who in 1818 left Constantinople to visit the islands in the Sea of Marmora, and there met an educated Greek named Yacobaki Rizo Néroulos. Rizo, who spoke French as well as he spoke Greek, acquainted the Count with the great Dionysiac epic of Nonnos, which the Count later translated and had published. Let us suppose that we on our island have met a similar Greek, who recounts to us the mythology of his ancestors. All that he knows of it is what is to be read in the classics or to be learnt from the monuments. He calls it "our" mythology, and when he says "we" he means the ancient Greeks.

This "we" is simply a convenience of narration, whereby the mythology can be more easily translated back into its original medium. The author makes no claim to any higher authority than that which scholars habitually claim when they use the word "we". Every account of a mythology—unless it reproduces its sources in the original text and in their frag⁄ mentary condition (a procedure, by the way, that would offer the reader merely "dead matter")—must be an interpretation. And every interpretation is conditioned by the degree of recep⁄ tivity of the contemporary presenter of the material—that is to say, it is conditioned by a subjective factor. Would a lack of receptivity towards music, poetry or painting conduce towards a satisfactory interpretation of the products of these arts? The subjective factor cannot be eliminated, but it must be com⁄ pensated for by the vigilance of the interpreter and by his faithfulness to his material.

In an attempt to achieve such faithfulness, the author has endeavoured to make these tales adhere—word for word, wherever possible—to the original texts. Varying versions— these variations on a theme that are characteristic of every mythology—have not been equated. The author proceeds on the assumption—which is generally confirmed by the sum of the material available, and entails only a minimal and inevitable generalisation—that every mythological theme has in every period been the subject of a number of different stories, each of them variously conditioned by the place, time and artistic powers of the narrator. On the proper treatment of these variations—which should be neither ignored nor over-emphasised —depends the answer to the question whether such a presentation of Greek mythology as is attempted here can be successful; whether it can be a genuine presentation of all that has been really handed down. One is, of course, much tempted to dwell on every variation, to explain where and when and from which author it first came, and to think up some more or less plausible explanation for it. This has hitherto been the usual practice, with the result that the stories themselves have been, so to speak, thrust into the background, as if Greek mythology were interesting only by reason of these valid or conjectural explanations. This shifting of interest from the ancient stories to the modern commentaries is something that the present author has done his best to avoid.

The original story-tellers of Greek mythology justified their variations simply with the act of narration, each in his own fashion, of the story. In mythology, to *tell* is to justify. The words: "It was told", which the reader of this book will so often encounter, are not intended to compensate for the fact that the tones of the original story-teller, and often, alas, the original narrative itself, are now extinct. They are intended to concentrate the reader's attention on the only thing that matters —namely, *what* was told. This, however it was shaped, was essentially and in all its forms, developments and variations the same permanent and unmistakable basic story. The *words* of the basic story have disappeared, and all that we have are the variations. But behind the variations can be recognised something that is common to them all: a story that was told in many fashions, yet remained the same. The author has sought in this book to avoid the stiffness of a strict terminology, which would to some extent do violence to the fluid material. He prefers, for example, the word "story" to "*mythologem*", a term used in the *Introduction to a Science of Mythology*. The latter expression would simply serve to emphasise—as was, indeed, at one time necessary—that the "basic texts" of mythology are, in fact, textual works, in the same way as poems or musical compositions, which cannot be arbitrarily dissolved into their elements or they would become something else—a mass of dumb "dead matter."

Attention must now be drawn to another aspect of the "basic texts" of Greek mythology. These texts, the perpetually repeated "stories", are also "works"—the creations of their narrators. But they are not wholly "works". Even the very first narrator did no more than take the characters of a drama—for a mythological tale is always a sort of drama—and put them on the stage. He made them appear and speak in the manner of his time and his art; the chief characteristic of mythology, however, is that its dramatis personae do not merely act the drama, but—like the figures of a dream—themselves actually construct it. To continue with the simile, and to explain its meaning more accurately, they bring with them on to the stage the plan of a little drama of their own, which usually has a certain necessary group of characters—a pair, a trinity or a quaternity. Thus the Great Mother appears with her two companions and her little darling: with three sons, who together with her constitute a quaternity. Even at this original stage, the mythological "work" contained—like every work of art— both conscious and unconscious elements. The dramatis personae are selected and simultaneously impose themselves. One brings another after it, and the story—*of its own will*—is in being: the narrator need only complete it. And his completion of it is all the time conditioned by his characters and by their wilful yet schematic behaviour.

Just as Goethe, in constructing the action of his Mephistopheles, was tied not only to the popular tale of Doctor Faustus, but also to a dramatic "plot" peculiar to the concept of the

Devil—a plot that called also for seduced and betrayed characters—so an ancient poet, even one so early as the poet of the Homeric Hymn for Hermes, was tied to a definite "plot" for any story that he wished to tell about the god. There is no justification for making any fundamental distinction between poetical works dealing with such figures as Hermes, and the prose texts in which the same figures appear. Mythology is everything that presents such figures as would be defined, in a history of religion, as gods or demons. They are historical data of a bygone culture. In the texts to be found in this book they will be presented under another aspect, too: that of their behaviour as *human* data in a situation in which such behaviour was still free from restriction. This ancient freedom from restriction has for us today the scientific advantage that the figures and their behaviour can be observed as one observes a play in a theatre—purely for entertainment, if one wishes. But the play contains a teaching concerning gods which is also a teaching concerning human beings.

It cannot be guaranteed that these stories will always have the complete directness of drama. Texts that have a directly dramatic effect—such as the Homeric Hymn to Hermes, the two Hymns to Aphrodite, the Hesiodic account of the Deed of Kronos—are rare. They are, indeed, poetical texts, but are nevertheless sufficiently archaic—being, moreover, freed from the stylistic strait-jacket of heroic verse—to allow unhampered effectiveness to the given "plot", the basic plan of the mytho-logical action. In the work of later poets—the Alexandrians or Ovid—it usually happens that even when the original basic text is followed, the basic plan is mostly replaced by the motivations of a new, personal psychology. The Deed of Kronos; Aphrodite's situation in the midst of a male pair; Hermes's need for discovery and invention—which means invention also in the sense of deceit: all these are not the products of a personal psychology of this sort; they are the products of humanity at a more general and impersonal level. These basic texts are examples of the more general human lessons that mythology teaches us: a teaching that accords with that of the psychology of the Unconscious, but is presented in its own manner of dramatic demonstration.

It is seldom possible to offer a direct, dramatic presentation which, at the same time—as the classical texts above mentioned have done—affords a glimpse of the underlying mythological drama. In addition to the dramatis personae, the cast presented in the present work must also comprise a fictitious character, who retells the stories of Greek mythology. This character will speak the Prologue before the larger and smaller sections of the narrative; he will, in the classical manner of the Greek tragedy, introduce the other characters on their appearance and describe their "costumes"—as he will for the Erinyes, for example.

A comparison with the Greek stage does not, however, explain the entire function of the "narrator" in this book. The story he retells has come down from various periods. The author had no intention of compiling fragments on a fictitious level, as if they all belonged to the same period or to a timeless, static antiquity. What he offers is a mosaic in which every little stone is separated from the next, and is even transposable. Although he does not thrust the student of history into the foreground—to do so would be to interfere with the style of the narrative and shatter its form with the interpolation of long, scholarly dissertations—he nevertheless makes his narrator move continually in the dimension of Time. The author has borne in mind the comparative chronologies assigned to the stories by historical research, even when he has felt constrained to modify these in the light of his own historical studies. (He has done this, for example, in his early dating of certain archaic tales of the followers of Orpheus—a dating that he sought to justify in a work of attempted reconstruction, "*The Orphic Cosmogony and the Origin of Orphism*", in his *Pythagoras and Orpheus*, 3rd edition, Albae Vigilae N.F. IX, and in the Eranos-Yearbook, 1949.)

The object of this book is to invest Greek mythology with

as much historical concreteness as it can nowadays be given: a concreteness such as Sir George Grey found in Polynesian mythology. This object cannot be achieved without reconstruction. But for the author "reconstruction" means only the concretising of what is to be found in the historical sources. He has imposed upon himself restrictions which perhaps will not always please the reader, who would doubtless like to pursue the stories beyond the bounds of the surviving texts. The author has not carried any story further away from the sources than his conscience as a scholar will permit. He has not, however, refrained from indicating possible continuations and combinations. The reader may, of course, choose to ignore these indications and content himself with the original texts, which he can look up, with the help of the notes provided, in the classical authors. He is also invited to make use of the Index if he wishes to discover at a glance what mythological information this book provides concerning any particular god or goddess.

The author has not followed the stories into the field of Greek heroic saga, in which the problems of distortion by retelling are even more difficult to solve than in mythology in its narrower sense. Gustav Schwab's *Sagas of Classical Antiquity* (translated as *Gods and Heroes*), and Robert Graves's account of the epic of the Argonauts represent two extremely opposite attempts to make a rich and resilient stuff available to men and women of the present day. The former author, who wrote for the young, attempted this in the old fashion; the latter, who writes for adults, attempts it in a new fashion. Neither one course nor the other could be followed as a continuation of the course chosen in this book. The name of Robert Graves, poetical rediscoverer of the Threefold Great Goddess, should be mentioned here also for the reason that his novel about the Argonauts—except, indeed, for its account of the rise of the Olympians—to some extent points the direction in which, although much more cautiously, a historian may attempt a reconstruction of heroic saga: a reconstruction, in a manner neither sentimental nor dry, of something that fired the Greeks. The liberties taken by the learned poet would not have been conceded, or even permissible, if taken by the author of the present work. What the latter hopes of his retold tales is that they have hampered the free movement of the gods as little as could be expected in a work based on scholarly research.

In conclusion, a still more personal message to the indulgent reader. This book presents the divine stories of Greek myth, ology, together with the stories concerning the origin and destiny of mankind, in such a form that they can be read from beginning to end, as if they were chapters of a single narrative. The author has done his best to facilitate this manner of reading. There was one thing, however, that he did not feel entitled to do. The archaic forms of so many tales have been lost that the whole body of what has reached us and can be presented has become exceedingly compact. This compactness should not be artificially loosened. Already in Ovid we find that the archaic spirit has been spoilt in a process of dilution. The author has decided against trying to provide any relief of this kind. The reader's best plan, therefore, is not to absorb too much of this solid fare at a sitting, but to read only a few pages at a time—and preferably more than once, as he would read an ancient poem. The words of the composer in Hof, mannsthal's *Ariadne on Naxos* may be quoted here: "The Secret of Life approaches you, takes you by the hand."

C.K.

Ponte Brolla, near Locarno, Switzerland
   Late autumn, 1950

CHAPTER I

The Beginning of Things

OKEANOS AND TETHYS

O u r mythology contains many tales of the beginning of things. Perhaps the oldest was that to which our most ancient poet, Homer, refers when he calls Okeanos the "origin of the gods"[1] and "the origin of everything".[2] Okeanos was a river-god; a river or stream and a god in the same person, like the other river-gods. He possessed inexhaustible powers of begetting, just like our rivers, in whose waters the girls of Greece used to bathe before marriage, and which were therefore supposed to be the first ancestors of ancient races. But Okeanos was no ordinary river-god, for his river was no ordinary river. Ever since the time when everything originated from him he has continued to flow to the outermost edge of the earth, flowing back upon himself in a circle. The rivers, springs and fountains —indeed, the whole sea—issue continually from his broad, mighty stream. When the world came under the rule of Zeus, he alone was permitted to remain in his former place—which is really not a place, but only a flux, a boundary and barrier between the world and the Beyond.

It is, however, not strictly correct to say that "he alone was permitted". Associated with Okeanos was the goddess Tethys, who is rightly invoked as Mother.[3] How could Okeanos have been the "origin of everything", if there had been in his person only a male original stream, unaccompanied by a conceiving original water-goddess? We understand, too, why it is told in Homer that the original couple have for a long time refrained from breeding.[4] It is said that they have quarrelled; an explanation that one might well expect to find in such ancient tales. The fact is that, had the original breeding not ceased, our world would have no stability, no rounded frontier, no circular course turning back upon itself. Begetting and bearing would have continued into infinity. So Okeanos was left only with his circular flux and his task of supplying the springs, the rivers and the sea—in subordination to the power of Zeus.

᾿ Of Tethys our mythology tells us little except that she was the mother of the daughters and sons of Okeanos.[5] The latter are the rivers, three thousand in number.[6] The daughters, the Okeaninai, were equally numerous.[7] Later on I shall mention only the eldest of them. Amongst the granddaughters was one whose name, Thetis, sounds rather like Tethys. In our language we make a clear distinction between the two names; but it may be that, for people who lived in Greece before us, they were closer together in sound and meaning, and meant one and the same great Mistress of the Sea. I shall shortly speak of Thetis again. The prevalence of this tale, and the dominance of these deities all over our sea probably go back to a time before peoples of Greek stock lived in these regions.

2

NIGHT, THE EGG AND EROS

Another story of the beginning of things was passed down in the sacred writings preserved by the disciples and devotees of the singer Orpheus. But latterly it is to be found only in the works of a writer of comedy, and in certain references to it by philosophers. At first it was more commonly told amongst hunters and forest-dwellers than amongst our sea-coast people. In the beginning was Night—so this story runs[8]—or, in our language, Nyx. Homer, too, regarded her as one of the greatest goddesses, a goddess of whom even Zeus stands in sacred awe.[9] According to this story, she was a bird with black wings.[10] Ancient Night conceived of the Wind and laid her silver Egg[11] in the gigantic lap of Darkness. From the Egg sprang the son of the rushing Wind, a god with golden wings. He is called Eros, the god of love; but this is only *one* name, the loveliest of all the names this god bore.

The god's other names, such of them as we still know, sound very scholastic, but even they refer only to pa ticular details of the old story. His name of Protogonos means only that he was the "firstborn" of all gods. His name of Phanes exactly explains what he did when he was hatched from the Egg: he revealed and brought into the light everything that had previously lain hidden in the silver Egg—in other words, the whole world. Up above was a void, the Sky. Down below was the Rest. Our ancient language has a word for the void, "Chaos", which simply means that it "yawns". Originally there was no word meaning turmoil or confusion: "Chaos" acquired this second meaning only later, after the introduction of the doctrine of the Four Elements. Thus the Rest, down below in the Egg, was not in turmoil. According to another form of this story, the earth lay down below in the Egg, and the sky and the earth married.[12] This was the work of the god Eros, who brought them into the light and then compelled them to mingle. They produced a brother and sister, Okeanos and Tethys.

The old tale, as told in our seagirt lands, probably went on to relate that originally Okeanos was down below in the Egg, and that he was not alone there but was accompanied by Tethys, and that these two were the first to act under the compulsion of Eros. As is stated in a poem by Orpheus:[13] "Okeanos, the beautifully flowing, was the first to enter into marriage: he took to wife Tethys, his sister by the same Mother." This Mother of them both was she who had laid the silver Egg: she was Night.

3

CHAOS, GAIA AND EROS

The third tale of the beginning of things comes from Hesiod, who was at once a farmer and a poet, and in his youth had pastured his sheep on the divine mountain of Helicon.[14] Eros and the Muses had sanctuaries there. The disciples of the singer Orpheus paid especial reverence to these divinities, and perhaps brought their cult to this place from more northerly regions. Hesiod's tale sounds as if he had simply omitted the eggshell from the story of Night, the Egg and Eros, and had sought, as a farmer would, to attribute the rank of senior goddess to Gaia, the Earth. For Chaos, whom he mentions first, was for him not a deity but merely an empty "yawning"—that which remains of an empty egg when the shell is taken away.

As Hesiod tells it:[15] First arose Chaos. Then arose broad-breasted Gaia, the firm and everlasting abode of all divinities, those that dwell high above, on Mount Olympus, and those that dwell within her, in the earth; likewise Eros, the loveliest of the immortal gods, who loosens the limbs and rules the spirit of all gods and men. From Chaos are descended Erebos, the lightless darkness of the depths; and Nyx, Night. Nyx, in love with Erebos, bore Aither, the light of heaven, and Hemera, the day. Gaia, for her part, bore, first of all and as her equal, the starry Sky, Ouranos, so that he should completely cover her and be a firm and everlasting abode for the blessed gods. She bore the great Mountains, whose valleys are favourite dwellings of goddesses—the Nymphs. She bore also that desolate, foaming Sea, the Pontos. And all those she bore without Eros, without mating.

To Ouranos she bore, besides the Titans and Titanesses (amongst whom, in Hesiod, are numbered Okeanos and Tethys), also three Kyklopes: Steropes, Brontes, Arges. These have a round eye in the middle of the forehead, and names that mean thunder and lightning. To Ouranos she also bore three Hekatoncheires—giants each with a hundred arms and fifty heads: Kottos, "the striker"; Briareos, "the strong"; and Gyes, "the bemembered". But the whole story of the mating of Ouranos and Gaia—although it must originally have been one of the tales concerning the beginning of things—already takes us into the stories of the Titans. It is the earliest tale of this particular sort in our mythology. I shall proceed to relate the other tales in their due order.

CHAPTER II

Stories of the Titans

THE stories of the Titans are about gods who belong to such a distant past that we know them only from tales of a particular kind, and only as exercising a particular function. The name of Titan has, since the most ancient times, been deeply associated with the divinity of the Sun, and seems originally to have been the supreme title of beings who were, indeed, celestial gods, but gods of very long ago, still savage and subject to no laws. We did not regard them as being in any way worthy of worship; with the single exception, perhaps, of Kronos; and with the exception also of Helios, if we identify the latter with the wilder, primordial Sun-God. These two did, it is true, have places of worship here and there. The Titans were gods of a sort that have no function except in mythology. Their function is that of the defeated: even when they win seeming victories—before the stories come to their inexorable conclusion. These defeated ones bear the characteristic of an older male generation: the characteristics of ancestors whose dangerous qualities reappear in their posterity. What sort of beings they were will be shown in the tales immediately following.

I

OURANOS, GAIA AND KRONOS

Ouranos, the god of the sky, came in the night to his wife, to the Earth, to the goddess Gaia.[16] The two bright children of Night and Darkness, the children Aither and Hemera, who appeared in daytime, have already been mentioned. Ouranos came every night to his mating. But from the very beginning he hated the children whom Gaia bore him.[17] As soon as they were born he regularly hid them and would not let them come out into the light. He hid them in the inward hollows of the earth. In this wicked work—so Hesiod expressly states —he took his pleasure. The gigantic goddess Gaia groaned under this affliction, and felt herself oppressed by her inner burden. Therefore she, too, invented a wicked stratagem. She quickly brought forth grey iron. She made a mighty sickle with sharp teeth, and took counsel with her sons.

The number of these was then already great. Hesiod names, besides Okeanos, also Koios, Krios, Hyperion, Iapetos, and, as the youngest, Kronos. These six brothers had six sisters: Theia, Rhea, Themis, Mnemosyne, golden-wreathed Phoebe and sweet Tethys. Gaia, in her woe, said to all her children, but especially to her sons: "Ah, my children—and children, too, of a nefarious father—will you not hear me and punish your father for this wicked ill-doing? He was the first who ever devised a shameful deed!" They were all afraid, and none opened his mouth. Only great Kronos, the tortuous thinker, took courage. "Mother," he said, "I give my promise, and I shall act thereon. I care nothing for our father, of hated name. He was the first who ever devised a shameful deed!" At this Gaia rejoiced. She hid her son in the place appointed for the ambush, gave the sickle into his hand and told him all her plot. When Ouranos came at nightfall and, being inflamed with love, covered the earth and lay all across it, the son thrust out his left hand from the place of ambush and seized his father. With his right hand he took the huge sickle, quickly cut off his father's manhood, and cast it behind his back.

Gaia received in her womb the blood shed by her spouse, and gave birth to the Erinyes—the "strong ones", as Hesiod calls them—also to the Giants and the Ash Nymphs, or Nymphai Meliai, from whom arose a hardy race of men. The father's manhood fell into the sea, and thus—according to stories that I shall tell later—Aphrodite was born. What Hesiod did not tell us (although it is a thing that all hearers of this story of the Titans will at once perceive), should now be added: namely, that since the bloody deed of Kronos the sky has no longer approached the earth for nightly mating. The original begetting came to an end, and was followed by the rule of Kronos. That is another of the stories of the Titans.

2

KRONOS, RHEA AND ZEUS

Out of the total number of twelve Titans and Titanesses, three brothers took their own sisters to wife—or, more correctly, three sisters took their brothers to husband. (In such cases Hesiod always mentions the female deity first.) The Titaness Theia bore, to her husband Hyperion, Helios, the sun, Selene, the moon, and Eos, the dawn.[18] Phoebe bore to Koios a superb race of gods,[19] comprising the goddesses Leto, Artemis and Hekate and one male god, Apollon. Rhea married Kronos,[20] to whom she bore three daughters and three sons: the great goddesses Hestia, Demeter and Hera, and the great gods Hades, Poseidon and Zeus. Just as Father Kronos was the youngest son of Ouranos, so Zeus—according to Hesiod, who when referring to deities anterior to Zeus's overlordship especially emphasises and extols their maternal origins—was the youngest son of Rhea and Kronos.[21] Those who attached importance to paternal origin—as Homer did, for example— believed Zeus to have been Kronos's eldest son. But in telling the stories of the Titans it is better to follow Hesiod than Homer, who, like all his school of poets, did not esteem tales of this sort, and referred to them only seldom and indirectly.

Great Kronos devoured all his children as soon as each of them had left its mother's sacred womb and fell to her knees.[22] He was king amongst the sons of Ouranos and did not wish any other god to succeed to his possession of this dignity. He had been told by Gaia, his mother, and by his father, the starry Sky, that he was fated to be overthrown by a powerful son. He was therefore continually on his guard, and swallowed his children. For Rhea this was an insupportable grief. So, when she was about to give birth to Zeus, the future father of gods and men, she turned in supplication to her parents, the Earth and the starry Sky, for good counsel as to how she might bring the child secretly into the world and also take vengeance for the children whom the great Kronos, the tortuous thinker, had swallowed.

Gaia and Ouranos heard their daughter's prayer, and revealed to her the manner in which the future of King Kronos and his son had been decided. The parents sent Rhea to Lyktos, on the island of Crete, where Gaia took charge of the newly born child. When Rhea brought the child to Lyktos, in the darkness of night, she hid him in a cave in the wooded mountain of Aegaeon. On the other hand she offered Ouranos's son, that first king of the gods, a great stone wrapped in swaddling-clothes. The terrible one seized the stone and thrust it into his stomach, not realising that his son, unvanquished and heedless of him, was only waiting for the time when he could overthrow the father, strip him of his authority and rule in his stead. Quickly grew the limbs and the courage of this new ruler (whom Hesiod calls, not *basileus*, or king, but *anax*, "Sir" or "Sire", as our gods have been addressed since the new overlordship) until in the fullness of time it really happened that Kronos was conquered by Zeus's force and deceitful cunning, and even yielded up from within himself his swallowed children. Zeus liberated not only his own brothers, but also those of his father, whom Ouranos still held in fetters. The most important of these were the Kyklopes, who in gratitude gave Zeus thunder and lightning, which are the emblems and instruments of his power.

Kronos has left to us, associated with his own memory, the memory of the Golden Age. His kingdom coincides with this happy period in the world's history, of which I shall speak later. The closeness of the connection between the two is indicated by the further story of Kronos, which other poets have told more fully than Hesiod. In that ancient Golden Age honey poured from oaks. The disciples of Orpheus were convinced[23] that, when Zeus enchained Kronos, the old god was befuddled with honey. (In those days there was no wine.) Zeus enchained the old god in order to carry him off to the place where he, Kronos—and with him the Golden Age—still exists: at the outermost edge of the earth, on the Isles of the Blest. Thither Zeus betook himself with his father.[24] There the breezes sent by Okeanos bathe the Tower of Kronos. There he is king, the husband of Rhea, the goddess enthroned supreme over all.

3

THE BATTLES OF THE GODS AND TITANS

At one time our mythology contained numerous stories of wars of the gods, stories which later were forgotten. Zeus, who had thrown his father Kronos into captivity, was himself threatened with the same fate. Mention is made in Homer[25] of how Zeus was once almost bound by his mighty sister and brother, Hera and Poseidon, and by Pallas Athene. But Thetis, in her quality of great goddess of the sea, fetched from the depths one of the three "Hundred-armed": him whom the gods called Briareos, but men called Aigaion. (At one time he must have shared with the goddess dominion over the depths of the Aegean sea.) The hundred-armed one stationed himself, delighting in his glorious office, as guardian over the son of Kronos. The blessed gods were afraid and laid no chains upon Zeus. Furthermore, it was thanks to the help of such benevolent monsters as Briareos that Zeus was able, after his victory over Kronos, to assert his power over the turbulent Sons of Heaven, who resembled their father more than Zeus did.

As Hesiod tells it:[26] for fully ten years the Titans and the children of Rhea and Kronos had been at bitter war. The old gods, the Titans, waged their struggle from the summit of Mount Othrys; Zeus and his brothers and sisters from Mount Olympus. There was no possibility of a decisive end to the struggle. Then Gaia revealed to the new gods the secret of victory. On her advice they fetched from the depths, from the outermost edge of the earth, the hundred-armed ones, Briareos, Kottos and Gyes; they strengthened them with nectar and ambrosia, the drink and food of the gods, and Zeus called upon them to show their gratitude by joining in the war against the Titans. Kottos promised, in the name of the three, that they would do so. Battle was re-engaged.[27] Gods and goddesses stood marshalled against each other. But the new allies had three hundred hands. In these three hundred hands they seized three hundred stones. With this deluge of stones they over-whelmed the Titans and sealed their doom. The vanquished were enchained and thrown into Tartaros, which is as deep below the earth as the earth is below the sky. An anvil dropped from the sky falls for nine nights, and on the tenth it reaches the earth; and likewise it falls nine nights and days from the earth, and on the tenth day it reaches Tartaros. Tartaros is surrounded by an iron wall. Three times this stronghold is encompassed by Night. Over it grew the roots of the earth and sea. Within it the Titans are hidden in darkness, and can never escape; for it was Poseidon who set the iron doors around them. As trusty guardians, appointed by Zeus, dwell there Gyes, Kottos and Briareos.

It is further told[28]—whether by Hesiod himself, or by someone else who made this addition to the story in order to protect Zeus's reputation, nobody knows—that the turn of fortune in the battle of the Titans was in fact caused by the lightning of the new ruler. But, as I have already related, Zeus had received thunder and lightning out of the depths, from the Kyklopes whom he had freed. In any case, the Sons of Heaven and Earth were defeated with the help of Gaia and her sons, who were Sons of Earth and Heaven.

4

TYPHOEUS OR TYPHON, ZEUS AND AIGIPAN

Another very old story is one that not even Hesiod, or those who expanded his poem of the origin of the gods, cared to tell us. It came back to us from Asia Minor. One is entitled to say "came back", for the cave named "Leather Sack" (*korukos*) —the *korukion atron*—is as well known to us at Delphi as it is over there in Cilicia; and so is a female dragon named Del-phyne, who in both parts of the world was associated with a male dragon named Typhon. The only difference is that in Asia Minor the dragon's opponent was Zeus, whereas in Delphi he was Zeus's son Apollon; and that Zeus defeated the male dragon, whereas Apollon defeated the female.

It was told[29] that after the overthrow of the Titans, the dragon Typhoeus—who is also called Typhaon, Typhon or Typhos, and is often confused with the Typhon of the Egyp-tians—was born to Gaia as her youngest son.[30] His father was said to have been Tartaros. (The Typhaon of Delphi, on the other hand, was born to Hera without a father.[31]) The Typhoeus of Asia Minor came into the world in Cilicia, and was half man and half beast. He surpassed all Gaia's other children in size and strength. Above the hips he was shaped like a man, and was so tall that he overtopped the highest mountain and his head often knocked against the stars. One of his arms extended to the sunset and the other to the sunrise. From his shoulders grew a hundred heads of serpents. From the hips downwards he was shaped like two wrestling serpents, which towered up to the height of his head and yelled hissingly. As for the voices of his hundred heads, it is reported[32] that the gods could often understand what he said, but he could also bay like a dog, or hiss so that the mountains echoed. The whole body of the monster was covered with wings. The wild hair of his head and chin waved in the wind, his eyes were afire. Hissing and bellowing, he flung fiery stones at Heaven,

ZEUS AND TYPHON

and from his mouth spurted flames instead of spittle. It was still uncertain whether or no Typhoeus would gain mastery over gods and men. But Zeus struck him from afar with light-ning, and at close range with the steel sickle, and pursued him to Mount Kasion. When he saw that the dragon was wounded, he went in to fight him at close quarters. But he was at once caught in the writhing coils of the huge serpents, and the dragon seized the sickle from his hand and cut the sinews from the god's hands and feet. Typhoeus picked Zeus up on his shoulder, carried him through the sea to Cilicia, and left him in the cave named "Leather Sack". Here, too, he hid the sinews of Zeus in a bear's pelt and set Delphyne, a female dragon who was half maiden, half serpent, as guardian over them. Hermes and Aigipan stole the sinews and secretly gave them back to the god. Zeus became strong again, and, appear-ing from Heaven in a chariot drawn by winged horses, pursued the dragon first of all to Mount Nysa. Here the fugitive was betrayed by the goddesses of Fate, the Moirai. He ate of fruit that they offered him, telling him that he would thereby regain his strength. The fruit, however, was that named "Only for a day". He continued his flight and fought again in Thrace, on the mountain-range of Haimos, flinging whole mountains around him and daubing them with his blood (*haima*), from which this range has its name. Finally he reached Sicily, where Zeus hurled Etna upon him. This mountain still spits forth the lightnings that fell upon the dragon.

In this story Hermes is clearly out of place. He was one of the youngest sons of Zeus, and was brought into the story only because—as will later be shown—he was a master-thief. The real participant in the story was Aigipan: the god Pan, that is to say, in his quality of a goat (*aix*). He must have been related by kinship to the dragon, and must therefore have betrayed him. For at Delphi, too, it is told of the dragon there —in a tale in which he is called Python—that he had a son named Aix.[33] In another, later form of the story[34] it was the hero Kadmos, disguised by Pan as a goat-herd, who first cast a spell over Typhoeus with the notes of Syrinx, and then tricked him. He persuaded the dragon that he would make from the sinews of Zeus a still more magnificent instrument, namely the lyre; and Typhoeus allowed himself to be deceived. He succumbed, as so often happens in the stories of the Titans, to a treacherous wile.

5

THE BATTLE WITH THE GIANTS

A tale in the manner of the stories of the Titans is that of the Giants, or, in our language, the Gigantes. They were born, it will be remembered, of the blood shed by the maimed Father of Heaven. "Glittering in their armour, with long spears in their hands"—so our Hesiod describes them.[35] But the most notable thing about them was that their mother was Gaia, the Earth; so that our painters also depicted them as savages dressed in the pelts of animals, hurling crags and trunks of trees, or as huge creatures shaped from the hips downwards like twin serpents. They are supposed to have appeared on the earth's

POSEIDON SLAYS THE GIANT POLYBOTES IN THE
PRESENCE OF GAIA

surface in one particular region: in Phlegra—that is to say,
"the burning plains"—or Pallene.[36]

Gaia's attitude towards the Giants was quite different from
her attitude towards the Titans in that war which the Olympians had waged against the Sons of Heaven, and had won
with the help of the earth-goddess and her brood of monsters.
In this new war even the hundred-armed ones are thought to
have sided with the Giants.[37] Their mother did the same: not,
perhaps, so much because she wanted to avenge her sons, the
Titans, or the dragon Typhoeus, as because the new gods had
now usurped the position of the Sons of Heaven, and Gaia
was always an adversary of Heaven. It began to be said[38] that
the Olympians were able to gain the upper hand over the
attacking Giants only with the help of a mortal—or, more
specifically, with the help of two gods born of mortal mothers.

It seems that the Olympians could never gain a victory without enlisting the aid of lower powers. Zeus had on his side not only his brothers and sisters, but also his children, amongst whom were two sons by mortal mothers: Dionysos and Herakles. It is they who are thought to have decided the issue of the battle against the Giants. It was said, furthermore, that even against these odds the Giants might have found salvation in a certain magic herb. Gaia sought to find this herb for them. Zeus forbade the dawn to rise, and the sun and moon to shine, until he had found the magic herb himself.

There were other remarkable stratagems in this battle. The Giant Alkyoneus could not be defeated as long as he was on his own home soil: so Herakles carried him, after having wounded him with an arrow, over the border of Pallene, and thus Alkyoneus perished. The Giant Porphyrion, who attacked Hera and Herakles simultaneously, was inflamed by Zeus with such a desire for the goddess that in his lust he tore off her robe. At that same moment he was struck by the lightning of Zeus and an arrow sped by Herakles. Ephialtes was wounded in the left eye by Apollon, and in the right eye by an arrow from Herakles. Pallas, in an encounter with the Giant who was likewise named Pallas, tore his skin off and used it as a shield or breastplate. Athene served Enkelados much as Zeus had served the dragon in the story of Typhoeus: she threw the island of Sicily at him.

This tale could be still further continued, as it was continued by the poets and painters of later times. It ended in victory for the Olympians. But the tale has much less significance in our mythology than the older stories of the Titans. These include a special group of tales: the tales of Prometheus and the Human Race, whose cause Prometheus espoused against Zeus. For after the fall of the Titans mankind set itself up in rivalry against the gods. But it would be premature to turn our attention immediately to these stories. There is much to be told first. Especially I must tell what deities existed at this time besides the children of Rhea and Kronos, and how they fared under the rule of Zeus.

CHAPTER III

The Moirai, Hekate and Other Pre-Olympian Deities

IN our tales concerning the beginning of things three great goddesses play the part of Mother of the World: the sea-goddess Tethys, the goddess Night, and Mother Earth. They constitute a Trinity; but this may well be a chance result of the fact that only three tales of such a Mother have come down to us. It may also be a result of chance that in the tale concerning the origin of the Trojan War, the most important event in the age of our heroes, three goddesses appear in the story of the Judgment of Paris.

All through our mythology one comes across *three* goddesses. What is more, they do not merely form accidental groups of three—usually a group of three sisters—but actually *are* real trinities, sometimes almost forming a single Threefold Goddess. Tales are also told of larger groups, of fifty goddesses or fifty daughters of the same father or couple. Let me at once state the association suggested by these numbers. Our lunar month was divided into three parts, and our moon had three aspects: as the waxing, the full and the waning sign of a divine presence in the sky. (It could naturally also be seen in two aspects: as waxing and waning, or as bright and dark.) On the other hand, our greatest festal period, the Olympiad, consisted of fifty moons, or, on every alternate occasion, of forty-nine: this alternation is sometimes reflected in our tales.

All this does not mean that the great threefold goddess, whom we will find spoken of under many names, is *nothing else but* the moon. The moon-goddess Selene will only come into my narrative later, in connection with the sun-god Helios and his tribe.

I

THE GODDESSES OF FATE (MOIRAI)

I have already mentioned that even Zeus stood in sacred awe of the goddess Night.[39] According to the tales of the disciples of Orpheus, an account of which I shall postpone until later, Nyx was herself a threefold goddess.[40] Amongst the Children of Night were the goddesses of Fate, the Moirai. This tradition concerning them is to be found in our Hesiod,[41] although he also states that these three goddesses were daughters of Zeus and of the goddess Themis.[42] According to the later devotees of Orpheus, they lived in Heaven, in a cave by the pool whose white water gushes from this same cave:[43] a clear image of moonlight. Their name, the word *moira*, means "part"; and their number, so the Orphists claim, corresponds to that of the three "parts" of the moon; and[44] that is why Orpheus sings of "the Moirai in white raiment".

We knew the Moirai as the Spinners, *Klothes*, although only the eldest of them is called Klotho. The second is called Lachesis, "the Apportioner", the third Atropos, "the Inevitable". Homer mostly speaks only of one Moira, a single spinning goddess who is "strong", "hard to endure" and "destroying". The Moirai spin the days of our lives, one day of which inevitably becomes the day of death. The length of the yarn that they assign to each mortal is decided solely by them: not even Zeus can influence their decision. The most he can do is to take his golden scales, preferably at noon, and measure—in the case, for example, of two confronted opponents—which of them is doomed to die that day.[45] The power of the Moirai probably comes down from a time before the rule of Zeus. And they do not always form a Trinity: in the famous old vase-painting of the marriage of the goddess Thetis with the mortal Peleus they are depicted as four in number. At Delphi, on the other hand, only two of them were worshipped: a Moira of birth and a Moira of death. They were

PLATE 1

a GORGO WITH A DARK FACE

b GORGO WITH A BRIGHT FACE

PLATE 11

a HESPERID STEALING A GOLDEN APPLE

b HERAKLES AMONGST THE HESPERIDES

two when they took part in the battle against the Giants—in which they wielded brazen pestles.[46] Young gods had little respect for them. Apollon—so we were told by an ancient dramatist—made the three grey-haired goddesses drunk, in order to save his friend Admetos from his appointed day of death.[47] It was told that they were present at the birth of the hero Meleagros in the house of King Oineus.[48] Klotho prophesied that the child would be of noble nature; Lachesis prophesied his status of hero; but Atropos prophesied that he would live only as long as the log which was at that moment on the fire. Whereupon his mother, Althaia, saved the log from the flames. It was also said[49] that, of the three Klothes, Atropos was the smallest in stature but the oldest and most powerful.

I shall do no more than briefly mention the Children of Night, a sinister brood only some of whom were deities, and whom Hesiod mentions[50] only in order to complete his genealogy of All Things. Death is mentioned under three names: as Moros, Ker and Thanatos. (The first of these names is the masculine form of Moira.) Mentioned with Moros are his brother Hypnos, Sleep, and the whole tribe of Dreams; Momos, Mockery; Oizys, Woe; the Hesperides, who guard their golden apples beyond Okeanos; and the goddess Nemesis, of whom, too, a special tale is told; Treachery and Intercourse (Apate and Philotes); Grey Old Age (Geras), and Strife (Eris). The Children of Eris do not enter at all into the stories of the gods. At a later time they dwelt at the entrance to the Underworld.

2

THE GODDESSES EURYBIA, STYX AND HEKATE

An account of the goddesses of Fate, whom Homer unites into the single *Moira Krataia*, the "strong Moira",[51] must be followed by an account of goddesses who were likewise noted for their strength or for their especial connection with beings

who signify strength. They form an accidental group of three
—but not entirely accidental, since Hesiod joins them in
kinship.

Eurybia, as her name signifies, was a goddess "of wide force".
Bia means "force" and is synonymous with *kratos*, "strength".
Eurybia was supposed to be a daughter of Gaia. But her father
was the Sea, Pontos.[52] Her brothers were Nereus and Phorkys,
two "Old Ones of the Sea" and Thaumas, whose name means
"Sea Wonder". Her sister was Keto, the goddess of the
beautiful cheeks, whose name means "Sea Monster". Eurybia
had a heart of steel. She bore children to Krios, whose name
means "The Ram of Heaven", and who was one of the two
Titans who did not marry Titanesses. She of the steely heart,
however, was herself almost a Titaness. Her sons resemble the
Titans in their nature: Astraios, "the Starry One"; Pallas, the
husband of Styx; and Perses, the father of Hekate.

Styx is to us a hated name; it is associated with *stygein*, "to
hate". It is the name of the river that nine times encircles and
confines the Underworld.[53] The chilly waterfall on high
Mount Araonios in Arcadia was named after the river of the
Underworld, and not the other way round. Of the goddess of
the same name it is said that Zeus begat by her the Queen of
the Underworld, Persephone.[54] In Hesiod the goddess Styx
is the mightiest of the eldest daughters of Okeanos and
Tethys.[55] It is told[56] that Styx bore to Pallas, besides Zelos
and Nike ("Zeal" and "Victory") also Kratos and Bia
("Strength" and "Force"). These two never left the side of
Zeus, either at home or on his journeys. Styx had arranged
this on the day when the Olympian called upon all gods to
help him against the Titans and told them that none who did
so would afterwards lack reward or honour: any who held a
particular rank or dignity would keep it, and any who had
had none such under Kronos would receive a befitting one.
Whereupon Styx was the first to rally to Zeus, with her children. Such was her wisdom, inherited from her father Okeanos.
And Zeus did really honour her, and rewarded her richly: she

THE "STRONG GODDESS" IN HER TRIPLE REIGN

became the great Oath of the gods. Not even mortals dare to perjure themselves by Styx. She remained associated with the Underworld, and never became an Olympian goddess. The significance of the oath taken by the waters of the Styx will be explained later, when I come to the tale of Iris. The Children of Styx became the constant companions of the Ruler. It will be remembered that in Aeschylus's tragedy, *Prometheus Bound*, Kratos and Bia appear as Zeus's retainers.[57] The winged goddess Nike, on the other hand, was more closely associated with Zeus's daughter Pallas Athene.

Hekate, the third of this group, was always closest to us— although her name perhaps means "the Distant One". It is not only her name that links her with Apollon and Artemis, who are also named Hekatos and Hekate, but also her family origin—if Hesiod is right in his account of it. She is elsewhere supposed to have been one of the Daughters of Night.[58] Hesiod, however, gives us the following genealogy:[59] the Titan couple Phoebe and Koios had two daughters: Leto, the mother of Apollon and Artemis, and Asteria, a star-goddess who bore

Hekate to Persaios or Perses, the son of Eurybia. Hekate is therefore the cousin of Apollon and Artemis, and at the same time a reappearance of the great goddess Phoibe, whose name poets often give to the moon. Indeed, Hekate used to appear to us carrying her torch as the Moon-Goddess, whereas Artemis, although she, too, sometimes carries a torch, never did so. Hesiod seeks further to distinguish Hekate from Artemis by repeatedly emphasising that the former is *monogenes*, "an only child". In this respect, too, Hekate resembled Persephone, the goddess of the Underworld. For the rest, she was an almighty, threefold goddess. Zeus revered her above all others,[60] and let her have her share of the earth, the sea and the starry sky; or rather, he did not deprive her of this threefold honour, which she had previously enjoyed under the earlier gods, the Titans, but let her retain what had been awarded to her at the first distribution of honours and dignities. She was therefore a true Titaness of the Titans, even though this is never expressly stated. On the contrary, she is said to be[61] that *Krataiis*, that "Strong One", who bore to Phorkys the female sea-monster Skylla. Tales are told of her love-affairs with gods of the sea: with Triton, in particular,[62] whom Hesiod calls *eurybias*, "of wide force". On the other hand, it was also said[63] that Hekate was mistress of the Underworld and every night led around a swarm of ghosts, accompanied by the barking of dogs. She was even called Bitch and She-wolf.[64]

She was literally "close" to us, in the sense that she stood before the doors of most of our houses under the name of Prothyraia, the goddess who helped women in childbed (or sometimes cruelly oppressed them), and was also to be seen at meeting-places of three ways, where images of her were set up: three wooden masks upon a pole, or a threefold statue with three faces looking in three directions. To describe how and with what purposes she was invoked by women would take us into the field of witchcraft; and I propose to confine myself as closely as possible to Mythology.

3

SKYLLA, LAMIA, EMPOUSA AND OTHER BOGIES

Hekate had a share of the sky, earth and sea, but never became an Olympian goddess. She was so closely connected with the life of our women, and therefore with mankind generally, that she seemed smaller than the wives and daughters of Zeus. On the other hand, her realm—especially the sea, where in primordial times she carried on her love-affairs—was so great that the Olympian could not possibly control it. When she was not walking on the highways, she dwelt in her cave. So did her daughter Skylla, a sea-bogy—according, at least, to the tales of our seamen, whose main object in telling them was to frighten landsmen. For they themselves knew the real nature of even the most dangerous parts of the sea, and did not associate the great goddess, who could appear in many shapes, with a single spot only.

Seamen told[65]—and the tale has been preserved in the Odyssey, where the goddess, who was, I suppose, originally three-fold, was further doubled—that there are two cliffs, one of them of smooth stone and so high that it rises to heaven and its summit is invisible. In the middle of this cliff is the cave of Skylla. The cave faces towards the west, towards the impenetrable darkness of Erebos. There dwells Skylla, barking horribly, like a young bitch. Her twelve feet—the necessary number for a doubled Hekate—remained undeveloped. Her six terrible heads are poised upon a long neck. In her mouths the death-dealing teeth are set in three rows. With these she fishes, thrusting her heads out of the cave and searching amongst the rocks for dolphins, seals or larger sea-monsters. When the ship of Odysseus came that way and the hero, upon the advice of Kirke, decided to avoid the other cliff, Skylla inadvertently swept up and devoured six of the crew.[66]

Under the other cliff lurked Charybdis.[67] She belongs wholly to seamen's tales, and scarcely at all to mythology, although Homer calls her "the divine Charybdis", using the same adjective, *dia*, as he applies to the beautiful cave-nymph Kalypso. Thrice daily Charybdis sucked the sea into herself, and thrice daily she spat it out again. On the top of the cliff, which was not nearly as tall as Skylla's cliff opposite, stood a wild fig-tree. Charybdis herself stayed out of sight. It was later told of her[68] that she was a daughter of Gaia and Poseidon, an all-devouring monster who stole the cattle of Herakles, and for this was hurled by Zeus's lightning into the depths of the sea.

A somewhat similar tale is told of Skylla[69]—that she, too, the wild bitch, stole the kine of Herakles, and for this was slain by the hero. Her father Phorkys brought her back to life by first burning her body with torches and then boiling it. For this reason Skylla has no fear even of Persephone, goddess of the Underworld. We must recognise in Skylla a great goddess resembling her mother Hekate. Probably the accounts of Skylla that are truest to her real nature are those that depict her in the shape of a beautiful woman down to the hips, but changing at the hips to a dog and from the hips downwards into a fish. Those accounts that speak of her as also having wings are equally true to her nature, in that, unlike Charybdis, she rules not only over the depths but also over the far distances both below and above. But perhaps she had this dominion more commonly amongst our western neighbours the Etruscans than amongst ourselves. If so, that must be why Skylla is also named *Tyrsenis*, "the Etruscan".[70]

The mother of this goddess—who is not to be confused with another Skylla, who was a human being, a daughter of Nisos —is called not only Hekate, but also Lamia.[71] At this point these stories wander off into tales that do not even form part of seamen's legend, but lie still further away on the outer fringes of mythology. They become such fables as nurses used to tell to children, both to frighten them into good behaviour and also to entertain them. Lamia, or Lamo, is by name "the Devourer": *laimos* means "gullet". The shortened form of the

SKYLLA

name, Lamo, was probably that used by nurses talking to children, like the shortened names they gave to other bogies such as Akko, Alphito, Gello, Karko, or as Mormo for Mormolyke. It was told[72] that Lamia was a queen and ruled in Libya. Her cave was actually pointed out to visitors. Zeus loved her[73]—for she was beautiful—and begat children by her. These fell victim to the jealousy of Hera. Since then Lamia has been ugly with grief and enviously steals the children of other mothers. She can take her eyes out of her head, so that they remain watchful even when she herself is asleep. And she can change into any shape. But if she is seized and held fast, the children can be taken alive from her belly.[74]

A similar story of the Titans was also told to children. The tale in some ways resembles the story of Kronos. Lamia, like Kronos, possessed a tower[75]. It is not clear whether she was a goddess or a god, or both. The comic poet Aristo⁄phanes,[76] who has preserved, but also distorted and burlesqued, so many ancient tales, mentions parts of Lamia's body which are certainly not female. (Similarly the Gorgon sometimes has a phallus attached to her.) On the other hand, she was noted for having the lustfulness of a harlot, and sometimes a harlot would be nicknamed Lamia. Her ability to change her shape reminds one of the threefold shapes of Hekate and of the mixed bodily structure of Skylla. Lamia had this gift in common with certain divinities of the sea, and also with another bogy, Empousa. Sometimes this last name is simply another name for Hekate,[77] but sometimes Empousa appears as a separate being.

People also used to speak of Lamiai and Empousai in the plural, and when they did so the two names were synonymous. When Empousa was encountered in the entrance to the Under-world, as in a play by Aristophanes,[78] she appeared now as a cow, now as a mule, now as a beautiful woman, now as a bitch. Her whole face glowed like flame. One of her feet was of bronze. (But obviously the poet is exaggerating. Other narrators speak only of her brazen sandal, which later Hekate wore in her quality of *Tartarouchos*, "Ruler of Tartaros".[79] In her quality of bright goddess she wore golden sandals.) Empousa's other foot was so befouled with the mule's dung that it seemed to be not a mule's foot, but a foot of mule dung. At this point, however, mythology has given place to mere ribaldry.

4

THE ELDEST DAUGHTERS OF TETHYS AND OKEANOS

I shall now tell the names of the eldest daughters of Tethys and Okeanos, as they are told by Hesiod.[80] Besides Styx, who was the mightiest of them and has already been mentioned, there are forty others. Hesiod included in his list the names of well-known great goddesses such as Perseis, the "daughter of Perses", i.e. Hekate and Urania, i.e. Aphrodite; also the names of wives of Zeus such as Dione and Europa, Metis and Eury-nome, of whom only the last-named continued to be a sea-goddess comparable with Tethys and Thetis. Thus Hesiod is in some degree acknowledging the correctness of that tale of the beginning of things which makes Okeanos and Tethys the parents of other deities besides those of the sea and the rivers.

Of the other Okeaninai whom Hesiod names, only nine have to do with water, wind and wave, with their mobility and speed, with rocks and caves and ships. Kallirhoe and Amphiro stand for flux; Plexaura and Galaxaura for the whipping wind and for calm; Thoe and Okyrhoe for speed and mobility; Petraia for the rocks; Kalypso for the sheltering cave; Prymno for the ship's stern. Of the other names, the following refer to gifts and wealth (*doron* and *ploutos*), which can also sometimes be granted by the sea: Doris, Eudora, Polydora, Plouto. The first of these was supposed to be the mother of the younger generation of sea-goddesses, the daughters of Nereus, whom I shall later speak of in connection with the "Old Ones of the Sea". But most of the names of the daughters of Tethys I have yet to tell, and these are amongst the most puzzling: Peitho, Admete, Ianthe, Elektra, Hippo, Klymene, Rhodeia, Zeuxo, Klytia, Idyia, Pasithoe, Melobosis, Kerkeis, Ianeira, Akaste, Xanthe, Menestho, Telesto—she of the saffron-yellow raiment —and lastly Chryseis, Asia and Tyche.

One could make many conjectures concerning the goddesses hidden behind these names; but I shall make only the most obvious interpretations. Peitho, the goddess "Persuasion", was clearly only one particular name of the Goddess of Love, and she therefore became a companion of Aphrodite. Admete, on the other hand, was, like Artemis, an "untamable". Hippo and Zeuxo had to do with horse and cart. Idyia was a goddess of magical knowledge, Xanthe a fair-haired goddess, Telesto a goddess of initiations into mysteries, and Tyche was a goddess whose name means "what may hap" or "Chance", a deity of whom no particular stories are told, but whose power —like that of the three Moirai and the threefold Hekate— proved stronger than the rule of Zeus.

5

THE OLD ONES OF THE SEA—PHORKYS,
PROTEUS AND NEREUS

In tales like those of Eurybia, Styx and Hekate, or of Skylla, Lamia and Empousa, one can never tell whether all these names do not refer to a single deity, the "Strong Goddess" whose realm of power and dominion comprises sky, earth, sea and even the Underworld. Nor can one tell whether Tethys, Thetis and Eurynome were not manifestations of the same deity—or, indeed, merely three different names, originating in various places and times, for her manifestation as Goddess of the Sea. It is the same with the three male deities, Phorkys, Proteus and Nereus, each of whom Homer describes as "The Old One of the Sea".

Readers of the sacred books of Orpheus were familiar with a tale[81] according to which Phorkys, Kronos and Rhea were the eldest children of Okeanos and Tethys—who, in turn, were the offspring of Earth and Sky; or, as I have already said, of the upper and lower halves of the original Egg. According to another tale[82] told in these books, Gaia and Ouranos had as their children seven Titanesses and seven Titans. In addition to those I have already mentioned, the books included amongst the Titanesses the beautiful Dione, and amongst the Titans they included Phorkys, whom they surnamed *krataios*, "the strong". According to Hesiod,[83] Phorkys was a son of Gaia and Pontos. One of his sisters was Eurybia: I need not repeat the names of the others. He was married to the beautiful-cheeked Keto, whose name is the feminine form of *ketos*, "sea-monster". This word can also be used to describe "The Old One of the Sea"—as when Herakles wrestles with him and he assumes various shapes. It is true that tricks of metamorphosis are more commonly attributed to Proteus and Nereus than to Phorkys, and the story of the wrestle with Herakles is told only of Nereus. Essentially, however, it is always the same "Old

One of the Sea" who is meant. Phorkys—also called Phorkos —was in a way the eldest of them, the leader of the chorus of all sea-divinities. And he must have been a cunning and wonder-working god, if, as I have already told, he was able by his arts to bring his daughter Skylla back from death to life!

Proteus is the most easily explicable name of the "Old One of the Sea". It is an archaic form of Protogonos, "the first-born". No mention is made of Proteus's parents, but only of the waters in which he can be encountered. He frequented a sandy island off Egypt, which was known as Pharos; whereas Phorkys was more at home in the west, in a bay of Ithaca, or still further westwards, where his daughter Skylla also dwelt. It is told,[84] in the style of the seamen's legends that Homer loves to tell in the Odyssey, that Proteus had a daughter called Eidothea, and that she betrayed him. "A greybeard of the sea frequents this region," this goddess told the hero Menelaos, "the sea-greybeard of Egypt, the immortal Proteus. He knows the depths of all the sea, and is a subject of Poseidon. They say that he is my father, who begat me. If you could lay an ambush for him and capture him, he would be sure to tell you your course and the number of days of your voyage home, so that you may cross the fish-teeming sea. And, if you so desire, he will also tell you everything—evil or good—that has happened in your house while you were away upon your long, toilsome voyage."

To which Menelaos: "Tell me then how I can lay an ambush for the aged god, that he may not espy me or be otherwise forewarned and escape me. For it is hard for a mortal to gain mastery over a god." To which the goddess: "I shall tell you, stranger, exactly what to do. When the sun is at noon the greybeard of the sea comes out of the water, the greybeard who tells the truth. He comes in the gust of the west wind, in the dark ripple of the waves. Once he is out of the water he lies down beneath the cavernous cliffs. Around him sleep the seals, the brood of the beautiful sea-goddess, in herds, just as they rose from the grey-white water and still exhaling the bitter

smell of the deep sea. I shall lead you there at dawn and hide
you in ambush. You must choose out only three of your companions, the best men for the task. Now I shall tell you the
dangerous wiles of the Old One. First of all he counts the
seals, five by five. Then he lies down in their midst, like a
herdsman in the midst of his flock. As soon as you see that
he has fallen asleep, use force and strength. Hold him fast,
however he may strive to escape. For this he will do. He will
take on the shapes of all the beasts on earth. He will even
change into water and fire. But hold him dauntlessly, tie the
bonds upon him all the more closely. Only when he begins
to beseech you, and has the same shape as that in which you
saw him fall asleep, only then cease using force, set the Old
One free and ask him . . ." And so it came about. Proteus
took on the shapes of a lion, a serpent, a leopard, a pig, then
also of water and of a tree, and finally gave truthful answers
to all that was asked him.

It was told that Nereus used similar tricks of metamorphosis.
These tales were told also by our ancient painters, sculptors,
vase-painters and goldsmiths. They created for us men with
the bodies of fish, and this at a far earlier time than they created
women with such bodies: which is evidence that the power
of the great goddesses of the sea was not confined to the watery
element, whereas the "Old One of the Sea" was always
associated with the depths. The pictures also show him with
a lion, a buck and a serpent thrusting their heads out from his
fishlike body. These were the creatures into which Nereus
changed himself when Herakles wrestled with him, bound
him in the manner advised by the goddesses of Fate, and thus
questioned him. This happened much earlier than Menelaos's
adventure with Proteus, and earlier even than Herakles's
wrestling-match with the Triton, who in our mythology is
one of the younger sea-gods. We will come across him as the
son of Poseidon and Amphitrite. The "Old One of the Sea"
was, however, also a spectator at that wrestling-match, in
threefold shape, as he is shown on one of the earliest pinnacles

of the Acropolis at Athens, where he is most often referred to mistakenly as "Typhon".

Under one name or another, the "Old One" ruled our seas before Poseidon. Unlike that still earlier sea-ruler, the hundred-armed Briareos, he was famed for his wisdom and truthfulness. In the words of Hesiod:[85] "The eldest son of Pontos was Nereus, who never lies but always tells the truth. For this reason he is called 'the Old One', because he is truthful and kind. He never departs from what is seemly, but is always full of justice and kindness." Doris the Okeanine bore him fifty daughters, all of them sea-goddesses, whose names I shall tell later.

6

THE GREY GODDESSES (GRAIAI)

To the Greybeard of the Sea, Phorkys, were born, in our mythology, daughters who were likewise grey. Hesiod tells:[86] "Keto bore unto Phorkys the beautiful-cheeked Graiai, who came into the world with white hair. That is why they are called Graiai by both gods and men." In our tongue *graia* means an old woman. So that these grey ones may not be confused with other grey goddesses, they have always been more exactly named the Graiai of Phorkys, or of Phorkos, or the Phorkides, or in later times the Phorkyades. This name they share with their sisters the Gorgons, whilst at the same time it distinguishes them from the Moirai, who likewise are grey goddesses. Whether the Graiai and the Moirai were, nevertheless, closely related to each other is a question that we late-comers cannot answer.

Hesiod tells the names of only two Graiai: Pemphredo, of the beautiful raiment, and Enyo, of the saffron raiment. He also extols their beautiful faces, although they were grey-haired. Enyo is a warlike name and would be suitable for a goddess of battle. Pemphredon is our name for a species of wasp. (Soothsaying goddesses—such as might also be taken for

Moirai—appear in the Homeric Hymn to Hermes in the guise of bees.) To the third Graia—for, according to other tales, there were three of them—tradition assigns two names: Deino, "The Terrible", and Perso, which is merely another form of Persis or Perseis, the name Hekate got from her father. It was further told[87] that the Graiai were grey-haired maidens resembling swans. They had between them only one eye and one tooth, which they shared. In the place where they lived there is no light of sun or moon. It is a cave at the entrance to the land of the Gorgons, which lies beyond Okeanos and is called Kisthene, "the land of rock-roses".

The story of the one eye and one tooth goes on to relate that the Graiai were strict guardians of the way to the Gorgons. Like the Moirai, however, they were capable of betraying the secret of the way and of the means of getting there. Perseus stole their eye when one of them was handing it to another, so that none of the sisters could see. In this manner the hero compelled them to betray the secret of the way and the means. This story belongs to mythology more than any other of the heroic sagas, and I shall come back to it.

7

THE ERINYES OR EUMENIDES

The third group of Grey Goddesses—besides the Moirai and the Graiai—is composed of the Erinyes. They are old: older than the gods who came to power with Zeus. They say this themselves[88] when they appear on the stage—for example, in the play by Aeschylus whose title is their other name, the *Eumenides*. They have serpents in place of hair. Their skins are black, their raiment is grey. It is told that another name for them is Maniai,[89] or Furies, and that when they appeared to Orestes, whom they were pursuing for having slain his mother, they were at first black; but, when the fugitive had gnawed off a finger in his torment, they turned white. In the region where this tale was told, in the neighbourhood of Megalopolis in Arcadia, sacrifices were made to the Eumenides and the Charites simultaneously. The other name of the Erinyes, the Eumenides, means "the Benevolent"—whether it was that they really became benevolent, or simply that people wished they would do so.

Whenever their number is mentioned, there are three of them. But—like the Moirai, of whom they are associates and almost doubles—they can all be invoked together as a single being, an Erinys. The proper meaning of the word is "a spirit of anger and revenge". It will be remembered that the Erinyes, these "strong ones", were born to Mother Earth, Gaia, when she was made fruitful by the blood shed by her punished husband, the maimed Ouranos (whose maiming, in its turn, called forth punishment and revenge)—so it was told by Hesiod. Others told other tales. The Erinyes were daughters of Night;[90] or else, if they were indeed daughters of Earth, then their father was Skotos, Darkness.[91] Epimenides, the sage of Crete, was convinced that the following were amongst the children of Kronos: Aphrodite, the Moirai and the Erinyes.[92] It is also said that the mother of the Erinyes was named Euonyme,[93] which may be taken to mean the Earth. It is more likely that the correct name is Eurynome—which is also the name of the mother of the Charites, who, as I recently remarked, received sacrifices in Arcadia simultaneously with the Eumenides. The Erinyes are also described as daughters of Phorkys;[94] who is an appropriate husband for Eurynome, as will later be seen from the story of this goddess. The disciples of Orpheus supposed that the parents of the Erinyes were Hades, the Zeus of the Underworld, and Persephone.[95]

The Erinyes were not always winged. Even when they had no wings, however, they bore a resemblance to those predatory female spirits, the Harpies.[96] The smell of their breaths and bodies was intolerable. From their eyes poured a poisonous slaver. Their voice was often like the lowing of cattle;[97] but usually their approach was heralded by a sound of barking, for they were bitches, like Hekate.[98] The whips they bore were brass-studded thongs.[99] They carried torches and serpents. Their home was below the earth, in the Underworld. One of them was called Allekto, "the Never-Ending"; the name of the second, Tisiphone, contains the word *tisis*, retaliation; and the name of the third, Megaira, means envious anger. All three were virgins, but above all they represented the Scolding Mother. Wherever a mother was insulted, or perhaps even murdered, the Erinyes appeared. Like swift bitches they pursued all who had flouted blood-kinship and the deference due to it. They defended the rights of the father, and also of the elder brother; but especially they supported the claims of the mother, even when these were unjust.

All this is made plain in the story of Orestes as put on the stage by Aeschylus. Orestes, at the command of Apollon, slew his mother, the adulteress and husband-slayer Klytaimnestra, in order to avenge his father. And these revengeful spirits of the mother would have been stronger than the whole new theocracy founded by Father Zeus, had not the Father's daughter, Pallas Athene, espoused the cause of the sons—that is to say, of Orestes and her own brother, Apollon. The hero was saved and purified. Nevertheless the worship of the "Old Goddesses", the Eumenides, remained as strong as that of the Moirai.

8

THE GORGONS STHENNO, EURYALE AND MEDOUSA

After the third group of Grey Goddesses it is appropriate to describe the daughters of Phorkys, whom Hesiod mentions directly after the Graiai:[100] the Gorgons, whom we call *Gorgones* or *Gorgous*, as the plural of Gorgo. They are not to be likened to old women, but to masks: rather similar to the masks that were set up to Hekate and also depicted her.

Anyone who wanted to go to the Gorgons needed the help of their sisters, the Graiai. For the Gorgons lived—so Hesiod

PLATE III

a EUROPA ON THE TRICOLOURED BULL

b WINGED GODDESS WITH LION (RHEA OR ARTEMIS)

PLATE IV

a LEDA, THE DIOSKOUROI AND THE EGG OF THE NEMESIS

b HERMES AND MAIA WITH THE STOLEN COWS

tells—even farther away than the Graiai, in the direction of
Night, beyond Okeanos, with the clear-singing Hesperides.[101]
They were three in number. One of them was called Sthenno
or Stheno—a name connected with *sthenos*, "strength". The
second was called Euryale, whose name (from *eurus* and *hals*)
means that she appertained to the wide sea. The third,
Medousa, may also, to judge by her name, have appertained
to the sea: *medousa* means "ruleress"; and how often was the
"Ruler of the Sea" (*halos medon, pontomedon, eurumedon*) invoked
—what though his usual name was Phorkys or Poseidon—by
the masculine form of the name Medousa! Gorgides and
Gorgades were names for sea-goddesses. One cannot believe
that "Gorgo" meant only something ugly and terrible; for
the same name used to be given to little girls, whose
parents certainly did not expect them to turn into terrifying
creatures!

It is told[102] that, of the three sisters, Medousa was the only
mortal one. Both the others were immortal and ageless, like
the rest of the goddesses. Poseidon, the dark-haired god, lay
with the mortal sister in soft grass, under spring blossom. This
tale brings Medousa quite close to Persephone. She, too, the
goddess of the Underworld, was ravished by a dark god and
went, as if she were a mortal, down among the dead. She
sends the Gorgon's head,[103] "the gigantic shape of fear", to
meet those who seek to invade her Underworld. This head is,
in a sort, the other aspect of the beautiful Persephone. And
this is the most remarkable thing about Medousa: although
she, too, was "beautiful-cheeked", like her mother the sea-
monster Keto, she and her sisters also resembled the Erinyes.
The Gorgons had golden wings, but their hands were of
brass.[104] They had mighty tusks like a boar's, and their heads
and bodies were girdled with serpents.[105] If anyone looked at
the terrible face of the Gorgon, his breath left him, and on the
spot he was turned to stone.[106]

As for the question of how the Gorgon's head could appear
by itself—which it did, according to one version, in the

Underworld as a self-protection by Persephone; and, according to another version, which is adopted in many tales, on the breast of Pallas Athene—this was explained in the story of Perseus.[107] This hero was named by his mother Eurymedon, as if he were a "ruler of the sea" and Medousa's husband, not merely her slayer. It was chiefly Athene who protected and guided Perseus in his task of winning the Gorgon's head. She had instructed him[108] not to look at the Gorgon when he advanced upon her, but to see only her reflection in his bright shield. (The same procedure was followed by our youths in certain initiation rites, in which they were required to look at a mask mirrored in a silver vessel.) In this manner Perseus succeeded in seeing the Gorgon's head without confronting it face to face. He struck the head off with the sickle which he had received from Athene—or, according to other accounts, from Hermes or Hephaistos.

From the Gorgon's head sprang the winged horse named Pegasos,[109] which is told of in the story of the hero Bellerophon. But not the horse alone: with it was also born Chrysaor, the hero whose name means "he of the golden sword". The mask-like Gorgon's head, the *gorgoneion*, was thenceforth worn by Athene, either as a sign on her shield or attached to her breast-plate, which was her sacred goatskin named Aegis. It was even supposed that the Gorgon had been the original owner of this goatskin,[110] and that she was a child of Gaia whom Athene had flayed. The goddess Artemis, and very probably also the scolding Demeter—Demeter Erinys, as she was called —wore the mortally terrible countenance as if it were their own, set on their necks. The disciples of Orpheus, however, used the word *gorgoneion* for the face in the moon.

9

THE ECHIDNA, THE HESPERIDEAN SERPENT
AND THE HESPERIDES

I have already spoken, in the story of Typhoeus, Typhaon or Typhon, of a female dragon, a serpent-shaped goddess who in Asia Minor and at Delphi was called Delphyne. The name suggests that she was more like a dolphin, the sea-creature with a womb (this is the meaning of the syllable *delph*). In the stories, as told in our oldest mythology, of any god or goddess of the great family of Phorkys, Proteus and Nereus—or of the corre-sponding old gods of the earth, such as Typhon or the Athenian Kekrops or the Kychreus of Salamis—it is always difficult to make out whether the deity concerned was believed to resemble, in the parts below the hips, a serpent, a dolphin or a fish. Hesiod told us of a goddess named Echidna, "the Serpent", a daughter of Phorkys and Keto. Later on I shall mention still another serpent, a son of the same couple, who was guardian of the Apples of the Hesperides, and shall thus complete my account of the children of Phorkys as listed by Hesiod. But first let me tell his tale of the goddess.[111]

She was born in a cave, the divine Echidna, with a mascu-line disposition and a gigantic frame resembling neither a human being nor an immortal god. In half of her body she was a beautiful-cheeked, bright-eyed young woman; in the other half she was a terrible, huge snake, thrashing about in the hollows of divine Earth and devouring her victims raw. Her cave lay beneath a rock far from gods and men: this dwelling had been assigned to her by the immortals. The name of the place was Arima, and it is described by Homer as "the couch of Typhoeus"[112]—that is to say, of Echidna's husband, to whom she bore a whole brood of monsters. Before I give an account of these, let me explain how our old vase-painters used to depict such a being: as a winged and beautiful goddess, with the body of a serpent from the hips downwards. There

is a lovely old vase-painting which depicts goddesses or
nymphs of this sort, without wings, but with mighty serpents'
bodies below the hips. Four of them, in two couples, are
performing sacred rites in a vineyard, whilst on the other side
of the picture goats are attacking the vines. The tale of the
Garden of the Hesperides mentions similar goddesses or
nymphs, and at least one serpent, the brother of Echidna. But
of Echidna there is more to be told.

Her children were, according to Hesiod,[113] above all those
Hounds who are the most terrible creatures of their kind in
our mythology: Kerberos, the three-headed or even five-headed
hound of the Underworld; and Orthos, or Orthros, the hound
of the three-headed Geryoneus, son of Chrysaor. Orthos had
two heads of his own, but also had seven serpent-heads, or at
least a serpent's tail—which, incidentally, is sometimes also
attributed to Kerberos. Herakles slew Orthos on the occasion
when he killed Geryoneus and drove off the latter's herds of
kine. Orthos lay with his own mother, Echidna, and begat
the Phix, or Sphinx, a winged monster, half maiden and half
lioness, which is mentioned in the story of Oidipous; and begat
also the Lion of Nemea, which, too, was slain by Herakles.
Echidna also bore to Typhaon the Hydra of Lerna, a water-
serpent with many heads which, when they were cut off, at
once grew again. The Hydra is often described in very much
the same fashion as its mother. Another child of Echidna was
the fire-spitting Chimaira, whose body was a combination of
a lion, a goat and a serpent. It was vanquished by Bellerophon.
According to some tales,[114] Echidna suffered a like fate to
that of most of her children: Argos, who had eyes all over his
body, killed her in her sleep. Hesiod, however, expressly states
that she is an immortal and ageless nymph.[115]

There is also a variety of tales concerning Echidna's brother,
the serpent Ladon, and concerning the Hesperides. Ladon,
whose name is the same as that of a river in Arcadia, is more
often referred to as a serpent (*ophis*) than as a dragon (*drakon*).
It is said of him, as also of his sister Echidna, that his mother

ECHIDNA

was really Gaia,[116] or, alternatively, that Echidna was his mother, and, in this case, his father was Typhon. Ladon was appointed guardian of the tree that bore the Golden Apples. He lurked in the hollows of the dark earth,[117] or in the night that stretches out from the west beyond Okeanos, where also dwell the Hesperides,[118] guardians of that same tree. Or is another story true, that the Hesperides were thieves who stole the golden apples, and this was why the serpent had to coil around the tree?[119] The tale is told sometimes in one way, sometimes in the other, according to the needs of the particular story in which the apples, the tree and the garden occur.

In a story concerning the wedding of Zeus and Hera—which I shall tell later—Mother Earth produced the miraculous tree as a wedding-gift for the bride,[120] and it was Hera who appointed Ladon its guardian.[121] According to another tale, the apples belonged to Aphrodite,[122] who furthermore had sacred gardens of her own amongst us mortals. In any case, the divine garden of the Hesperides contained the serpent Ladon, whose ability to speak with various voices is mentioned in the tales[123] as frequently as the bright song of the female guardians.[124] There is no knowing how many throats Ladon had for the utterance of these voices, or whether they were like those of Typhon. Usually the Serpent of the Hesperides has two heads, but often he has three, and in one tale he even has a hundred. Against the tales in which Herakles slew Ladon can be set other tales in which the hero—or, on his behalf, the giant Atlas, who in the west supports the arch of Heaven—obtained the apples in a friendly manner: either from the serpent, or from the Hesperides, or with the help of the Hesperides, according to the taste of the story-teller.

The Hesperides were supposed to be daughters either of Night,[125] or of Phorkys and Keto,[126] or of Atlas:[127] not to speak of that mistake of identity—a confusion with the Horai—by which they are made out to be daughters of Zeus and Themis.[128] Three or four names are usually mentioned—and either three or four seems to have been their actual number, although in paintings many more of them are depicted. The names given to them are widely various. Their joint name, the Hesperides, is connected with Hesperos, the star of evening, the star of Aphrodite. They were sometimes supposed to have had a father called Hesperos.[129] It is unnecessary to suppose this, since the Hesperides, like Hesperos, are directly associated by name with evening, with sunset and the approaches towards Night—although, indeed, to a Night that harbours golden fruit. One of them is actually called Hespera, or Hesperia, "the Vespertinal"; the second is called Aigle, "the Luminous"; and the third Erytheia or Erytheïs, "the Crimson". The fourth is Arethousa, who is elsewhere a goddess of springs.

Another lovely quaternity of names for the Hesperides is the following: Lipara ("of soft radiance"), Chrysothemis ("golden law and order"), Asterope ("star-brilliant"), Hygieia ("health"). Medousa, the Gorgon's name, is also found as a name of one

SERPENT‑NYMPHS

of the Hesperides. Mapsaura, still another name, describes a goddess who snatches like a gust of wind, a Hesperide like a Harpy. Others besides the sage Epimenides have identified the Hesperides with the Harpies; and let us not forget their "bright voices", which gives them an especial resemblance to the Sirens. The tales of the Sirens and Harpies must, however, be distinguished from those of the Hesperides, by reason of the former creatures' peculiar bodily shape and functions. The Hesperides have a closer link with Echidna and Ladon; also with those nymphs whom I recently mentioned, the serpent‑nymphs in the vineyard. One of these nymphs plays the double flute. And when our forbears heard the notes of a flute at dusk or by night, they knew that such notes were often an enticement to secret rites and initiations: they knew, too, that the secrets of these ceremonies could sometimes be repulsive and terrifying.

10

ACHELÖOS AND THE SIRENS

Any account of the Sirens must include a mention of Achelöos, the most revered of our river-gods, to whom, as well as to Phorkys,[130] is attributed the paternity of the Sirens. Hesiod[131] numbers Achelöos, him of the silver eddies, amongst the sons of Tethys and Okeanos—that is to say, amongst the river-gods —but not as the principal of these. Homer,[132] on the other hand, sets him even above Okeanos, the "origin of everything". Achelöos could beget seas and streams, springs and fountains, just as Okeanos could. When Okeanos was portrayed as an old man with the horns of a bull, the prototype for this por-trayal was Achelöos. In other pictures and descriptions, the shaggy head of Father Okeanos—which was finally only a mask, a countenance of deep, almost sorrowful gravity— sprouted a lobster's claw and feeler. The bull's horn played a special part in the tales concerning Achelöos. Herakles fought with this water-god, as well as with the Old One of the Sea and with Triton. Like these latter, Achelöos had a lower body consisting of a serpent-like fish. But his head was horned, and one of the horns was broken off by Herakles.[133] From the blood that dripped from the wound the Sirens were born: a birth similar to that of the Erinyes.

In our ancient tongue the Sirens were called *Seirenes*. This word, in its masculine form, was also the description of a species of bees or wasps—as also was the name of Pemphredo, one of the Graiai. Our ancient painters and designers upon vessels depicted the Sirens not only as female beings, but some-times as male and bearded. That the beings depicted are Sirens, either male or female, is shown by their having predominantly a bird's body, to which a human head is added, and often also a woman's breasts and arms. The talon-feet are often very powerful, and sometimes end in a lion's pads, as if to reveal a close kinship between Siren and Sphinx. The lower part

ACHELÖOS AND HERAKLES

of the body is sometimes shaped like an egg. Closely akin to the Sirens are also the Graiai, as "swanlike maidens", and likewise Medousa, at least in that picture in which a bird with a Gorgon's countenance and two pairs of wings seizes up a struggling youth in each hand and snatches them away. Such snatching creatures, however, are more properly Harpies, whose name means "Snatchers". The distinguishing charac-teristic of the Sirens, on the other hand, is—apart from their birdlike shape—their talent for music; and this connects them with the Muses. They play on the lyre or on the double flute; or, when two of them are portrayed together, one of them plays on the former and the other on the latter. And as they play they sing. To all this both the tales and the Sirens' own names bear witness, and so do the pictures of them. These pictures, which appear on the tombstones of our classical age, are of marvellous beauty, and clearly were inspired not by our seamen's fables, but by other old stories that are now forgotten.

The Sirens did, in fact, find their way into seamen's legend
—as did the great goddess Skylla. Homer puts a tale of them
into the mouth of the great liar Odysseus, who speaks of two
Sirens but does not tell their names. One of these names,
however—Himeropa, "she whose voice awakens desire"—is
to be found in an ancient vase-painting. Later on we find
mention of two trinities of Sirens. One of these is thought to
correspond to the Sirens of Homer. Their individual names
have been passed down in various forms: Thelxiepeia,
Thelxinoe or Thelxiope is "the enchantress", for *thelgein* means
"to enchant"; Aglaope, Aglaophonos or Aglaopheme is "she
of the glorious voice"; Peisinoe, or Pasinoe, may mean "the
seductive", if the former version is correct. A second trinity
is that of the Sirens who were worshipped in Graecia Major,
on the southern Tyrrhenian coast of Italy: Parthenope, "the
Virginal", in Neapolis, which is now called Naples; Leucosia,
"the White Goddess", and Ligeia, "she of the bright voice",
south of Naples.

As mothers of the Sirens, who bore them to Achelöos, are
mentioned Sterope[134] (which means the same as the Hesperi-
dean name Asterope) or, alternatively, one of the Muses.[135]
Older story-tellers had knowledge of another mother; and they
also knew of a close link between the Sirens and Persephone.
It was told[136] that the Sirens were companions of the Queen
of the Underworld; that they were daughters of Chthon,[137]
the "depths of the earth", and that Persephone sent them into
this world. An ancient vase-painting shows two Sirens singing
before a great goddess and gazing towards the ship of Odysseus,
which is being attacked from the air by two huge birds. It
was the Sirens' task to bring all approaching travellers before
the great Queen, to entice them into her presence by the sweet
tones of their music and song. And this they did not only
to unlucky seamen, but to all who must enter the realm of the
dead. By their art the bitterness of death is alleviated and disguised. Perhaps the male Sirens had the task of making death
sweeter for women.

ODYSSEUS AND THE SIRENS

Odysseus's story of the Sirens is as follows: Kirke had warned him[138] that he must steer clear of the voices and the flowery meadows of the Sirens; or, if he could not do this, then he alone might hear their bright voice, but first he must fill his shipmates' ears with wax and have himself bound to the mast. The Sirens sat in their meadow. It seemed to be covered with flowers; but—and here the story turns into a real bogy-tale, obviously a sailor's yarn—it was full of mouldering human bones and dried-up human skins. The words they sang to Odysseus, as he stood erect and bound, are also reported:[139] "Come hither, Odysseus famed in song, great glory of the Greeks! Bring your ship to, so that you may hear our voice. Never has any man voyaged past this place in his black ship without listening to our song. It flows like honey from our mouths. He who has heard it finds delight and gains wisdom. For we know all that the Greeks and Trojans suf-fered, by the will of the gods, for Troy. And we know all that happens on the earth, everywhere and at all times!" At these words Odysseus, according to his own story, wanted to be set free of his bonds; but his shipmates bound him all the more firmly. It is not to be wondered at that Odysseus felt thus: the Sirens made themselves out to be oracular goddesses, which perhaps, at the place where they had their shrine, they really were.

Nevertheless they were always goddesses of death and love, servants of the Goddess of the Underworld, Persephone. The goddess of the realm of the dead is, to a certain degree, herself also dead. The Sirens served death, and were themselves

doomed to die—or so one tale informs us[140]—if ever a ship
came by and the crew did not fall victim to them. When
Odysseus and his shipmates had escaped, the Sirens com-
mitted suicide. Hesiod told that Zeus gave the Sirens the island
of Anthemoessa, "rich in flowers", as their dwelling-place.[141]
This accords with the fact that they served not only death, but
also love. A carving in relief, of a later date, shows a Siren,
only the lower parts of whose legs are those of a bird, amorously
approaching a sleeping man who resembles a Satyr. The scene
is reminiscent of Selene's approach to Endymion. There was
something amorous also about the egg-like shape of the Sirens
as shown in early pictures of them: the more so as they often
clasped small human figures against their bodies. They served
not only the goddess of death, but also served human mortals
in that they carried men—or, at any rate, men's desires—on
golden wings to Heaven.[142]

II

THAUMAS, IRIS AND THE HARPIES

Thaumas, the great son of Pontos and Gaia,[143] brother of
Nereus and Phorkys, is probably only another name for the
Old One of the Sea.[144] For this reason he is said to be a
son of Tethys. *Thauma* means a "wonder", and Thaumas
must have been a "sea-wonder" in the same sense as that in
which his brothers were or Proteus was. The tricks of metamorphosis and magic practised by these three have already
been described. The Okeanine Elektra bore Thaumas the
following daughters:[145] Iris, a goddess whose name means
"Rainbow", and all the Harpies. All these daughters were
goddesses who intervened in the affairs and destinies of mortals.

Iris, the fleet-footed, but also having great wings, held the
office of Messenger. In our language, she was an *angelos*. There
was a cult-worship of her on Hekatesnesos, the island of
Hekate, near the island of Delos. Hekate herself was at one
time known as Angelos. In her capacity of Messenger, Hekate

was thought to be the daughter of Hera and Zeus. It was told[146] of her that she stole her mother's beauty-salve and gave it to Europa, Hera's rival. When Hera sought to punish Hekate for this, she fled first to the bed of a woman in childbirth, then to a funeral procession, and lastly to the Acherusian Sea in the Underworld, where she was purified by the Kabeiroi: an adventure, one would say, entirely typical of her! But Iris too, as I shall shortly relate, was in the habit of visiting the Under-world. Another figure with which Iris can perhaps be identi-fied is Eidothea, the daughter of Proteus, whose name refers to an *eidos*, a visible phenomenon such as the rainbow. To explain why Iris, the formally named Messenger of Heaven, used to be sent by the gods to the Underworld, let me tell the story as Hesiod told it.[147]

Far distant from the gods lives the Hated Goddess, Styx, in her famous palace beneath a high rock. There the sky is sup-ported by pillars of silver. Iris seldom journeys thither, over the wide plains of the sea. But if dissension and strife break out amongst the immortals, and if some dweller on Olympus takes refuge in a lie, then Zeus sends Iris to fetch the mighty Oath of the gods. She fetches it from afar, in a golden goblet, that cold water, known by many names, which gushes down from the high rock. It is the water of Styx. Like all other waters, this water, too, pours beneath the earth, in deep night, from the horn of Okeanos. Its stream is divided into ten parts. Nine arms encompass the earth and sea: the tenth arm flows from this rock, to the hurt of the gods. For whoever of them perjures himself by this water, he is at once struck down and lies unbreathing a whole year long. He comes no more to the ambrosia and nectar, to the food and drink of the immortals, but remains dumb and aswoon in his abode. After the end of the year, other and heavier punishments await him. For nine years he is banished from the councils and revels of the gods. Only in the tenth year may he again take part in their assemblies.

The Harpies are, like Iris, fleet-footed and winged. They

seldom appear in so birdlike a form as that of the Sirens. But
even when they have human fingers, these are bent like claws
for clutching and snatching. Indeed, their name means "the
Snatchers". The word *thuella* or *aella*, "the tearing wind", has
almost the same meaning. If any man disappeared at sea as
utterly as Odysseus, people would say: "The Harpies have
snatched him away."[148] Of the well-known story of the
daughters of Pandareos, which was told in the Odyssey, it is
further said[149] that the unhappy maidens, snatched from the
house of their dead father, were set by the Harpies to serve the
Erinyes. We already know that the Erinyes and the Harpies
were so alike that they could be mistaken for one another. A
further resemblance that the Harpies bear, a resemblance to
Medousa, is indicated by the Gorgon's countenance of the
Harpy with four wings; and it is also indicated by the fact
that, according to Homer,[150] a Harpy named Podarge, "the
fleet-footed", was raped, whilst "grazing" on the shores of
Okeanos, by Zephyros, the West Wind, and became mother
of the immortal horses of Achilleus, the horses Xanthos and
Balios. It will be remembered that a magic horse also sprang
from the neck of Medousa; and she herself was depicted by
ancient painters as having a horse's head or body. It seems that
at some time in our history our ancestors learnt to admire the
speed of the horse as much as they had admired the speed of
the wind and of the birds.

Hesiod gave us the names of two Harpies:[151] Aello, who
is also called Aellopus, "the wind-foot", and Okypete, "the
swift of flight", who is also called Okythoe or Okypode, "the
swift" or "the swift-footed". But the Harpies, just like the
Sirens and the Graiai, vary in number from two to three; and
we have record of a third name, Kelaino, "the dark one":[152]
a name that is also borne by one of the daughters of Atlas,
the Hesperides, another of whom was named Mapsaura, "the
Blast of Wind". Enemies and defeaters of the Harpies were
the winged sons of Boreas, the North Wind. These sons were
named Kalais and Zetes. They defeated the Harpies in the

THE HARPIES

story about the blind seer Phineus, on whose food the Harpies descended like great birds and stole or befouled it. In the version of this story told by the poet Apollonios Rhodios,[153] Iris also appears. She called out to the sons of Boreas that it was contrary to "the law of Nature"—contrary to Themis—to pursue "the Hounds of great Zeus" with swords. So pursuers and pursued halted and turned about at the islands that had formerly been called the Plotai, "the Swimmers", but were thenceforth called the Strophades, "the Isles of the Turning-point". The Harpies returned to the depths of the earth under the island of Crete, and Iris returned to Olympus.

12

THE DAUGHTERS OF NEREUS

Nereus had by Doris, the Okeanine,[154] fifty daughters, our famed sea-goddesses whose alluring forms—in earlier times clad, in later times naked—are so often seen riding on miraculous sea-monsters or on the back of a Triton. The oldest monster of this sort—that is to say, the oldest of which we have a picture—is a dog-fish, i.e. a dog in its fore part and a fish in its hind part. But no Nereids are riding upon it, and for the present we shall confine our attention to these beautiful goddesses, famous for their rosebud faces.[155]

That the daughters of Nereus were fifty in number we are expressly and repeatedly told—by Hesiod[156] amongst others, although he actually lists fifty-one of them: but his list, it should be added, includes a second Doris. The names of the Nereids are not exactly the same in all the accounts. Our poets loved these names for their sound and for the pleasant images and sensations that they evoked. That is why ever since Homer they have filled many lines of their poems with these names, without any fear that a mere recital of them might weary an audience. I may therefore be permitted, as a conclusion to my tales of the older, pre-Olympian divinities, to quote the list of Nereids as given by Hesiod. To this I shall add an explana-tion—whenever a clear explanation seems possible—of the names' meanings as our ancestors may have understood them.

The following, then, were the daughters of Nereus:[157] Ploto, "the swimmer"; Eukrante, "the bringer of fulfilment"; Sao, "the rescuer"; Amphitrite (who, as I shall later tell, became the wife of Poseidon); Eudora, "she of good gifts"; Thetis (of whom I have spoken and shall speak again); Galene, "calm weather"; Glauke, "the sea-green"; Kymothoe, "the wave-swift"; Speio, "the dweller in caves"; Thoe, "the nimble"; Halia, "the dweller in the sea"; Pasithea; Erato, "the awakener of desire" (which is the name also of one of the Muses); Eunike, "she of happy victory"; Melite; Eulimene, "she of good haven"; Agaue, "the noble"; Doto, "the giver"; Proto, "the first"; Pherousa, "the bringer"; Dynamene; Nesaia, "the dweller on islands"; Aktaia, "the dweller on coasts"; Protomedeia, "the first ruleress"; Doris (who, like Eudora, whose name has the same meaning, is also one of the Okeaninai); Panopeia; Galateia (that Aphrodite-like sea-goddess who was wooed by

NEREUS, DORIS AND THE NEREIDS

the Kyklops Polyphemos—the enemy, later on, of Odysseus
—and was loved by the beautiful Akis); Hippothoe, "swift
as a mare"; Hipponoe, "unruly as a mare"; Kymodoke, "the
wave-gatherer"; Kymatolege, "the wave-stiller"; Kymo, "the
wave-goddess"; Eione, "the shore-goddess"; Halimede, "the
sea-goddess of good counsel"; Glaukonome, "the dweller in
the green sea"; Pontopereia, "the seafarer"; Leiagora and
Euagora, "the eloquent"; Laomedeia, "ruleress of the people";
Polynoe, "giver of reason"; Autonoe, "giver of inspiration";
Lysianassa, "the redeeming mistress"; Euarne; Psamathe, "the
sand-goddess"; Menippe, "the courageous mare"; Neso, "the
island-goddess"; Eupompe, "she of good escort"; Themisto (a
sort of double of the great goddess Themis); Pronoe, "the
provident"; and Nemertes, "the truthful", who in knowing
and telling the truth resembles her immortal father.

That is the entirety of Hesiod's list of the Nereids. In other
lists other names were also mentioned. Not all of those named
were thought to be daughters of Doris.[158] In more recent
antiquity an attempt was made to distinguish between Nēreides
and Nērēides, and thus to prove that only the latter were
children of Doris. This distinction derives no authority from
any ancient tale. Amongst other Nereids not mentioned by

Hesiod is one previously named by Homer, Apseudes, "she who never lies":[159] she, like Nemertes, inherits her father's quality of a god who tells the truth. The sea-goddesses were also oracular goddesses. The oldest of them, Tethys, had an oracular shrine amongst the Etruscans. Her granddaughters, the daughters of Nereus, could often—or so it was believed—rescue seamen in danger of shipwreck. It was they, too, who revealed to men the mysteries of Dionysos and of Persephone.[160] A hymn attributed to the singer Orpheus contains a reference to this tale: but the tale itself has not been preserved. The tradition concerning a son of Nereus, Nerites, with whom Aphrodite first practised her amorous sport, has its proper place in the stories of the great Goddess of Love. These stories I shall now relate.

CHAPTER IV

The Great Goddess of Love

OUR great Goddess of Love was never ours alone. She is the same deity as our oriental neighbours worshipped under such barbarian names as Ishtar or Ashtaroth, which we later reproduced as Astarte. In the East she was a goddess who made peculiarly strong amorous demands, but was also abun⁄ dantly generous with the pleasures of love. In the heavens the star of morning and evening—the planet Venus—belonged to her; and amongst earthly creatures her especial possession was the dove. The stories that are told of her are not the same as our stories, but remind us of them. Here is one such story:[161] The fish in the river Euphrates found a marvellous great Egg. They pushed it ashore, a dove hatched it out, and thus was born the goddess of whom it is said that she is the kindest and most merciful to mankind. The oriental story of the goddess's young lover Thammuz (or, as we call him, Adonis, using the Semitic vocative form of his name, Adoni, "My Lord", as it were) was the original story concerning him. In this story the goddess may perhaps have caused his death, but only through excessive love.

With us the corresponding tale attached itself to Aphrodite, whose name is still faintly reminiscent of "Ashtaroth". In this story, which I shall presently tell, Aphrodite is still outside the ranks of the Olympian deities, and continued to be so, as far as this story is concerned, even after she was received amongst them. One reason why she remained aloof from Olympus was her great sphere of dominion elsewhere: as, for the same reason, did Hekate, to whom she becomes closely similar when she is found, under the name of Aphrodite Zerynthia on the Thracian coast, or of Genetyllis on the Attic coast, receiving sacrifices of dogs. For the Athenians she was "the oldest Moira".[162] Elsewhere, too, she was thought to resemble the

67

Moirai and the Erinyes, in being, like them, a daughter of Kronos.[163] On the other hand, the tale of her being directly begotten by Ouranos connected our great love-goddess for all time with the sea. For us she was the Anadyomene, the goddess who "emerges" from the salt waves; and she also had the additional name of Pelagia, "she of the sea".

Two other of her surnames afforded an opportunity for certain persons in Athens, who preferred the love of boys and whose views were expressed by Plato, to distinguish between an Aphrodite Pandemos, as "common love", and Aphrodite Ourania, as "heavenly love". The truth of the matter is that the name Pandemos expresses the presence of the goddess amongst all ranks and conditions of a people, whom she binds together in peace and amity; and the name Ourania bears witness to her origin as an oriental sky-goddess, in honour of whom her worshippers—as in Corinth, for example—made pilgrimages to a shrine on the summit of a mountain, where they were received in friendly fashion by the temple's hand-maidens.[164] These two surnames appear to be associated with a third name, and thus to form a trinity: as in the very ancient cult at Thebes, where the goddess had a third form as Apostrophia, "she who turns herself away".

Moreover, Aphrodite was not the love-goddess's only principal name. She also had the Greek name of Dione: this is the feminine form of Zeus, which in its formation resembles the Latin Diana and means a "goddess of the bright sky". Dione was also recognised as a water-goddess. At Dodona she was worshipped together with Zeus in his quality of a god of springs, being regarded as wife of the supreme god and herself a spring-goddess and giver of oracles. Hesiod numbered her amongst the Okeaninai,[165] and according to the followers of Orpheus she was a daughter of Ouranos.[166] The inaugura-tion of the oracle of Dodona was ascribed to a dove.[167] Those who sought to make the great goddess Aphrodite entirely subordinate to Zeus, as Homer did, declared that she was a daughter of the Olympian and of Dione.[168]

Running parallel with the tale that makes Aphrodite out to be a daughter of Zeus and Dione, that other tale whereby she was directly begotten by Ouranos continued to find accep⁄tance. It is with this tale that I shall begin the stories of the Great Goddess of Love.

I

THE BIRTH OF APHRODITE

The tale of Aphrodite's birth is preserved in Hesiod, and forms the continuation to the story of Ouranos, Gaia and Kronos. It begins with the goddess's first journey to the island of Cyprus, home of her oldest and most powerful shrines, those at Paphos and Amathus. The story was amplified in a hymn that was attributed to Homer. But first I shall tell the original tale.[169]

The excised manhood of Father Ouranos fell into the restless sea, into which Kronos had cast it from the firm earth. For a long time it was tossed hither and thither. White foam— *aphros*—gathered round it, formed from the immortal skin. A maiden sprang up and grew within it. She swam first to the island of Cythera, but afterwards to Cyprus. Here the beautiful, shy goddess arose from the water, and young grass sprouted at her feet. She is called Aphrodite by gods and men, because she was fashioned of foam. She is also called Kythereia, because it was to Cythera that she first swam. Eros and Himeros ("Desire", the double of the love⁄god) began to accompany her as soon as she was born and became a goddess. From her very beginning she was awarded charge and office, amongst both gods and men, over the following: the whisper⁄ing of maidens, laughter and hoaxes, sweet lust, love and loving kindness.

The Homeric hymn further tells[170] how on Cyprus Aphro⁄dite was received and clothed by the Horai. The Horai are the daughters of Themis, the goddess of the law and order proper to the natural relations of the sexes. Contemplation of the complete nakedness of the goddess would have been contrary to Themis—or such was the notion of our ancestors in ancient times, excepting the Dorians. Only when she had been clothed, wreathed and adorned could Aphrodite be brought amongst the gods. As soon as they saw her, they all kissed her, firmly grasped her hand, and sought to take her to wife in permanent wedlock. The stories of her marriage I shall tell presently, but shall conclude this part of my narrative with mentioning the tale of how Aphrodite was born from a cockle and landed in a cockle-shell on the island of Cythera.[171] In the town of Cnidus on the coast of Asia Minor the cockle was regarded as a creature sacred to the love-goddess. It was in this town that men of pure Greek stock, and not Orientals, first dared to set up a naked Aphrodite: the famous statue by the sculptor Praxiteles.

2

APHRODITE AND NERITES

The love-affair that Aphrodite is supposed to have had whilst yet in the sea, before her introduction amongst the gods of Olympus, has to do with a cockle. The narrator, who is of a late period, calls Aphrodite a daughter of Zeus. But even this story indicates that the pre-Olympian days of the goddess were passed in the sea.

It is told[172] that there exists a cockle, small but of marvellous beauty, living in the purest water, in the reefs beneath the sea-surface. Its name is Nerites, who formerly had been the only son of Nereus. (Hesiod knows only of the fifty daughters, and Homer of no more. The story of Nereus's son was told by people of the sea-coast.) Nerites was the fairest being of men and gods. As long as Aphrodite lived in the sea, she took pleasure only in him, and lived with him as with a lover. The time came, as was fated, when she was to be admitted amongst the Olympians, and the Father summoned her. She wanted to take her comrade and playmate to Olympus with her. But he preferred to live in the sea with his sisters and parents. She wanted to bestow wings upon him, but he had no desire for these, either. So the goddess changed him into the cockle, and took as her companion and servant the young love-god Eros; to whom, furthermore, she gave the wings.

Another story made Nerites out to be a darling of Poseidon and a double of Phaethon. As the lovely boy drove in his chariot over the waves, Helios was angered. But this is an even later story than the one I have just told.

3

APHRODITE, ARES AND HEPHAISTOS

There were tales in which Aphrodite took to husband the war-god Ares. In other tales she was the wife of Hephaistos. Lastly there is a story, made famous by Homer, in which the love-goddess betrays her husband Hephaistos with Ares. Her union with the war-god resulted, according to the tales of the Thebans,[173] in the birth of the beautiful Harmonia, "the uniter", who was a second Aphrodite. Her husband was Kadmos, the dragon-slayer and founder of Thebes, whose name will reoccur in the story of Europa. Other children attributed to Ares and Aphrodite were, on the one hand, Phobos and Deimos, "Fear" and "Terror",[174] and, on the other hand, Eros and Anteros, "Love" and "Answering Love".[175] All this, however, is scarcely mythology, but mere genealogy. According to another genealogy, Eros's father was Hephaistos.[176]

I shall have much to say about Hephaistos. Let it suffice for the moment to say that he was, according to most tales, a skilled and sturdy master metalworker, yet at the same time only a crippled craftsman dwarf. He created young virgins made of gold,[177] who moved as if they were alive, and thought and talked and worked. He fashioned the first woman,

Pandora.[178] She was not his wife, but the wife of beings closely resembling him. Hephaistos's wife—according to Homer, in his Iliad,[179] and according to Hesiod—was the youngest of the Graces, Aglaia, "the glorious".[180] Did more ancient tales (which these poets knew) mean that she, too, was a living work of art? It may be so, for *charis* ("grace") also means the delightfulness of art. Or was it their purpose to give the smith-god a lesser Aphrodite for wife, instead of the great one? In any case, in our tongue the love-goddess could also have been called Charis. In the Odyssey, the spouse of Hephaistos was Aphrodite, and Ares was her lover.

A singer of the people of the Phaeacians,[181] who were still closer to the gods than we were, sang how Aphrodite and the war-god first fell in love with one another. It happened in the palace of the husband. None knew of it, and Ares had given much to be able to violate the marriage of Hephaistos. The Sun saw them in the act of love, and at once informed the famed master-smith. The latter was grieved by the news, and quickly went into his smithy and thought dark thoughts. He set up the great anvil and wrought chains that could be neither torn asunder nor unfastened, but were invisible, delicate as cobwebs. He hung them over the bedposts and departed, or so he pretended, for Lemnos, his beloved island with its beautifully built city. This was the opportunity for which Ares had been waiting. Full of desire for the beautiful Aphrodite, he entered the master-smith's palace. She had just returned from a visit to Zeus, her father, and was sitting indoors. Ares entered, seized her hand and cried: "Come, beloved, let us lie down and rejoice in our love! Hephaistos is far away, he is gone to Lemnos, to his foreign-tongued people the Sintians!" She, too, yearned to lie with him. So they went to bed, and then they fell asleep. The skilfully wrought chains of Hephaistos closed in upon them, so that they could not move a limb, much less stand up. Then for the first time they knew that they were trapped.

In came the sturdy master-smith—for the Sun was still on

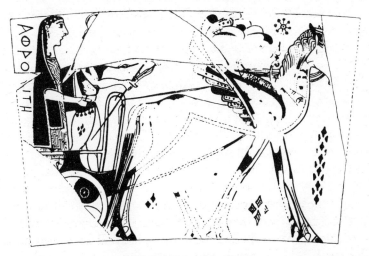

APHRODITE AND ARES

the watch and had betrayed the lovers. In the doorway stood
the husband, wild with rage, and called in a terrible voice to
all the gods: "Father Zeus and all the rest of you, blessed and
eternal gods! Come and see what mockery and shame we
have here! See how Aphrodite, the daughter of Zeus, continually brings shame upon me, because I am a cripple! She
loves the baleful Ares, because he is fair and his feet are alike,
whilst I go limping. Yet only my parents are to blame for that:
they should never have begotten me! But see how those two
sleep there, drowsy with love, in my own bed! They offend
my sight. For a long time yet, I think, they shall lie there, for
they love each other so dearly—yet they shall have no wish to
go on lying: my chains will hold them fast, until the father
decides to pay me back the gifts that I gave him for the shameless
hussy! For his daughter is beautiful, but she is not chaste!"

So he spoke, and the gods assembled in his palace, in the
house with the brazen threshold. In came Poseidon, Hermes
and Apollo. The goddesses stayed modestly at home. The gods
stood by the door, and unquenchable laughter seized hold of
the blessed ones as they perceived the artifice of cunning

Hephaistos. They said one to the other: "No good comes of a wrongful deed. The slow catches the swift. He who is taken in adultery must make atonement!" Apollon asked Hermes: "Would you like to lie in such chains with the golden Aphrodite?" And Hermes answered: "Ah, if only I might, I would willingly be bound in chains three times as strong! And all you gods and goddesses might come and look at me —so gladly would I lie beside the golden Aphrodite." The immortals laughed, all but Poseidon. He besought the master-smith to set Ares free, and promised on behalf of all the gods that fitting atonement should be made to him. Unwillingly Hephaistos consented and unchained the pair. They sprang away: Ares to the land of the Thracians, Aphrodite to Cyprus, to her temple in Paphos. There the Graces welcomed her and bathed her. They anointed the goddess with that immortal oil whose fragrance always clings to the gods, and they wrapped her again in her marvellously beautiful and delightful raiment.

4

THE STORY OF PYGMALION

In Cyprus Pygmalion was thought to have been a king and one of Aphrodite's lovers. We do not know how his name was pronounced amongst the non-Greek worshippers of the goddess, or what it meant to them: amongst us it also took the form "Pygmaion", which may have had for us the same meaning as *pygmaios*, a dwarf. (In primitive times other islands in the eastern Mediterranean besides Cyprus were inhabited, according to our ancient tales, by beings who can be described equally well as dwarfs or as great gods. Amongst these were the Kabeiroi of Samothrace and the craftsmen Telchines of Rhodes. In Lemnos Hephaistos was another such.)

It was told[182] that King Pygmalion fell in love with the naked, ivory idol of Aphrodite; for a cult-image of this sort was not uncommon amongst the non-Greek peoples of ancient times. He sought to take the statue to wife, and laid it in his bed. This, of course, is only a fragment of a story. But it was also told[183] that Pygmalion himself fashioned the beautiful woman's figure in ivory, and fell deeply in love with it. In his desperate love he prayed to Aphrodite, and the goddess took pity on him. The statue came alive, and Pygmalion married it. It bore him Paphos, whose son Kinyras founded the city of Paphos, where Aphrodite's shrine is.

According to this tale the worship of the love-goddess began only with Pygmalion and his creation of the naked idol. Of Pygmaion it is said[184] that he was, like Adonis, Aphrodite's lord and loved one.

5

THE STORY OF ADONIS

The story of the lord and loved one of the great Goddess of Love was connected—amongst us, and presumably also in the eastern countries where it was adopted, in Syria, Cyprus and Asia Minor—with the story of a tree, of that Arabian shrub whose strongly fragrant gum the peoples of antiquity prized most of all their congealed saps. The gum was called "myrrh" or "smyrna".

The tale goes[185] that Myrrha (or Smyrna) was a king's daughter; a daughter of King Theias of Lebanon, or of King Kinyras of Cyprus, founder of Paphos—or variously a daughter of other kings whom I need not mention. Myrrha fell mortally in love with her father. (Various reasons were given for this: the wrath of the sun-god, or the wrath of Aphrodite. Myrrha was supposed to have thought her hair lovelier than that of the goddess; and there are other similar stories.) The daughter succeeded in deceiving her father, or in making him drunk—an occurrence also found in a Biblical tale. She slept with him as an unknown wench for twelve nights, or for less. At last her father discovered, by the light of a hidden lamp, who his bedmate was, and pursued her with a drawn sword. Myrrha had already conceived a child of this forbidden love, and was full of shame. She prayed to the gods that she might be nowhere, neither amongst the living nor amongst the dead. Some deity, possibly Zeus or Aphrodite, took pity on her, and she was turned into the tree that weeps its fruit in spicy gum, the fruit of the wood: Adonis. For he, the future lover of Aphrodite, was born from the riven bark of the myrrh-tree.

Adonis was beautiful, so beautiful that as soon as he was born Aphrodite hid the child in a chest and gave the chest to Persephone for safe keeping. The Queen of the Underworld opened the chest, saw the beautiful boy and did not want ever to give him back. The dispute between the two goddesses was brought before Zeus. The king of the gods shared out the possession of Adonis as follows: for a third part of the year he was to dwell by himself; for a third part with Persephone; and for a third part with Aphrodite. Of the death of Adonis, which every year carried him off to Persephone in the Underworld, it was most commonly said that he was wounded by a boar while hunting. His blood ran down, red anemones sprang up from it, and the brook Adonis in Lebanon ran red.[186] It is thought that Artemis or Ares sent the boar against the lad.[187] Aphrodite was thus compelled to mourn for Adonis before she could truly possess him. The festivals at which her woeful love was celebrated were held in commemoration of the day of the love-goddess's parting from her young lord. He lay there wounded unto death, loved and wept over by Aphrodite.[188] In vain she tried to hold him back. On the next day he soared away through sea and air. It used to be said, however, that he was still alive. Women brought him little "gardens"—a symbol and picturesque expression, which was common in our tongue, as in others, for their own femininity. In eastern shrines they gave themselves to strangers. Whoever did not do this must at least sacrifice her hair to Adonis.

6

APHRODITE AND ANCHISES

The stories concerning the great love-goddess that I have hitherto been telling had their settings on the south-eastern edge of our Greek world—in Cyprus and in Syria. The scene of the next story is the region of Troy, in Asia Minor. Aphrodite appears accompanied by wild beasts: this connects her with the "Mother of the Gods", whom I shall presently describe, thus concluding my account of the deities who either were pre-Olympian or at least remained aloof from Olympus. The story was passed down to us in a hymn attributed to Homer.[189]

There were three goddesses over whom Aphrodite had no power: Athene, Artemis and Hestia. All other gods and goddesses succumbed to her, and she even compelled Zeus himself to fall in love with mortal women and to neglect his own wife-sister Hera, daughter of Kronos and Rhea. This was why Aphrodite, in her turn, was compelled by Zeus to fall in love with the herdsman Anchises. He pastured his cattle on the heights of Mount Ida, and was as beautiful as the immortals. Aphrodite beheld him, and love seized hold of her. She hastened to Cyprus, to her temple in Paphos. She shut the temple doors behind her, the Graces bathed her and anointed the great goddess with the oil of the immortals, whose fragrance clings to the eternal gods. In beautiful raiment and adorned with gold she returned swiftly to Troy, to Mount Ida, to the mother of wild beasts.

She made her way through the mountains to the cattlesheds. Behind her came, waving their tails, grey wolves, fiercely staring lions, bears and swift leopards, insatiable in their hunger for gazelles. The goddess rejoiced at the sight of them and filled the hearts of the beasts with love, so that they all lay down in couples in the shade of the forests. Aphrodite entered the herdsmen's tent and found Anchises alone. He was walking to and fro and playing on a lute. Aphrodite stood before him in the form of a beautiful, tender mortal maiden. Anchises beheld her and was astonished at her beauty, her stature and her splendid clothing. She wore a robe whose redness was more dazzling than fire; her breasts shone marvellously, as if they were bathed in moonlight. Love seized upon Anchises, and he spoke to the goddess. He hailed her as an immortal, promised her an altar and sacrifices, and besought her blessing upon himself and his posterity. Thereupon the goddess lied to him, telling him that she was a mortal maiden, a Phrygian princess who could also speak the language of the Trojans. Hermes had carried her off, so she said, from the choir of Artemis, in which she had been dancing with her playmates and with nymphs, and had carried her to Mount Ida through the air from Phrygia. For she was summoned—so the divine messenger had said—to become the wife of Anchises. But she desired the herdsman to leave her untouched until he had shown her to his parents and brothers, whose daughter-in-law and sister-in-law she was to be; and she wished also, before the wedding was celebrated, to send a message to her parents concerning the dowry.

These words of the goddess provoked Anchises to still greater love. "If you are a mortal maiden, and destined to be my wife, then neither god nor man shall hold me back from you. Even though Apollo should thereafter slay me, I wish to love you now, at once, and then die!" So the herdsman cried, and seized Aphrodite's hand. She followed him to his bed, repeatedly turning back as if she sought to retreat and casting down her lovely eyes. On soft sheets lay hides of bears and lions that Anchises himself had made his prey. He took off his bride's adornments, loosened her girdle and uncovered her. In accordance with the will of the gods the mortal lay with the immortal goddess, without knowing what he did. Not until the hour when the other herdsmen were due to return did Aphrodite awaken her sleeping lover and show herself to him in her true form and beauty. Anchises was dismayed when he saw her lovely eyes. He turned away from her, covered his face and begged her to save him. For no mortal man remains in good health for all the rest of his life, when he has slept with a goddess.

It is further told that Aphrodite prophesied the utmost good for the son whom she conceived of Anchises, and for his descendants. The son was Aineias, who was later to be famed amongst our Italian neighbours as founder of the Latin nation. For her own part the goddess lamented that she had given herself to a mortal. Anchises was not to reveal to anyone that she was the mother of the son, whom the nymphs would bring to him as if the child belonged to one of themselves. If he did so, Zeus's lightning would strike him. It is reported[190] that Anchises was later lamed by a lightning-stroke. But there was also a tale that he was punished with blindness for having seen the goddess naked. Bees stung out his eyes.[191]

7

APHRODITE'S SURNAMES

Our mythology has lost all too many stories concerning just those deities who are best known to us. The gist of the tales was contained in the figure of the deity itself, but no single tale could present the whole figure in all its aspects. The gods lived in the soul of our ancestors, and did not enter completely into any one story. Nevertheless each story—now as then—contains some living part of them, a contribution to their entirety. The tales, for their part, cannot be completely contained in a single word, in the name or in one of the surnames of the divinity concerned. Yet they are to some extent comprised in these names: as, for example, the tale of Aphrodite's birth is contained in her surname of Anadyomene. For this reason such surnames as have been preserved are necessary to an understanding of our mythology. In the case of Aphrodite, a few more, at least, of her names must be mentioned, so that all aspects of our great love-goddess may be brought to light.

In our language the word *aphrodite* acquired the meaning, "pleasure of love". In the ancient poets this gift of the goddess is accompanied by the adjective *chruse*, "golden". This must not, however, be understood in too narrow a sense, for it also expresses the whole atmosphere of Ourania, the Oriental "Heavenly One", who in Cyprus also bore the surname of Eleemon, "the merciful". This atmosphere already becomes restricted when we find the courtesans of old worshipping the goddess as one of themselves, as Aphrodite Hetaira or Porne. In this restricted atmosphere arose the works of art that portrayed the beauty of the goddess as "Kalligloutos" or "Kallipygos", "she of the beautiful buttocks", with her dress lifted high around her: this occurred at a time when our sculptors had generally succeeded in dispelling the awe with which the nakedness of the bathing goddess had formerly been regarded. In Sparta, where women enjoyed great freedom in matters of love, Aphrodite had the surname "Mistress", which was also the name of Zeus's wife-sister: she was called Aphrodite Hera. In a shrine amongst the Spartans she was worshipped under two surnames: either, bearing weapons, as Aphrodite Enoplios; or, in chains, as Aphrodite Morpho, "the shapely" or "she of various shapes", which was probably another name for that Eurynome, the mother of the Graces, who, as I shall presently relate, was two-shaped and enchained. In Sparta Aphrodite was also called Ambologera, "she who postpones old age". At Athens she had her own gardens as *Aphrodite en kepois* and was worshipped as Ourania and as the oldest Moira. On Cape Colias, on the Attic coast, she was also Genetyllis, which is the same as the *Venus Genetrix* of the Latins, a patron-goddess of childbirth. She was the chief of a group of three goddesses, and received, like Hekate, sacrifices of dogs. A beautiful vase-painting shows her riding on a swan, and as Epitragidia she sat on a buck.

Another aspect of Aphrodite, with which the buck also must have had something to do, is expressed in such surnames as Melaina and Melainis, "the black one", and Skotia "the dark one". In so far as this refers to the darkness that love seeks, this aspect is connected with the aspect already described. But the black Aphrodite can equally well be associated with the Erinyes, amongst whom she was also numbered. Such surnames as Androphonos, "Killer of Men", Anosia, "the Unholy" and Tymborychos, "the Gravedigger", indicate her sinister and dangerous potentialities. As Epitymbidia she is actually "she upon the graves". Under the name of Persephaessa she is invoked as the Queen of the Underworld. She bears the title of Basilis, "Queen". Her surname of Pasiphaessa, "the far-shining", associates her also with the moon-goddess. All these characteristics are evidence that at one time there were tales which identified the goddess of love with the goddess of death, as a being comparable to the *Venus Libitina* of the Romans. The masculine form of Aphrodite's name, Aphroditos, leads us to presuppose another group of tales. The goddess was worshipped under a similar name at Amathus in Cyprus, where she was depicted as having a beard. We shall presently deal with the double sex of the Mother of Gods in Asia Minor, and later with the Hermaphroditos, a figure which was a product of this characteristic of the great goddess of love.

CHAPTER V

The Great Mother of the Gods and her Companions

THE title of Great Mother, or Mother of the Gods, or of both names at once, was given to only one of the daughters of Gaia and Ouranos: namely, to Rhea, who had borne to Kronos the three world-ruling gods Zeus, Poseidon and Hades, and the three goddesses Hera, Demeter and Hestia. This was the origin of the entire younger generation of Olympian gods, so that the goddess from whom all these were descended might well be called the Great Mother of the Gods. An even better right to this title, of course, is possessed by Mother Earth, Gaia, who produced even Father Ouranos from within herself. In fact it was only in the Hesiodic genealogy that so strong a distinction was made between Gaia and Rhea that the former became the latter's mother. The stories concerning Rhea pre-suppose that it was she who was the First Mother and herself produced her male helpers and comrades, either extracting them from the earth or, in other stories, being made fruitful by the sky-god.

Rhea was, admittedly, no more *our* Great Mother than the great love-goddess was ours alone. (Amongst our Oriental neighbours, in Asia Minor and Syria and in regions still farther east, it is not always easy to distinguish between the two.) In Asia Minor, especially, Rhea was worshipped as *Meter oreia*, "Mountain-mother", to mention one of her many names, which were almost always formed from the name of a mountain and indicated a relationship to a mountain land-scape—such names as Berekyntia, Dindymene, Idaia. In the territory of Asia Minor, from which her cult was spread and, indeed, often came back to us, she was called, in Phrygia, Matar Kubile, which in our language is Kybele. She can be recognised in the Cretan Mistress of the Beasts, who appears, flanked by two lions, on the summit of a mountain. Her well-known enthroned figure, however, she first acquired as Phrygian Mother of the Gods. She usually wears a rampart-crown, like a city on her head, and plays with a lion or drives a chariot drawn by lions.

Her festive procession included male beings who accompanied her in wild, ecstatic dance, to the shrill tone of "highland instruments"—flutes, cymbals, hand-drums, rattles, and, in the oldest times, also bull-roarers. These beings may originally have been men, but they imitated spirits of gods such as in our language are called *daimones*, "demons". In Phrygia the divine servants of the goddess were called Berekyndai. Their best-known name was "Korybantes". I shall presently mention the names given to similar gods amongst ourselves: these names are almost all that has survived from the tales of the Great Mother. For the most part her attendant beings were identified with the Korybantes, who will not, therefore, play any particular part in the tales I shall now relate.

I

IDAEAN DAKTYLOI AND KOURETES

I have already told how Rhea, when she was in process of bearing Zeus, the future father of gods and men, came to Crete and hid the child in a cave of Mount Aigaion, near Lyktos.[192] Other places besides this mountain and this cave had claims to having been the birthplace and nursery of our supreme god: Mount Dikte and Mount Ide—each of which has a sacred cave—were both thought to have had this honour. The latter mountain, which is in Crete, had the same name as Mount Ida in Asia Minor, haunt of the Great Mother of the Gods. The Cretan mountain is the scene of the following story:

On Ide Rhea awaited the time of her delivery.[193] When the due time came and the birth-pangs began, in her torment she supported herself with both hands on the soil. The mountain at once brought forth as many spirits, or gods, as the goddess had fingers. These beings stood around her and assisted at the birth. They were called the Daktyloi Idaioi, the "Idaean Fingers", from Mount Ide and from the fingers of Rhea, but were also called Kouretes or Korybantes. (I have already mentioned that the companions of the Mother of the Gods in Asia Minor were called Korybantes.) The name Kouretes means "youths": they were commonly three in number, armed with sword and shield and performing a weapon-dance around Rhea's newborn child. They made a din with their iron weapons, to drown the wailing of the child so that Kronos might not hear it. It was also told[194] that they grew from the earth after rain, or from the tears of the divine child.[195] They were closely associated with the divine boy (the *kouros*), and were also supposed to be sons of the Daktyloi.[196]

Daktulos means literally "finger", and for this reason there are ten of them in the story I have just related, whereas the Kouretes are three in number. There were, however, also tales of nine Kouretes, or of whole peoples of Kouretes, of nine or ten Korybantes, and of a hundred Idaean Daktyloi. In still other stories the number of Daktyloi Idaioi was different, and they also varied amongst themselves in nature. It was told[197] that there were twenty right-hand and thirty-two left-hand Daktyloi; that the right-hand ones had been smiths and the left-hand ones magicians; or that the left-hand ones had laid spells and the right-hand ones had broken spells; or that the right-hand ones were men who discovered iron and invented metallurgy, and the left-hand ones were their sisters.[198] Elsewhere five Idaean Daktyloi are mentioned. Of these, three bear names appropriate to men skilled in healing—Paionios, Epimedes, Iasios. A fourth was called Idas. The chief of them was Herakles—not the son of Zeus and Alkmene, so we were assured, but the Idaean Daktylos who inaugurated the Olympic Games by setting his four brothers to race against each other. Again, there was a tale of only three Daktyloi, who served the Phrygian Great Mother: and this exact number has—as on so many other occasions—a particular significance in their story.

The three Idaioi Daktyloi, servants of Adrasteia (for in this story[199] the Phrygian Great Mother is so named), were Kelmis, Damnameneus and Akmon. They were the first smiths, savage, earth-born, primitive men, and at the same time tools. Akmon means "anvil"; Damnameneus means "the compeller"—that is to say, in this case, the hammer; Kelmis most probably means "knife". This last was the unfortunate one of the three brothers, between the anvil and the hammer. It was told[200] that the boy Kelmis had been a loyal comrade of the little Zeus, but had insulted Rhea, who was his mother as well as Zeus's. As a punishment he was turned to steel—which is what happens to iron between anvil and hammer, if it is to be made into a good knife. It is also said[201] that the two other brothers were hostile towards the third. The same relationship is found in a certain story of three Korybantes, which I shall tell presently.

In the tale that mentions two Daktyloi,[202] it is especially stressed that they sat beside the Idaean Mother, shared her throne and were the "leaders of the Moirai" amongst all the many Kabeiroi. The names of these two were Titias and Kyllenos. It may be that these names refer to the pronouncedly phallic character of the Daktyloi, and described two figures that were simply phalluses. It was told[203] that the nymph Anchiale—which is still another name for the Great Mother —caused them to spring up in the Dictaean cave by clutching the earth with both hands in her torment. (As will be remembered, she had leant heavily on the soil in her birth-pangs.) According to this tale, however, not ten but only two "Fingers" sprang up beneath the hand of the goddess, whom they thenceforth accompanied. In all these stories the Daktyloi were servants and instruments of the Great Mother, obstetricians, smiths and magicians, who may also be described, by reason of their seemingly small stature, as craftsmen-dwarfs.

2

KABEIROI AND TELCHINES

The Kabeiroi, too, were servants of the Great Mother. It was known in ancient times[204] that they were called Kabeiroi after Mount Kabeiros in the country of Berekyntia, which be‑longed to the Phrygian Great Mother, and came thence to Samothrace, their sacred island. Their name always sounded foreign to us, and must have belonged to the same barbarian language as was preserved in Samothrace as the language of the religion and mysteries of the Kabeiroi. It was perhaps akin to the language of the ancient inhabitants of Lemnos, the foreign‑speaking worshippers of Hephaistos. It was said of the Kabeiroi[205] that they were the Idaioi Daktyloi, who had come westwards from Phrygia and whose magical practices had made the inhabitants of Samothrace the first converts to their secret cult. It was also believed that Orpheus had been one of their pupils at that time. It is said that the Mother of the Gods herself had settled her sons, the Korybantes, on Samo‑thrace;[206] but nobody was allowed to reveal who their father was, since this was told only in the secret cult. In these stories the Daktyloi, the Kouretes, the Korybantes and the Telchines are sometimes only a few primitive beings and sometimes entire primitive peoples—who, in comparison with the great size of the Mother, were, as I have said, of dwarfish stature.

Nevertheless the Kabeiroi were called amongst us *megaloi theoi*, "great gods". This was how our seamen invoked them, as rescuing gods in moments of danger. They were also called Kouretes and Korybantes, and in Lemnos also Hephaistoi, in the plural. On the mainland opposite—that is to say, in Macedonia—the following tale was told about them:[207] there were once three Korybantes, three brothers, two of whom murdered the third. They wrapped the head of the murdered brother in a purple robe, wreathed it and carried it on a brazen shield to the foot of Mount Olympus, where they buried it.

The same two brothers also carried the basket of mysteries, containing a phallus, the male member of Dionysos, to the country of the Etruscans. Of the stories told on the islands we now know almost nothing but names and genealogies. Kabeiro, mother of the Kabeiroi, she whose name was trans-lated in our language as Rhea, Demeter, Hekate or Aphrodite, was a daughter of Proteus:[208] or so, at least, it was said in Lemnos. Kabeiro bore to Hephaistos the boy Kadmilos. The latter begat three Kabeiroi and three Cabirian Nymphs. This genealogy makes no special mention of two brothers. In Samo-thrace, on the other hand, there stood on both sides of the entrance to the All-Holiest two brazen phallic statues like our statues of Hermes. They were said[209] to be twin brothers, sons of Zeus, the Dioskouroi. In the All-Holiest itself stood—so much even an uninitiate may guess—the third brother, who was worshipped both as a small and as a great Kabeiros, as a small Kadmilos and as the great and mysterious Korybas. His relationship with the Great Mother was kept secret. But it has been said that the father of the Korybantes was also kept secret, and yet it was revealed in a genealogy that the Kabeiroi and their Nymphs were descended from Kadmilos. "Kory-bantes" and "Kabeiroi" are well known to be two names for the same beings. The boy Kadmilos and the father of the Kabeiroi seem to have been one and the same person. You here recognise an identification by which the Great Mother is doubly connected with her youngest son: he is both her husband and her child. This relation between the two is often to be found in tales concerning our mysteries. The four names of divinities that reached us from Samothrace—Axieros, Axiokersa, Axiokersos and Kadmilos—were said[210] to be identical with Demeter, Persephone, Hades and Hermes respectively.

The Kabeiroi of Lemnos were smiths: that is why they were called Hephaistoi. Of beings of this quality, and also of their quality as sea-gods, which is common to them all, the tales concerning the Telchines tell us more, although the stories of the latter, too—and especially the ancient stories—have for the most part disappeared. On the island of Rhodes "Telchines" was the name of beings similar to those whom I have already mentioned under so many names. The Telchines had a more markedly Underworld character: they were famed as evil magicians, and they jealously guarded the secrets of their art.[211] On the other hand, it was they who made the first images of the gods.[212] It was furthermore told[213] that they were nine in number, and that they came to Crete with Rhea to rear the child Zeus. They were more widely known, however, as the rearers of Poseidon.[214] In this latter task they were helped by Okeanos's daughter Kapheira—a name that reveals the ancient identity of these divinities with the Kabeiroi. Kapheira and the Telchines were entrusted by Rhea with the charge of the child Poseidon. (I shall come back to this story.) There were also tales of hostility between the Telchines and Apollon,[215] as a result of which hostility the younger god destroyed the older ones. For us the sun-god ruled as supreme deity over Rhodes, which Zeus had given him as his portion.[216] According to one tale,[217] the Telchines foresaw the coming of the Flood, and thereupon departed from Rhodes. They, too, like the rest of the Daktyloi, are represented as an entire primitive people, although they were originally a small group of servants of the Great Mother.

3

THE STORY OF ATTIS

I must not omit the only known detailed story of a servant of the Great Mother—even though the tale is not Greek. The Mother of the Gods to whom it refers is entirely Phrygian. She is called Agdistis, from the rock named Agdos, near Pessinus, a town sacred to her. Her lover Attis was even less Greek than Aphrodite's lover Adonis. In other respects the two couples betray certain similarities—especially when one bears in mind that in Amathus the great love-goddess was likewise double-sexed. The hermaphroditism of the Great Mother of Asia Minor is reflected, amongst us, in the fact that, on the one hand, she was identified with our virgin huntress, the goddess Artemis, and was actually known as Megale Artemis, "the great Artemis"; and that, on the other hand, she could also be depicted with many breasts, as a Great Mother. In the version in which the Phrygian story of her was told to us, our gods, too, played a part. But this is merely a matter of nomenclature. When "Zeus" occurs in the story, the name may be taken to mean the Phrygian sky-god Papas.

The Agdos rock—so the story runs[218]—had assumed the shape of the Great Mother. Zeus fell asleep upon it. As he slept, or as he strove with the goddess, his semen fell upon the rock. In the tenth month the Agdos rock bellowed and brought forth an untamable, savage being, of twofold sex and twofold lust, named Agdistis. With cruel joy Agdistis plundered, murdered and destroyed whatever it chose, cared for neither gods nor men, and held nothing mightier on earth or in heaven than itself. The gods often consulted together as to how this insolence could be tamed. When they all hesitated, Dionysos took over the task. There was a certain spring to which Agdistis came to assuage its thirst when it was overheated with sport and hunting. Dionysos turned the springwater into wine. Agdistis came running up, impelled by thirst, greedily drank the strange liquor and fell perforce into deepest sleep. Dionysos was on the watch. He adroitly made a cord of hair, and with it bound Agdistis's male member to a tree. Awakened from its drunkenness, the monster sprang up and castrated itself by its own strength. The earth drank the flowing blood, and with it the torn-off parts. From these at once arose a fruit-bearing tree: an almond-tree or—according to another tale—a pomegranate-tree. Nana, the daughter of the king or river-god Sangarios (Nana is another name for the great goddess of Asia Minor), saw the beauty of the fruit, plucked it and hid it in her lap. The fruit vanished, and Nana conceived a child of it. Her father imprisoned her, as a woman deflowered, and condemned her to death by starvation. The Great Mother fed her on fruits and on the foods of the gods. She gave birth to a little boy. Sangarios had the child left out in the open to perish. A he-goat tended the suckling, who, when he was found, was fed upon a liquor called "he-goat's milk". He was named Attis, either because *attis* is Lydian for a handsome boy or because *attagus* was Phrygian for a he-goat.

Attis was a boy of marvellous beauty. The tale goes on that Agdistis fell in love with him. The savage deity took the grown lad out hunting, led him into the most inaccessible wildernesses and gave him spoils of the chase. Midas, King of Pessinous, sought to separate Attis from Agdistis, and to this end gave the boy his own daughter to wife. Agdistis appeared at the wedding and drove the participants mad with the notes of a syrinx. Attis castrated himself beneath a pine-tree, crying out: "Unto thee, Agdistis!" And thus he died. From his blood sprang the violets. Agdistis was repentant and besought Zeus to bring Attis back to life. All that Zeus, in accordance with Fate, could grant was that Attis's body should never putrefy, his hair should evermore continue to grow and his smallest finger should remain alive and move of its own accord.

CHAPTER VI

Zeus and his Spouses

IN order to avoid giving an entirely strange picture of Greek Mythology, I must now pass on to tales of Zeus and his spouses. Only with Zeus's accession to power, with the appearance of his male visage, did this mythology become *ours*—the mytho﹍logy that in later times was always recognised as Greek. One must not, of course, forget the tales dominated by the figures of the great goddesses—of the Strong Threefold One (usually called Hekate), of the Merciful Aphrodite and of Mother Rhea: without these stories the picture would be equally false.

Zeus did not come to power simply by means of his victory over the Titans: a victory which he owed, indeed, to Mother Gaia and some of her children. His dominion was founded much more upon marriages, upon alliances with Gaia's daughters and granddaughters. Of these Hesiod gives first mention to his union with Metis, and mentions last of all his marriage with Hera. In the following account of these mar﹍riages I shall start with Hera, adopting an old story to which Homer refers, although the story itself is now forgotten. The stories of Metis and of another famous wife of Zeus, Leto, will follow somewhat later, together with the tales concerning their still more famous children. Before telling the stories of Zeus's marriages, however, let me first speak of Hestia, who was the eldest daughter and first child of Kronos and Rhea, but after﹍wards became also their youngest child, since she was the first to be devoured by her father and the last to be yielded up again.

Hestia was wooed by one of the three brothers, Poseidon, and by one of the younger gods, Apollon.[219] They wooed her in vain, for after the defeat of the Titans she had asked of Zeus the dignity of remaining a virgin and of receiving the first victim of every sacrifice; and Zeus had granted her this. She obtained as her sacred place the central point of the house, the hearth—which is also the meaning of her name. Moreover, she received not only the first, but also the last sacrifice at every ceremonial assembly of mortals. Here and there a tale was told[220] of her having been attacked by Priapos or some other phallic god; but there is no story of Hestia's ever having taken a husband or ever having been removed from her fixed abode.

I

ZEUS'S BIRTH AND CHILDHOOD

I have spoken more than once of the birth of Zeus. But one cannot help noticing that such stories of his birth as have been preserved pass all too quickly on to the care and feeding of him as a divine child. The birth begins with the pangs of the great Mother of the Gods, but she remains wrapped in the darkness of night—a story in contrast with that of the birth of Apollon, which takes place, so to speak, in full public view. Rhea came in deep night[221] to Lyktos in Crete and hid her child in the cave of Mount Aigaion. According to another story,[222] Zeus was born in Arcadia, on Mount Lykaion, on whose summit, in the sacred region of Zeus Lykaios—"wolfish Zeus"—no creature cast a shadow.[223] Rhea bathed the newborn child in the spring of the Arcadian river Neda,[224] which gushed forth specially for the purpose, and hastened with him to Crete, where three Dictaean Ash-nymphs, Diktaiai Meliai, became the divine child's nurses. These nymphs were the companions of those Kouretes or Korybantes who took charge of the Zeus-child in other tales. There were, of course, several other caves in Crete which were said to have played a part in the story of Zeus's birth and childhood. Besides the cave in Mount Aigaion, "Goat-Mountain", mention was also made of the Dictaean and Idaean caves. One of these was the scene of the child's birth, the other of its feeding and protection. Besides the goddesses who appeared in the various tales as Zeus's wet-nurses, certain animals could also claim to have fed the god:

ZEUS

a she-goat and a sow,[225] bees and doves.[226] Of the many stories on the subject I shall tell first the only one whose scene is not set in a cave.

Rhea's three daughters, Hestia, Demeter and Hera, were already in existence when the Great Mother bore her three sons. The story continued as follows:[227] when Rhea bore to Kronos their youngest son Zeus, Hera besought her mother to leave the child in her charge. According to this tale, Kronos had by this time flung Hades into Tartaros and Poseidon into the depths of the sea. When he now asked Rhea to show him what she had born, she offered him a wrapped-up stone. This he devoured; but he at once perceived the trick that had been played on him, and began searching for Zeus all over the earth. Meanwhile Hera had brought her future husband to Crete, and Amaltheia (the being most frequently named as Zeus's nurse) hung the cradle on the branch of a tree, so that the child should not be discoverable either in heaven or on earth or in the sea. Furthermore, so that Kronos should not hear the wailing of his son, she assembled a number of boys, gave them brazen shields and spears and set them to dance round the tree and make a loud noise. The boys were called Kouretes—or in other stories Korybantes.

In another version of the same tale, Adrasteia laid the child in a golden cradle[228] and gave him a golden ball.[229] Adrasteia and Ide were the child Zeus's wet-nurses and guardians.[230] These were two names of Rhea herself, who was also called Meter Idaia. Adrasteia, "the inescapable"—this was a possible meaning of the name in our language—will be mentioned again, in one of the Orphic stories. Her golden gift referred to Zeus's future mastery of the world. According to another tale,[231] the child was fed by Amaltheia and Melissa, daughters of the Cretan king Melisseus. Melissa fed him with honey, for her name means "bee"; and there was a story, as I have already mentioned, in which Zeus was suckled by bees.

People told[232] of a sacred cave of bees in which Rhea bore Zeus. No god or man might enter the place. Every year, at a certain time, a great flame broke forth from the cave. This occurred at times of the fermentation of the blood shed at the god's birth. The cave was inhabited by sacred bees, the nurses of Zeus. Once upon a time there were four bold men, named Laios, Keleos, Kerberos and Aigolios, who tried to enter the cave to steal as much honey as they could get. They clad themselves in brazen armour and helped themselves to the bees' honey. Then they saw Zeus's swaddling-clothes and the blood: at this the armour fell from their bodies. An old vase-painting shows the four naked men being attacked by gigantic bees. It was said that Zeus first gave these bees their bronze-golden colour, and their remarkable vigour, in gratitude to them for having fed him. He turned the four men into birds of the same names. He could not slay the robbers with his lightning, because in that cave nobody might die.

It is said that Amaltheia gave the divine boy to drink from her famous horn. To judge by its shape, it was the horn of a bull, the prototype of the vessel called a *rhyton*, which one was expected to empty at a draught, but never could. It originally belonged to Amaltheia's goat.[233] In some stories Amaltheia herself was the goat, and fed Zeus on her milk. Musaios,[234] who is alleged to have been a son and pupil of Orpheus, told of the goat that she was a daughter of the Sun, but was so horrible that the gods around Kronos besought Gaia to hide the dreadful creature in a Cretan cave. It was entrusted to Amaltheia's charge, and with the milk of this goat she fed Zeus. When the divine boy grew up, so that he could fight against the Titans, he possessed no weapons. On the advice of an oracle, which he must have had from Gaia, Zeus slew the goat, whose skin lent him invulnerability and which also had on its back the dreadful Gorgon's countenance. It was further told[235] that a son of the goat, named Aigipan—that is to say, the god Pan in his quality of a he-goat, in which we have already come across him in the story of Typhoeus—was fed together with Zeus. He helped Zeus against the Titans, by sounding his conch-horn and filling them with Panic terror.

There is a story of Zeus's eagle which should be told at this point.[236] There was a boy named Aetos, "eagle", who was born of the earth, like the Idaean Daktylos, Kelmis, of whom I have already spoken, and who, like the last-named and like the above-mentioned Aigipan, was supposed to have been a playmate of the child Zeus. He was beautiful, and Hera turned him into an eagle because she suspected that Zeus loved him. A kindred story was told[237] of Ganymedes, a beautiful Trojan king's son who because of his beauty was stolen by Zeus's eagle, the carrier of lightning, and was made cupbearer to the gods.

2

ZEUS AND HERA

According to most of the tales, Zeus's real spouse was his wife-sister Hera: a name that in our language must once have meant "the mistress". As I have recently said, Hera chose her youngest brother as her husband as soon as he was born. A reference to the leading part played by the goddess in the match-making is contained in that song of Homer's[238] in which Hera entices Zeus to a repetition of their wedding, on Gar-garos, the highest crest of Mount Ida in Asia Minor. This story of the seduction and putting to sleep of Zeus also has a place in our mythology, but Homer puts it to a special purpose. I shall not therefore now tell the story as Homer tells it, but only those parts of his story that recall older tales.

The seduction required a love-charm. Hera therefore visited Aphrodite and obtained from her the *kestos himas*, a magic girdle that the love-goddess wore around her breast. The story of this visit contains a description[239] of the time when Zeus caused Father Kronos to sink beneath the earth and sea. At that time Zeus and Hera lived in the palace of Okeanos and Tethys, who had received the divine children from the hands of Rhea and were keeping them hidden. The brother and sister went to their marriage-bed secretly, without the know-ledge of their elders. According to another tale, the wedding took place in the region of Okeanos, on the western edge of the earth, but not in secret. There stood Zeus's palace and his bed.[240] Thither came all the gods with their wedding-gifts.[241] Earth gave the golden apples that are known as the Apples of the Hesperides. She brought the marvellous tree, with its fruit, to the young bride. Hera admired the fruit and had it guarded by the serpent, in the garden of the gods. According to this story the Hesperides sought to steal the apples.

However, the tales that tell of a secret wedding of the supreme divine couple are in a preponderance. There were also stories and pictures of ineffable love-services rendered to Zeus by Hera.[242] The inhabitants of Samos told that the mating took place on their island and lasted, in complete secrecy, for three hundred years.[243] Afterwards, when Zeus had established his supremacy by defeating the Titans and took up his abode on Olympus, Hera sat beside the ruler at the councils and revels of the gods. She was the mistress "with the golden throne", and was also enthroned on other peaks. There was a mountain in the country of Argolis in the Peloponnese, a mountain that was formerly named Thronax, "Throne-Mountain", or Thornax, "Stool-Mountain", but later Kokkyx of Kokkygion, "Cuckoo-Mountain". The following tale[244] was told of it:

Zeus once perceived Hera by herself, apart from the other gods, and sought to seduce her. He therefore turned himself into a cuckoo and alighted on the mountain. On that day he had sent a terrible storm. The goddess wandered alone up the mountain and sat down at the place where later stood the temple of Hera Teleia, "Hera fulfilled". When the cuckoo saw her, he descended trembling and numb into her lap. The goddess took pity on the bird and covered him with her robe. At once Zeus assumed his own shape and sought to make her his paramour. Hera struggled against him, since they were children of one mother, until he promised to take her to wife. It is said[245] that Hera was the only sister who ever had a man of exactly equal rank—that is to say, her own brother—as a husband. Amongst us mortals the consanguinity through the mother would have been an obstacle to this.

According to another tale[246] the sacred wedding occurred on Mount Cithaeron, in Boeotia. Thither Zeus carried off his bride from the island of Euboea. This long island, named "the good cow-country", belonged to Hera, whose sacred animal was the cow and of whom it was said that she herself had beautiful cow's eyes. She appeared in Euboea as a small girl under the care of her nurse Makris, "the long one"—another name for Euboea. Makris sought for the abducted maiden on the mainland opposite, and came near to the place where the divine couple had hidden themselves. The mountain-god Kithairon falsely told her that Zeus was in hiding with Leto. (As already mentioned, I shall have more to say later concerning this other great wife of our supreme god.)

There were special tales concerning Hera's solitude, her

separation from the other gods and from her husband. Homer is referring to these tales[247] when, in a description of the matrimonial quarrels of the Olympian ruling couple, he makes Zeus say: "I do not heed your anger: what though you were to flee to the utmost end of the earth and sea, where Iapetos and Kronos abide, without sunshine or breath of wind; what though you were to travel even so far in your wandering, I would not heed your anger!" Hera's wanderings, during which she was wrapped in deepest darkness, repeatedly ended in her returning to her husband. It was told[248] that when she bathed in the spring of Kanathos, which is near Argos, she always regained her virginity. Her bathing there must on each occasion have been a preparation for her mating with Zeus.

Of all the goddesses, Hera was the wife who sought fulfil- ment with her husband. She could, however, also bear children of herself, without Zeus. Thus she bore the Typhaon of Delphi, in anger when Zeus brought Pallas Athene into the world, and likewise Hephaistos and perhaps also Ares, as I shall later tell. Hephaistos and Ares were quite especially the sons of Hera, even when they were also supposed to be sons of Zeus. There were also tales of two daughters born by Hera to Zeus: Hebe and Eileithyia. The latter was the goddess who helped women in their birth-pangs. If other goddesses were invoked on such occasions—either Hera herself or Artemis—then in this capacity they too were called Eileithyiai. Hebe's name, on the other hand, means "Flower of Youth". She was another version of her mother in the latter's quality of Hera Pais, "Hera the young maiden". The hero Herakles, son of Zeus and of the mortal queen Alkmene—a hero who was very closely connected with Hera by his name, "Hera's glory", and by his deeds and sufferings—was finally given Hebe as his wife when he became a god on Olympus.

3

ZEUS, EURYNOME AND THE CHARITES
OR GRACES

Zeus's quality of victor and conqueror is less emphasised in his relations with his wife-sister Hera than in the other stories of his marriages. Eurynome, who bore him the Charites, was certainly one of the defeated, oldest gods—although no story to that effect has been preserved. It is reported[249] that a goddess named Eurynome had a temple in Arcadia, in a spot difficult of access. This temple was open only once a year. The cult-image of her showed a woman with a fish's tail and in golden chains. The inhabitants of the region supposed her to be Artemis, but better educated people remembered that, according to Homer and Hesiod, Eurynome was a daughter of Okeanos, and that she and Thetis received Hephaistos in their lap, in the depths of the waters, when he was flung into the sea: I shall tell this story later. Eurynome had a lovely countenance, she was a worthy mother of the Charites, and, I presume, identical with the Aphrodite Morpho of the Spartiates.

It was told[250] that Eurynome and Ophion, or Ophioneus, whose name means that he was a god with a serpent's body, like "The Old Ones of the Sea", ruled over the Titans before Kronos and Rhea. They had their abode on Olympus. But Ophion had to yield to Kronos, and Eurynome to Rhea, in accordance with a pact[251] whereby the victor in each case should be the one who could throw the other into Okeanos. Ophion and Eurynome fell into the depths. This happened while Zeus was still in the Cretan cave. Thereupon the Son of Kronos took Eurynome, daughter of Tethys, as another wife, and begat by her the Charites. In a story[252] in which her name was corrupted into "Euonyme", Kronos begat by her Aphrodite, the Moirai and the Erinyes.

For us the Charites were a sort of threefold Aphrodite. Like her, they were not portrayed naked until later. They are familiar

to us in a naked group in which two of them face towards the
onlooker and the third shows her back. In earlier times they
were clad. In their old temple in Boeotian Orchomenos they
were to be seen in the form of three stones, which were said[253]
to have fallen from heaven into the possession of King Eteokles.
It was said[254] that the Charites were threefold, whether the
name is taken to refer to a flower, to the goddesses or to mortal
maidens. Eteokles had three daughters, who were called
Trittai, "the threefold ones". As they were performing a dance
for the Charites, they fell into a well which they had failed to
observe. Earth took pity on them and brought forth a flower
which has the same name—Trittai—and has three parts, as
their dance had. The story of the three stones that fell from
heaven preserved the memory of their heavenly origin, whereas
the story of their disappearance in a well preserved their connection with the deep waters and the Underworld. The latter
is preserved also in genealogies, such as those according to
which the Charites are daughters of Night and Erebos,[255] or
daughters of Lethe,[256] the river in the Underworld whose
name means "Oblivion". The daughters of Hekate and Hermes
of whom there was also a story,[257] were probably likewise
these threefold Charites.

They were three in number in Boeotia, where Hesiod and
another great Boeotian poet, Pindar, both sang of them. The
three "Queens" of Orchomenos,[258] whose visible shape was
that of three uncut stones,[259] were named Aglaia, "the
glorious", Euphrosyne, "Joy", and Thalia, "Plenty". Pindar
celebrated "the pure light of the Charites"[260] and also called
them *keladennai*, referring to the tumult that accompanied their
festivals.[261] In Laconia, where two Charites were worshipped,
one of them was called Kleta,[262] "the invoked", the other
Phaenna, "the brilliant". These were names for goddesses who
appeared in the phases of the moon; for during the dark nights
of the festivals of the new moon the moon was tumultuously
invoked, and the "brilliant one" was tumultuously welcomed.[263] The Athenians, too, knew only two Charites:

Auxo, "the waxing", and Hegemone, "the precursor"; for in
the second half of the month the moon precedes the sun. These
names were still another expression of the heavenly origin of
the Charites. They were also called daughters of Heaven, of
Ouranos,[264] or daughters of the Sun and of Light,[265]
especially of Moonlight: of Helios and Aigle.

The word *charis* describes what was brought into the world
from heaven by the Charites, or by the union of Zeus with
Eurynome. *Charis* is the word from which *chairein*, "to rejoice",
is derived. It is the opposite of *erinus* and the Erinyes. The two
aspects—*charis* on the one hand, anger and revenge on the
other—must have been the manifestations of one and the same
great goddess. The Latins needed two words to translate
charis: *venus*, "beauty", which was their name for the love-
goddess, and *gratia*, "favour" and "thankfulness", which
became their name for three goddesses, the *Gratiae*, or Graces,
who danced together by the light of the moon.[266]

<h1 style="text-align:center">4</h1>

ZEUS, THEMIS AND THE HORAI

Zeus took to wife two of the daughters of Gaia and Ouranos,
two sisters of Mother Rhea. One of them was Themis. Her
wedding was described to us by Pindar.[267] In the story as
he retold it Themis was Zeus's first wife. First of all—as the
poet tells the tale—the Moirai brought the heavenly Themis,
she of good counsel, behind gold-gleaming mares from the
springs of Okeanos on the brilliant path up to Olympus, to be
the primordial, first wife of the saviour Zeus. She bore him
the truthful Horai, the goddesses with golden fillets, who bring
the glorious fruits of the earth. In another tale,[268] a story of
the birth of Zeus, Themis played the same part as was played
by Adrasteia: she received the child after his birth and
brought him to Amaltheia. (This does not mean that she
could not later have been his wife.) In this story Themis, like

Adrasteia, seems to have been merely another name for
Mother Rhea.

Themis is a name I have already more than once had occasion to mention. The word *themis* means in our language a law
of nature, the norm of the living together of gods and of beings
generally, especially beings of both sexes. It is easy to obey,
but it also forbids many things. The goddess Themis unites
the gods in assemblies[269] and does the same for human,
beings. It is *themis*, also, that men and women should come
together and be united in love.[270] It would have been contrary
to *themis*, however, had women not wished to protect themselves with modesty and clothing. As I have related, the Horai,
the daughters of Themis, even swathed Aphrodite as soon as
she had arisen from the sea. *Hora* means "the correct moment".
Its goddesses are the three Horai, who do not betray or deceive,
and are therefore rightly called truthful. They bring and bestow
ripeness, they come and go in accordance with the firm law
of the periodicities of nature and of life. They were entrusted
with the guardianship of the gates of Heaven and of Olympus,[271] through which Hera entered and departed. Themis
received Hera when she came in anger to Olympus.[272] The
two goddesses were friends. It was told that the Horai had
brought up Hera as a child.[273] They were named:[274] Euno-
mia, "Lawful Order"; Dike, "Just Retribution"; and Eirene,
"Peace". Such were the gifts that these goddesses, whom Zeus
begat upon Themis, brought into the world.

There was a special story concerning Dike. She was the
virgin likeness of her mother, just as Hebe was the maidenly
version of Hera. A fiercer form of Dike is Nemesis, of whom
I shall soon speak and who in Attic Rhamnus was worshipped
together with the maternal Themis. Hesiod prophesied to us[275]
that the goddesses Aidos and Nemesis, clad in white raiment,
would forsake mankind at the end of our wicked epoch—
after which still worse things would follow. But that is really
the story of Dike. It was told of her[276] that she had already
withdrawn into the mountains when mankind ceased to heed

dike—which in our language means not only just retribution, but also justice generally. When still worse things thereupon followed, Dike forsook the earth, and can be seen in the sky as the constellation Virgo.

5

ZEUS, MNEMOSYNE AND THE MUSES

The other daughter of Gaia and Ouranos with whom Zeus allied himself was Mnemosyne, the goddess whose name means "Memory". But she also gave us, through her daughters the Muses, forgetfulness of sorrows and cessation of cares, *lesmosyne*[277] or *lethe*. I have already said that Lethe, as a river, is part of the Underworld, which was called "The Lethaean fields" or "The House of Lethe". But in that infernal region there was also a spring of Mnemosyne, as I shall later tell. In Boeotia two springs were pointed out to visitors,[278] one called Mnemosyne and the other Lethe. Not far from these springs Mnemosyne was worshipped as a goddess. The Muses, too, had sacred places and springs in Boeotia, on Helicon, as well as others outside Boeotia, especially on Mount Olympus, in Pieria. Hesiod was pasturing his herds on Helicon when the Muses spoke to him and told him[279] that they knew both how to lie and how to reveal the truth. They gave him a spray of laurel and initiated him as a poet. Thereupon he told us of the ancestral origins of the gods.

He told us of the marriage of Zeus with Mnemosyne.[280] For nine nights the two lay together in their sacred resting-place, far from the other gods. When a year had passed, Mnemosyne bore nine daughters, all of the same nature, addicted to song and concerned with nothing else. She bore the Muses at a place not far from the summit of snow-covered Mount Olympus: here they were thought to have their dancing-grounds and palace.[281] With the Muses dwelt the Graces and Himeros, the double of Eros. From their dancing-grounds they would

go in procession to Olympus, with immortal song. The black
earth echoed with their hymns, and lovely was the tread of
their feet as they went to their father. They also had a dancing-
ground on the summit of Helicon, near the *hippou krene*, "the
fountain of the horse", and the altar of Zeus. Whenever they
went thence in procession to Olympus, they were wrapped in
clouds. One could only hear their wondrously beautiful voices
in the night. Their names were:[282] Kleio, "the giver of fame";
Euterpe, "the giver of joy"; Thaleia, "the festive"; Melpomene,
"the singer"; Terpsichore, "she who enjoys dancing"; Erato,
"the awakener of desire"; Polymnia, "she of many hymns";
Ourania, "the heavenly"; and Kalliope, "she of the beautiful
voice". He whom they loved, from his mouth poured sweet
the speech, and sweet the song.

The Muses were not always or everywhere described as being
nine in number. Various numbers were attributed to them,
and they also had another collective name, being called not
only Mousai, but also Mneiai,[283] a plural of Mnemosyne,
"Memory". And in Hesiod's own country there was a story[284]
that the Muses were originally three in number. The names
given to these three do not come from mythology, but from
the poet's practice. They were supposed to have been called:
Melete, "practising"; Mneme, "remembering"; and Aoide,
"singing". Amongst the parents ascribed to the Muses were
Ouranos and Gaia,[285] who were also the parents of Mnemosyne. Our poets claimed that whatever they said was a
repetition of what the Muses had told them, and they gave the
Muses all the credit. They often invoked "the Muse", in the
singular, either by this name or by that of one of the nine
Muses. She was expected to come down from heaven.[286]

It was also told,[287] however, that a man named Pieros, a
man of Macedonia, which lies to the north of Mount Olympus,
came to the region of Mount Helicon and there instituted the
cult of nine Muses, instead of the former three. He himself, so
the story goes, had nine daughters, the Pierides, who had the
same names as the nine Muses, and in fact had originally

themselves been these nine. Or, in another story,[288] they were only false Muses, but set themselves up as rivals to the true ones and, having been defeated in a singing contest, were turned into birds. When they sang, all grew dark and nobody listened to them. When the true Muses sang, everything stood still: sky, stars, sea and rivers. Mount Helicon itself began in its rapture to grow up to heaven, until the winged horse Pegasos, on Poseidon's command, struck the mountain with its hooves: whereupon arose the fountain *hippou krene*. This tale of a singing contest and of two sorts of Muses, the true and the false, may be of a late period. From their very beginning the Muses could assume the shape of birds, as also could the Sirens, who likewise were beautiful singers. In other respects the Muses were very close to the fountain-nymphs, just as their mother Mnemosyne was associated with springs, both in the Underworld and in the upper.

The names of the nine Muses were not at first assigned to the various musical arts; and even later the assigning of them was unclear and far from certain. To Kleio was awarded the art of history; Euterpe was mistress of the flute; Thaleia of comedy; Melpomene of elegies and tragedy; Terpsichore of the lyre; Erato of the dance; Polymnia of story-telling; Ourania of astronomy; Kalliope of heroic song. This last was the most glorious of the Muses, so Hesiod assured us;[289] and so she must have been, for otherwise she would not have been associated with that most glorious form of poetry.

6

ZEUS, NEMESIS AND LEDA

I have already said that one of the children of the primordial goddess Night was a daughter named Nemesis.[290] The name means righteous anger, which is directed against those who have violated order, especially the order of nature, and have disregarded nature's law and norm. Should Themis be dis-regarded, then Nemesis is there. She was winged, at least in later portrayals of her: it may be a matter of chance that no earlier portrayals have been preserved. Aidos, her companion, the goddess "Shame", who in Hesiod's prophecy forsakes mankind together with Nemesis,[291] is given wings in much earlier depictions. Artemis, to whom both Aidos and Nemesis are very close, was winged even in the most ancient times.

The Erinyes, the spirits of anger and revenge, are so like Nemesis—or the Nemeseis; for her name is to be found also in the plural[292]—as to be capable of being mistaken for her. But the Erinyes had a more limited function: they took vengeance when blood was shed, especially a mother's blood. Nemesis, on the other hand, appeared whenever Themis was in any way offended. It is not surprising that images of the Charites, who represented the opposite principle to that of the Erinyes, were to be found in a temple of the Nemesis.[293] It was told[294] of the famous cult-image of Nemesis in Rhamnus that the sculptor Agorakritos wrought it as an Aphrodite and then, in a moment of anger, reshaped it into a statue of Nemesis. The head was adorned with a wreath of winged girls and stags.[295] In her hand the goddess held a branch laden with apples, as if she were a Hesperide. She has also been taken for an Okeanine.[296]

When Zeus coupled with Nemesis he did not intend to beget goddesses who would bring into the world beauty, order and memory, which were the gifts of the Charites, Horai and Muses. It was told[297] that the goddess fled. She did not wish to couple in love with the King of the Gods, the Son of Kronos. She was tormented by shame and righteous anger. She fled over firm land and through the black sea. Zeus pursued her and sought to catch her. In the sea she turned herself into a fish. Zeus ploughed up the waters behind her, as far as Okeanos and the edge of the earth. On land she sought to escape the pursuing god by taking the shapes of land-creatures. Finally she turned herself into a goose: Zeus assumed the shape of a swan, and coupled with her. Afterwards she bore the egg from which sprang that beautiful woman who brought disaster

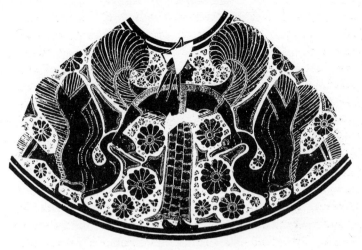

THE "WINGED ARTEMIS"

to mankind by being the cause of the Trojan war: Helena, daughter of Zeus. The egg had the colour of the blue hyacinth, so a woman poet told us.[298] It was found by Leda, wife of King Tyndareos of Sparta.[299] In another story[300] it was found in a wood or marsh by a herdsman, who brought it to Leda. In still another story Hermes threw the egg into Leda's lap, and she hid it in a chest until Helena was born from it.

Was it a different story that tells how Zeus took the shape of a swan and coupled with Leda,[301] or was it the same story with only the name of the bride altered? Leda is not a Greek name. Amongst the Lycians in Asia Minor *lada* meant "woman". Perhaps Zeus celebrated the swan-marriage with a goddess who—except for Mother Earth—was the world's first female being, and could therefore be called simply Leda, "the woman". It was told[302] that under the summit of Taygetos Zeus begat by Leda Kastor and Polydeukes. These twin brothers were the Dioskouroi, *Dios kouroi*, the "sons of Zeus", and rescued many men, especially in battle and at sea. In a story perpetuated by the vase-paintings they were already striplings—two handsome horsemen—when their mother bore an egg. The family wished to sacrifice it to the gods, and laid it on the altar: whereupon the child Helena sprang from the egg.

There were also tales of twin eggs,[303] from one of which the Dioskouroi came into the world and from the other Helena—and perhaps also, as Helena's twin sister, Klytaim-nestra, the husband-slayer who was slain by her son. There is also a stucco of Helena and her brothers springing from a single egg. The brothers were the subject of many stories, of which I shall briefly tell only one:[304] Polydeukes was immortal, Kastor was mortal. When the time came for Kastor to die, his brother did not wish to be parted from him. They therefore always spent one day together in the Underworld and the next day up above with their father. Such tales, however, already lead us into the fields of heroic saga; as do the love-stories in which Zeus coupled with mortal women.

7

CRETAN TALES

Our mythology contained many stories similar to that of Zeus and Leda. In the form that these stories have usually taken since Homer and Hesiod, the heroine who conceived a child of Zeus was only a king's daughter or a queen. Thereafter the doings of the child, like the love-story itself, more properly belonged to heroic saga. A son born to Zeus by a mortal woman was only a demigod, like Herakles; or else, in the case of twins such as Kastor and Polydeukes, only one of them was immortal. Herakles, it is true, finally achieved immortality. But he was certainly not a mortal hero in the original form of the story: as a Daktylos he must have had a divine mother. Similarly, most of the love-stories concerning Zeus originated from more ancient tales describing his marriages with god-desses. This can especially be said of the story of Europa. Her name occurs in the list of daughters of Okeanos and Tethys, together with the names of other wives of Zeus.[305] It means "she of the wide eyes" or "she of the broad countenance". The story told of her opens in Phoenicia, an eastern country, but continues with an account of her marriage and progeny in Crete. These are Cretan tales, but they were received into our mythology, and I shall therefore tell them, at least briefly.

The narrators did not agree[306] as to whether Europa was the daughter or the sister of King Phoinix, from whom Phoenicia took its name. Her mother was called Telephaessa, "the far-shining", or Argiope,[307] "the white-faced". In other words, the face of both mother and daughter was that of the moon, whereas the word *phoinix* means the reddish colour of the sun. It was told[308] that Zeus beheld Europa as she was picking flowers by the seashore. He came to her in the shape of a bull, and ravished her. The bull was certainly no ordinary beast: on an old vase-painting it is tricoloured. Poets said that the bull's breath smelt of crocus. The beast must have had a peculiar power of enchantment, for Europa set herself on its back and allowed herself to be carried over the sea. Our vase-painters depicted her as a real goddess riding on the bull: winged, or with a fish or a flower in her hand. She often carries vine-branches laden with grapes, as if the enchantment exercised upon her by Zeus had been the same as that exercised by the bull-god Dionysos. Or else she holds in her hand a hoop—probably a necklet—which was said[309] to have been Zeus's wedding-present to her, wrought by Hephaistos. Thus she journeyed to Crete. One place believed to have been the scene of the marriage was the Dictaean cave.[310] Near the town of Gortyn, however, there is a plane-tree in the crown of which Zeus is thought to have coupled with Europa after having assumed the shape, not of a bull, but of an eagle.

There were tales of other presents given by Zeus to his bride: a spear that never missed its target,[311] and magic creatures appointed to serve as Europa's guardians. One of these was a brazen dog. (There was also a Cretan tale[312] of a golden dog that guarded first of all the Zeus-child's goat, and later on his sanctuary.) The other magic creature was Talos,[313] a brazen giant who wandered round the island, either thrice daily or thrice yearly. He hurled stones at strangers, was com׳ posed entirely of metal, and had only a single vulnerable spot in his body: a knuckle, or a vein that ran from nape to knuckle and was closed with a brazen nail. His name, in the language of the ancient Cretans, who had not yet learnt Greek, meant the Sun, and in Crete Zeus also had the same name, as *Zeus Tallaios*. In the story of Europa, "Zeus" obviously means the Cretan sun׳god. This god also appeared in the shape of a bull —or perhaps, more exactly, it was the Cretan sky׳god in his darker aspect as god of the night sky. For it was further told[314] that Europa was espoused in Crete to a King Asterion, or Asterios, which means "King of the Stars". The bull׳god of the Cretans bore this name not only as father of the kings whom Europa bore to Zeus, but also—as I shall presently relate—as a bull׳shaped son in the same family.

The names are recorded of three sons of Zeus and Europa. One of these was the Lycian King Sarpedon, who, according to one tale, went from Crete to Asia Minor. Cretan stories dealt more fully with the other two sons: Minos, Crete's wise earthly king and lawgiver, and the just Rhadamanthys, who ruled over the Isles of the Blest. In the story of Minos's family[315] we once again find the marriage with a bull. Minos took to wife Pasiphae, "the all׳illuminating", the daughter of Helios and of Perseis, whose name we already know as a designation of the Moon׳Goddess. It was told[316] that Pasiphae fell in love with a marvellously beautiful, radiant bull whom a god— either Zeus or Poseidon—had sent to Crete. It is certain that the bull came out of the sea: that is why Poseidon is mentioned in this connection. But it was also stated[317] that this bull had been still another manifestation of Zeus himself. It is obvious that for the ancient Cretans the bull was a manifestation of their supreme god. In our own, better׳known tales, Pasiphae was in love with a real bull. She got the master׳craftsman Daidalos to construct the image of a cow, and hid herself in

it. The bull was deceived, and begat by the Queen the Mino⁄
tauros, the "bull of Minos", named Asterios. This latter was
a child with a bull's head, and it had to be hidden away. It
grew up in the Labyrinthos, a maze of masonry that Daidalos
built for this purpose. Theseus of Athens finally slew the man⁄
bull—another story from heroic saga. Inasmuch as the story
is interwoven with the tale of Ariadne, a daughter of Minos
and Pasiphae—a tale that has its place in the stories concerning
the god Dionysos—I shall tell it in its proper place.

Minos and Pasiphae had a son called Glaukos, "the sea⁄
green". Of him it was told[318] that as a small child he was
playing with a ball, or chasing a mouse, and in so doing fell
into a great cask full of honey and was suffocated. Nobody
knew what had become of him. An oracle was consulted and
answered: "A marvellous creature has been born amongst you:
whoever finds the true likeness for this creature will also find
the child." In Minos's herds was born a calf that thrice daily
changed its colour: it was first white, then red, and finally
black. A soothsayer from Argos, a man named Polyidos, "the
much knowing", found the true likeness: blackberries. For
the blackberry, too, is first white, then red and finally black.
Since he was now destined to find the child, Polyidos observed
that an owl was driving away bees from the entrance to a wine⁄
cellar. In the cellar he found the cask of honey and drew from
it the corpse of Glaukos. Minos now demanded of him that
he should bring the child back to life, and incarcerated him
with the child in an empty tomb. Here Polyidos observed a
serpent approaching the corpse. He killed the serpent. Another
serpent came, and, when it saw that the first serpent was dead,
fetched a plant and laid it on the slain serpent, which came
back to life. Polyidos took the plant and with it resuscitated
little Glaukos. Minos thereupon sought to compel the sooth⁄
sayer to teach Glaukos his art, and would not let him return to
his own country. Polyidos did as he was told, but when at last
he left Crete he asked the boy, at parting, to spit into his mouth.
Thus Glaukos unwittingly gave Polyidos back his wisdom.

So ends the Cretan story of Glaukos and the progeny of
Europa. On the mainland, in Boeotia, various further tales are
told of a certain Glaukos.[319] They offer the first explanation
of why he was called "the sea-green". The explanation has to
do with a magic plant, a flower that bestows immortality.
Glaukos ate of the plant, leapt into the sea and became a sea-
god. (Previously he had been only a fisherman, not a Cretan
prince.) According to one story,[320] when Europa, the family's
female founder, came from Phoenicia she arrived not in Crete
but in Boeotia. Here Zeus created a cave for her, so that no one,
not even the gods, might learn where he was hiding his beloved.
King Phoinix sent Europa's brother Kadmos to look for
her.[321] It was on this occasion that Kadmos, while following
a cow branded on both flanks with a full moon,[322] founded
the city of Thebes.

This brings us to the story of the wandering moon-cow,
whose heroine in another tale was Io, another woman whom
Zeus loved. Hera turned her into a cow,[323] and many-eyed
Argos guarded her. Zeus nevertheless continued to love her,[324]
even when he had to assume the shape of a bull in order to do
so. Hera had her driven by a gadfly from the country of Argos,
in Greece, to Egypt. There Io bore to Zeus her son Epaphos,
of whom it was said[325] that he was none other than the
Egyptian divine bull, Apis. It was also stated[326] that Io was
identical with the Isis of the Egyptians, and that this great
goddess had been turned into a tricoloured cow. Sometimes
she was white, sometimes black, sometimes of the colour of the
violet (*ion*), whose name sounds in our language like that of Io.
All these stories touch only the outermost edge of our mythology; although the rape of Europa is clearly reminiscent of the
carrying-off of Persephone.

8

ORPHIC STORIES

There was also a tale that, of his own sisters, the three daughters
of Rhea, Zeus also took to wife the second, Demeter. Elsewhere
it was supposed—as I shall later tell—that Demeter's husband
was Poseidon. But no other god but Zeus is named as the
father of Demeter's only daughter, Persephone. The story of the
union of Zeus and Demeter was well known, and yet at the
same time not so well known. Hesiod mentions it,[327] and it
was rumoured[328] that it was enacted by the priest and priestess
in the Mysteries of Eleusis: perhaps this is the reason why it was
one of the more secret tales and could never be told except in
the Mysteries. Or the story was given another turn, with another
name for the goddess's lover. It was told[329] of a Cretan youth,
or hunter, named Iasion or Iasios—an Idaios Daktylos, to judge
by his name—that Demeter gave herself to him in the furrows
of a thrice-ploughed field. The goddess bore him the child
Ploutos ("Wealth"), and the earth thereupon brought forth a
manifold harvest. Nevertheless Zeus smote the goddess's lover
with his lightning—or such, at any rate, was the public
story,[330] not the one told in the Mysteries.

I shall pass over the stories that were kept secret, and shall
relate instead the tales preserved by the disciples of Orpheus,
who entrusted to the written word much that was scarcely
spoken of—including a number of quite ancient stories that they
had woven into the weft of a newer account of the ancestry of
the gods. One of these more ancient stories was that in which
Rhea appeared in the rôle of Demeter. It was told[331] that Rhea
had forbidden Zeus to marry. At this Zeus sought to rape his
mother. Rhea turned herself into a serpent. Zeus did likewise,
and as serpent with serpent, entwined in an indissoluble knot,
he coupled with her. The commemorative emblem—in our
language, *symbolon*—of this union is the staff of Hermes, around
which two serpents coil and cling together. Afterwards Zeus

ravished his own daughter Persephone, who had been born of this same union. In this rôle, too, he was shaped like a serpent. The child born to him by his daughter was called, by one name, Dionysos. But both deities—Zeus, the ravisher of Perse, phone, and Dionysos, her son—were also called Zagreus, which in our language means "mighty hunter". I shall later say more of this matter, but the stories of the Daktyloi and the Kabeiroi have already made it plain that father and son could be identical.

I have already related the older tales, as told by the disciples of the singer Orpheus, concerning the beginning of things. At the very beginning of this tale appeared the goddess Night, in the shape of a black bird. But she did not appear entirely by herself. With her was the Wind whereby she was made fruitful, so that she laid the Egg, which in turn contained within itself a moving, winged being: Eros, or—as he was later more com, monly called—Phanes. Into the more recent tale[332] the later disciples of Orpheus introduced Chronos, "Time", who was not a Greek divinity. Our Kronos should not be confused with the never-ageing Chronos, who produced from within himself the calm Aither and likewise Chaos, the empty space which had no firm bottom and was filled with darkness. For Aither, a name that also means the light of heaven or the bright daytime sky, Chronos created a silver Egg, which spun around upon itself. But Aither and Chaos became distinct from one another only with the appearance of Aither's son Phanes, otherwise known as the Protogonos Phaethon, the "firstborn shining one". His dazzling white robe was the silver Egg. He had four eyes, four horns and golden wings; he bellowed like a bull or roared like a lion; he was double-sexed, being a woman before and a man behind; and he was also called Erikepaios, Eros and Metis. As Phanes he was "he who appears" and "he who reveals"; as Eros he was "Love"; and as Metis he was "Wise Counsel"—a deity who, to judge by the name, was female, but of whom it was said that she carried the semen of the gods. Of the foreign-sounding name Erikepaios there is no known translation.

It was further told[333] that nobody could look the Protogonos in the face, except holy Night. All other beings were merely bewildered by the light he shed. He created sky and earth, and he also created a second earth, the moon. As guardian over this first created and ordered world he appointed the Sun. This he did, the Father, as he dwelt in his cave with the threefold goddess Night. Properly speaking, there were three goddesses in the cave, daughters of the double-sexed Father Phanes. The first goddess, Night, gave the Oracle. The second "the bashful", became the Father's wife, whom he ravished. The third was the mother of justice, of *dikaiosune*, the high goddess Dike, who never came amongst men—unlike that daughter of Themis whom I have already mentioned. Before the cave sat the goddess Adrasteia. With the tones of her brazen drum—the instrument of the great Mother Rhea—she held men in the spell of justice. Phanes in his cave was the first king. He laid the sceptre in the hand of Night. From her it passed to Ouranos, from Ouranos to Kronos, from Kronos to Zeus, who was the fifth to rule the world. After Zeus came the sixth ruler, Dionysos, with whose reign the song of Orpheus ended. I shall not now carry the story so far, but shall only describe the deeds of Zeus as told by the followers of Orpheus.

Heaven and Earth were created by Phanes. In this story Ouranos and Gaia were a god and a goddess, and, like the other divinities, children of Night. Much the same stories were told of them as those I have already set forth in the tales of the Titans. The Titans were their children—fourteen in number, since Phorkys and Dione were included amongst them. I have also already told the story of how Kronos, King of the Titans, fell asleep drunk with honey—this was the first sleep in the world's history[334]—and was bound fast by Zeus. According to this story his son castrated him,[335] as he himself had castrated his father Ouranos. Meanwhile Rhea, after having at first been Zeus's mother, now turned into Demeter[336]—this is to say, into her own daughter and the wife-sister of Zeus, to whom she bore Persephone. Zeus frequently asked and obtained advice from the goddess Night, her of whom it was said that she gave the oracle. The new world-ruler and father relied upon her[337] and addressed her as "Grandmother and supreme goddess". It was on her advice that he had first bound Kronos, and thereafter he bound the whole progeny of Phanes, his first predecessor, with a golden cord. And he devoured them, together with their begetter, the double-sexed primordial father. When all this progeny "was *again* in Zeus"[338]—these are the words used in the tale, which thereby signifies that "Zeus" had also been one of the names of the first begetter[339]—the result, as the followers of Orpheus go on to exalt their supreme god, was as follows:

> "Zeus is the first, Zeus is the last, the god with the dazzling lightning. Zeus is the head, Zeus is the middle, of Zeus all things have their end. Zeus is the foundation of the earth and of the starry sky. Zeus is male, Zeus is an immortal woman. Zeus is the breath of all things, Zeus is the sweep of unwearying flame. Zeus is the roots of the sea, Zeus is the sun and moon. Zeus is the King, Zeus is the beginner of all things, the god with the dazzling lightning. For he has hidden all things within himself, and brought them forth again, into the joyful light, from his sacred heart, working marvels."

9

SURNAMES OF ZEUS AND HERA

Let me conclude by listing some of those many surnames of Zeus and Hera that either summarise stories I have already told, or amplify them with features to which I have not yet given sufficient prominence.

Homer's perpetually recurring surname for Zeus, *nephelegeretes*, means that he was the god who "assembled clouds". This is not a proper surname such as Ombrios or Hyetios, "the Rain-God", or Kataibates, "the Descender", Kappotas, "the Downpourer", or even Keraunos, "the Lightning"—all of which names preserve Zeus's quality of "god of the weather": a quality that was less emphasised in our mythology than his qualities of Gamelios, "God of Marriage", Teleios, "Giver of Completeness", or Heraios, "the Zeus of Hera". He was often called Pater, "the Father", also Patroos, Phratrios, Philios, Xenios and Hikesios, as the god of human communities, races and fellowships, even including those of hosts and of strangers seeking protection. As Polieus he was the god of cities. As Boulaios he was the *metietes*, the god of good counsel who helps those who consult him. As Basileus, "King", he had more to do with the depths than with the sky. As Soter, "the Saviour", Ktesios, "Protector of Property" and Meilichios, the god who could be appeased with honey, the kindly god of the depths, he appeared in the form of a serpent. The surname Chthonios, or Katachthonios, referred to Zeus's second, dark sphere, which was contrasted with his upper, bright realm of the sky and Olympus.

Of Hera's surnames there were three, all given to her at the same place, that expressed a threefoldness and a periodicity that recall the phases of the moon: Pais, "the Maiden", Teleia, "the Fulfilled", and Chera, "the Solitary". Under the second surname, especially, she was the Gamelia, Zygia, Syzygia, our great Goddess of Marriage.

CHAPTER VII

Metis and Pallas Athene

AMONGST the great spouses of Zeus there was one of whom we might perhaps have known nothing at all had she not appeared in the story of a great daughter of Zeus, Pallas Athene. Metis, "Wise Counsel", could perhaps also be a surname of Athene, of whom it was said[340] that she was Zeus's equal in wise counsel and courage. But it was told[341] that Zeus chose as his first wife that Metis who knew more than all other gods or men. She was a daughter of Okeanos and Tethys,[342] and she was already in alliance with Zeus[343] at the time when all his brothers and sisters were devoured by Kronos. She gave the potion that put the dreadful Father to sleep and compelled him to yield up again the gods whom he had devoured. Metis also had the art[344]—which was also attributed to the goddess Nemesis—of changing herself into many different shapes when Zeus sought to take her. Nothing more is told about this, except that Zeus took her nevertheless. What happened next comes into the story of the birth of Pallas Athene.

I

THE BIRTH OF ATHENE

One tale of the birth of Athene,[345] which is to be found in Hesiod after his statement that Zeus took Metis to be his first wife, runs as follows: When Metis was about to give birth to Athene, Zeus guilefully deceived her with flattering words and put her in his own belly. Gaia and Ouranos had advised him to do this, so that none of the eternal gods should achieve the dignity of a king in place of Zeus. For it was fated that Metis should bear exceedingly wise children. The first of these was the owl-eyed maiden Tritogeneia (a surname of Athene, the

THE BIRTH OF PALLAS ATHENE

meaning of which will be explained in a second tale), equal to Zeus in courage and wise counsel. After this maiden, however, she was to bear a boy of all-conquering heart, who would be king of gods and men. Zeus devoured Metis before this could happen, so that the goddess might practise for him her knowledge of good and evil.

The second tale was also to be found in Hesiod,[346] after his statement that Zeus gave birth from his head to the owl-eyed Tritogeneia—the terrible, the awakener of the din of battle, the chieftainess of armies, who rejoices in tumult, in wars and affrays—whilst Hera, of herself, bore the master-craftsman Hephaistos. It was a contest between the spouses, so the tale continues.[347] Hera bore Hephaistos without Zeus; but Zeus secretly took to himself a daughter of Okeanos, Metis. He tricked her, although she was very wise, seized her with both hands and put her in his belly. He feared that Metis would give birth to something stronger than lightning. That is why the Son of Kronos surprised and devoured her. At that time, however, she was pregnant with Pallas Athene. The father of gods and men himself gave birth to the daughter, beside a peak on the shore of the river Triton (hence the surname

Tritogeneia), whilst hidden within Zeus sat Metis, the mother of Athene, the encompasser of all righteous things, she who knew more than all other gods or men.

It is not stated in this particular tale that Athene was born from Zeus's head. Instead, a "peak"—which in our language is synonymous with "head"—is introduced into the story in order to disguise the strange manner of the birth. There were, however, tales in which Hephaistos[348] or Prometheus[349]—or Palamaon,[350] another name for Hephaistos—assisted at the birth and smote Zeus's skull with a double-edged axe or a hammer. Pallas Athene sprang forth with a far-echoing battle-cry, so that heaven and Mother Earth shuddered. In armour of gleaming gold[351] she was born from the sacred head of the Father. All the immortals were afraid and astonished at the sight of her, as she sprang out in front of aegis-bearing Zeus, from his immortal head, brandishing her sharp javelin. Mightily quaked great Mount Olympus beneath the weight of the owl-eyed maiden. Deeply rumbled the earth all round, and raging rose the sea in the riot of the purple waves. Over its shores rushed the salty flood, and long did Hyperion's splendid offspring halt the swift horses of the sun, until at last the virgin Pallas Athene lowered the divine weapon from her immortal shoulders. And much rejoiced the god of wise counsel, Zeus.

2

ATHENE'S FATHERS AND TUTORS

In our mythology Pallas Athene was the Father's daughter: a warlike virgin at whose birth the Father played a more impor-tant part than the mother. In our religion she took, at least since Homer, second place after her father Zeus. I have already mentioned, in my description of the battle with the Giants, a certain Giant named Pallas. This was also the name[352] of the son of the Titans Krios and Eurybia, and the same name is given[353] as that of a father of Pallas Athene. In our language

WINGED PALLAS ATHENE

the word *pallas* can be variously accented and inflected so as to have either a masculine or a feminine meaning. In the masculine it means a strong young man, in the feminine a strong virgin, a *virago*, as she would be called in Latin. The male Pallas was always the same figure, although given various genealogies, a wilder and even more warlike male version of Pallas the goddess. It is said of Pallas, the father of Pallas Athene, that he sought to do violence to his own daughter. The goddess overcame him, took his skin as booty (the same story is told of Pallas Athene and Pallas the Giant), and herself wore the skin. Pallas the father was winged, as also was Pallas the daughter in old portrayals of her.

Besides Zeus and Pallas, yet a third father of the goddess is mentioned. It was told[354] that when Zeus devoured Metis she was already pregnant. Brontes the Kyklops had begotten Athene upon her. Perhaps there is a reference to this paternity in the story I have recently told of Athene's birth, in the passage where it is stated that Zeus feared lest Metis might bear something stronger than lightning. The name Brontes means "the Thunderer". The Kyklopes are, as smiths, very close to the

Idaioi Daktyloi; who, as I have already said, were phallic primordial beings. Of other such beings, the first men and primordial kings of various countries, it was said that when Athene was born they took charge of her education. One of them, Itonos, was still another character believed to have been Athene's father.[355] This belief is associated with a tale that is also told of other families in which the goddess was said to have been brought up.

When Athene sprang forth from her father's head, on the banks of the river Triton, the river-god—so the tale ran[356]—took charge of her education. Triton had a daughter of his own, whose name was Pallas. Athene and Pallas played the war-game together. As Pallas was about to strike Athene with her javelin, Zeus feared for his daughter and held in front of her his fear-awakening goatskin, the Aigis. Pallas turned aside her gaze and was mortally hit by Athene. The goddess mourned for her and made an image of her, the Palladion. Around this statue she hung the Aigis, and set the Palladion beside the image of Zeus. Itonos, whom I have recently mentioned, had two daughters, Athene and Iodama. Athene slew her sister while they were playing the war-game. Itonos was a primordial king in Thessaly, ruler of a region where Athene was wor-shipped as Itonia. According to another story,[357] Athene was brought up by the Boeotian primordial man Alalkomeneus. He had emerged from the earth at lake Copais and was married to a certain Athenaïs—which is clearly a distorted version of the name of the goddess. Lastly, it was thought that Athene's tutor was a primordial king in Arcadia, also named Pallas.[358] This Pallas had two daughters, Nike and Chryse. I have already said that Nike, the winged goddess of victory, was in another tale[359] the daughter of that Pallas whose father was Krios the Titan. She became the companion of Athene, who was herself surnamed Nike. Chryse, "the golden"—but clearly not "golden" in the same sense as Aphrodite—was also one of Athene's surnames. The story is always the same, presenting two aspects of the one goddess under different names.

3

ATHENE AND HEPHAISTOS

In all the stories told of Athene she was styled Parthenos, "Virgin". But she was also invoked as Meter, "Mother".[360] There is a curious story of a mating of hers, a story in which she did not lose her virginity but nevertheless afterwards entrusted a child to the daughters of Kekrops, king of her beloved city of Athens. It was a sacred story and was often told in pictures. It can be marvelled at in Rome, on an altar that stood in the sacred precincts of a devout and deified empress.

It was told[361] that Hephaistos demanded, as a reward for the assistance he had lent with his hammer at Athene's birth, that she should become his bride. Indeed, she was given to him, and he actually led her into the bridal chamber. But when he lay down beside her,[362] the goddess vanished, and his semen fell to the earth. Of this the goddess Gaia—also called Chthon—bore Erichthonios, the divine child of the Athenian Acropolis, and handed over the newborn babe to Pallas Athene. According to another tale,[363] there was strife (*eris*) between Hephaistos and Athene, and that is why the child is called Erichthonios. According to yet a third tale,[364] the god pursued the goddess and finally overtook her (this is depicted on the altar in Rome), but could not take her virginity. Athene thrust him from her. There were several tales in which a part was played by the wool (*erion*)[365] with which the goddess wiped away the semen, or by the dust with which it became mingled.[366] In poetical diction there were references to "bridal dew".[367] Our language had two words for "dew": *herse* or *drosos*. Both words could also mean a newborn child. Even a god such as Apollon or Zeus was called, in his quality of divine child, Hersos or Erros.

Students of the more secret traditions[368] have preserved the memory of a story in which Athene bore to Hephaistos a son named Apollon, under whose protection—so said these ancient historians—stood the city of Athens. This story I must not forbear to mention, although nothing more has been heard of it. There were also tales,[369] told by the Athenians and Delians, in which Athene and Leto, the mother of Apollon, were closely connected. Athene helped Leto in her pregnancy when the latter came to Delos to bear her son.

4

THE DAUGHTERS OF KEKROPS

The Athenians told that their first king was Kekrops, an earthborn, primordial being, half man and half serpent. In this form the name must be a pun on "Kerkops", "the tailed one". When Pallas Athene and Poseidon disputed as to which of them should rule Attica,[370] which was later the country of the Athenians, Kekrops judged the dispute. Poseidon struck with his trident the rock on which later the Acropolis was to stand, and thus actually caused a "sea"—that is to say, a salt spring—to arise from it. It was also told[371] that on this occasion he caused the first horse to spring from the earth. Athene planted the olive, and for this Kekrops judged her the victor. It was further told[372] that Kekrops was the first to address Zeus by his name, the first to erect a statue of Athene, the first to discover that men have fathers as well as mothers,[373] and the first to introduce monogamy.

The wife of Kekrops was Aglauros or Agraulos, "the dweller on tilled land". (An epithet of her daughters is *drakaulos*,[374] "the housemate of the serpent".) It was told[375] that they had three daughters, the Aglaurides, named Aglauros, Herse and Pandrosos. The meanings of the last two names are, respec-tively, "dewfall" and "the all-bedewed" or "the all-bedewing". Probably the reference is to real dew—a gift, that is to say, of the moon. It was also told[376] that for the Athenians the Aglaurides were the Moirai. Of Aglauros it was told that she bore to Ares a daughter named Alkippe, "the bold mare".

There was also a love-story of Herse and Hermes, in which Aglauros played a tragic part—a part which she also plays in other tales. The three sisters dwelt on the Acropolis—so this story goes[377]—just as later did the Arrephoroi, the Athenian virgins, who served the city's goddess. Their house had three rooms. In the middle room dwelt Herse. Once upon a time Hermes espied the three as they were carrying the sacred baskets on their heads in the solemn procession, and he fell in love with Herse, who was the most beautiful. He asked Aglauros to give him access to her sister. She demanded gold for this service. But later she was so much overpowered by jealousy that she would not admit the god to her sister even for gold. Hermes was wroth, and with a touch of his magic staff he turned Aglauros into a stone image. Herse bore[378] to her divine lover a beautiful son named Kephalos, the darling of the goddess Eos. In the tale of the *kerukes*,[379] the "heralds" of the Eleusinian Mysteries, Herse bore the first ancestor of this family, the first herald, named Keryx.

Of all the stories of the daughters of Kekrops the best-known story[380] ran as follows: Athene received from Earth the child Erichthonios, whose father was Hephaistos, and she sought to bring it up in secret, so that the other gods should not know of it. She laid the child in a covered, round basket, probably such as those which are used in the Mysteries, and from which—as one can see in many pictures—a serpent crawls out. It was later said that Athene had borne a serpent.[381] In another version of the story,[382] Athene laid Erichthonios in a chest, as Aphrodite had laid Adonis. She entrusted the closed receptacle to the charge of the three daughters of Kekrops, and strictly forbade them to open it. When she was gone, the girls became inquisitive, especially Aglauros, of whom it is explicitly said that she opened the basket or chest. One of the other two sisters shared her guilt—but the narrators do not agree as to which of them she was. Aglauros and this other sister espied Athene's secret: but as to what it was, here again the narrators differ.[383] It was a serpent; or a child guarded by a serpent, or even by two serpents; or a child with serpent feet. Each of the girls who espied the secret—Aglauros, certainly, and either Herse or Pandrosos—went mad and leapt from the high rock on which later stood the Acropolis. Or were they pursued by the guardian serpents? They are so depicted in a vase-painting. The serpent that could be seen behind the shield of the famous statue of Athene Parthenos, a work of the sculptor Pheidias, was said to have been the serpent that emerged from the basket, and later took refuge with the goddess.

There was also a tale[384] of Athene's doings after she had entrusted the child to the three sisters. She went to Pallene in Attica and fetched a rock to fortify the citadel of Kekrops, which was to be the Athenian Acropolis. Just as the goddess was returning with the great stone, a crow flew to meet her and told her of the discovery of the secret. Until that time the crow had been a favourite bird of Athene, and in other parts of Greece it has continued to be so. Now, however, the goddess's first anger fell upon the crow. She dropped the great stone—which became Mount Lykabettos—and after that no crow might be seen on the Acropolis. In the sacred citadel where Athene is worshipped, and where her secrets are better kept than they were by the daughters of Kekrops, the office of favourite bird of the goddess was held by the owl. In ancient pictures the owl often represented Athene herself; and this bird, too, became the subject of stories. I shall conclude this part of my narrative by telling one of these.

Askalaphos was a son of Acheron,[385] a river in the Underworld, and of Gorgyra, whose name is a longer form of Gorgo. His mother was also called Orphne, "Darkness"; or else she was the Styx, which I have already mentioned as a river of the Underworld. Askalaphos saw and witnessed how Persephone, after she was carried off by Hades, ate of the pomegranate. By so doing she was lost to her mother Demeter, and was compelled perpetually to return to the Underworld. In her anger Demeter turned Askalaphos into an owl. According to one story,[386] the goddess first dropped a great stone on the culprit,

ATHENE RECEIVES ERICHTHONIOS FROM GAIA, IN THE
PRESENCE OF KEKROPS, HEPHAISTOS AND HERSE

and he lay beneath it until Herakles set him free. This story
seems to have nothing to do with Pallas Athene. It is known,
however, that the Athenians called the city's great goddess their
"Kore"—that is to say, their Persephone[387]—and that the
ancient Athenian statue of Athene Nike[388] bore in one hand
the goddess's helmet and in the other a pomegranate.

5

ATHENE'S SURNAMES

Like all our other great deities, Athene had numerous surnames, some of which expressed particular qualities of the
goddess whilst others summarised whole stories concerning her.
People even began to call her "Pronoia", "Providence": but
this must have happened later than the time at which the
surnames I shall now list were commonly accepted.

Athene's name of Aglauros indicated a darker, tragic,
Persephone-like aspect of the goddess. When called Pandrosos,
like that other daughter of Kekrops, she displayed herself under
another, bright aspect, which was associated with the olive. A
sacred olive grew on the Acropolis, in the temple of Pandrosos.

Selene, the name of the moon-goddess, was never one of Athene's surnames, any more than Metis was. But students of our ancient times—including, it is said, Aristotle himself[389]—have stated that disguised beneath the name of Athene was, in fact, the moon. The goddess Selene also had a father named Pallas—according, at least, to one account,[390] which deviates from that given by Hesiod; but Athene differs from the bright Selene in having various aspects, as sharply contrasted as full moon and darkness. She was also Gorgopis, "the Gorgon-faced", and bore the Gorgon's countenance upon her breast. But she was further called Hellotis, like Europa, "the broad-faced"—an expression that is associated with the name Selene. The poetical ephithet for Athene, *glaukopis*, was more of a play upon words: it can be translated as "owl-eyed", but it can also refer to the sea-green or olive-green colour of the goddess's eyes. The surname Tritogeneia did not originally mean that she came into the world on the banks of any particular river or lake, but that she was born of the water itself; for the name Triton seems to be associated with water generally. Under the surname Aithyia she was a sea-bird: the grey puffin or shearwater, also known as the sea-crow. It was told[391] that in this form she took under her wings the serpent-shaped primordial man Kekrops and carried him from Athens to Megara. As Hephaistia she was associated with Hephaistos, and as Areia with the war-god Ares. As Ergane, goddess of handicrafts, she came close to the former of these gods, and as Alalkomene, "the Parrier", she came close to the latter. Of all the handicrafts she most loved and protected the art of smiths and metal-founders, likewise the women's crafts—spinning and weaving and woolwork. She was also surnamed Hygieia and, in this quality, accompanied by a son of Apollon, Asklepios.

Of all our goddesses Athene was eminently the protecting goddess of a city, with such surnames as Polias or Poliouchos, and the protectress of heroes—but not of all heroes: she had her own especial protégés, such as Perseus, slayer of the Gorgon, Diomedes and Tydeus, the wild son and still wilder father, and

PLATE V

a APOLLON ACCOMPANIED BY TWO MUSES
ENCOUNTERS ARTEMIS

b APOLLON ON THE BEAKER OF A WINGED TRIPOD

PLATE VI

a SILENOI ATTACK HERA
IN THE PRESENCE OF HERMES AND HERAKLES

b TITYOS ATTEMPTS TO ABDUCT LETO
IN THE PRESENCE OF APOLLON AND AIDOS, *i.e.* ARTEMIS

the wise Odysseus. She also had priestesses bearing names that might have been used to describe herself: names such as Tritaia, a shorter form of Tritogeneia; Auge, "the lustrous"; or Aithra, "the bright". These priestesses bore heroes: Tritaia bore Mela-nippos, "the black stallion", to Ares; Auge bore Telephos, "the far-shining", to Herakles; and Aithra bore Theseus to Poseidon. All these stories lead over into heroic saga—like that oft-told story of Perseus, upon whose mother, Danae, Zeus notoriously descended in the form of a rain of gold. The inhabitants of the island of Rhodes[392] told that something similar happened at the birth of Athene: when the goddess sprang from her father's head, he let fall a golden rain.

CHAPTER VIII

Leto, Apollon and Artemis

A GREAT spouse of Zeus, a spouse who belonged much more to her children, especially to Apollon, than to their father, was Leto. It was justly said of her[393] that one of her offspring was the most glorious amongst all the great-grandchildren of Ouranos: namely, her son, the third-greatest deity of our religion, less only than Zeus and Athene. All the gods rose from their seats—so the scene was described to us[394]—when Apollon appeared amongst them and drew his bow. Only Leto remained peacefully seated beside Zeus and took the bow and quiver from her son's shoulders. She was swathed in dark raiment,[395] but was always gracious, mild as honey and the most pleasant divinity on Olympus. She rejoiced in her two children, who were called, after their mother, the Letoides. She rejoiced in Artemis,[396] her daughter, when she saw her stride over the mountain-ranges and take her pleasure, accompanied by the nymphs, upon boars and stags. Artemis, the everlastingly virginal, was a sister-figure in her relationship both with her brother and with her mother. All stories concerning Leto start with the birth of her son. His twin sister is usually already on the scene.

I

LETO'S WANDERINGS

Of Leto's birth no tale has been preserved. She was a grand-daughter of Ouranos and Gaia,[397] and a daughter of the Titan Koios, whose name means the same as *sphairos*—that is to say, "the Ball of Heaven". He was therefore also called Polos,[398] the god "Heaven's Pole". The people of Cos told[399] that Leto was born on their island. Of her mother, Phoibe, I have already

said that this name meant the moon-goddess—more exactly,
"the Pure" and "the Purifying". Phoibe's grandson Apollon
was called, with the use of the masculine form of her name,
Phoibos Apollon. It has been said[400] that Leto conceived her
children by Zeus at Didyma near Miletus. All the stories concerning the wanderings of Leto seem to have had their starting-
point in Asia Minor. In some versions, Leto still carried her
children within her and was seeking for a place in which to
bear them; in others she was already carrying the children on
her shoulders.

It was said[401] that Leto might give birth only in a place on
which the sun never shone. Jealous Hera had thus willed it—or
such was the explanation given. But it is possible to disregard
this explanation and simply remark the fact that the birth had
to occur in darkness—or, at best, during a time when only
wolves could see. Our language contained expressions that
described the dusk—the dusk, that is to say, before sunrise—
as "wolf-light", *lykophos* or *lykauges*.[402] One story of Leto's
wanderings tells us that Zeus turned her for twelve days into a
she-wolf. In this shape she came to the island of Delos from the
Hyperboreans, the fortunate inhabitants of a northern country
of the gods whither Apollon was thought to repair once a year.
This is the reason, it is said, why she-wolves bear all their cubs
within a space of twelve days in each year. The Delians actually
stated[403] that she-wolves suffered travail for twelve days and
twelve nights on end.

According to another story, Leto came to a country of wolves
—that is to say, to Lycia in Asia Minor; for in our language
Lycia means "wolf-country". On the river Xanthos, near
Araxa, visitors are shown the birthplace of Leto's twins—"two
lights of heaven", as they are entitled on an inscription. In a
third story[404] Leto, having borne her twins, came with them to
Lycia to bathe in the river Xanthos. First she came to the spring
Melite, from which she was driven away by cowherds, whom
she turned into frogs. Wolves escorted the family onwards to
the river Xanthos. Leto dedicated the river to Apollon and

gave the country, which was that of the Termiles, the name of
Lycia. These stories obviously came from Asia Minor. Leto,
Apollon and Artemis seem to have been worshipped there
earlier than amongst us. The account of Leto's parturition, as
told in Greece, contains another story that specially concerns
Delos: a story that I shall now relate.

2

LETO AND ASTERIA

In some tales Leto has a sister named Asteria, "Star-Goddess".
According to Hesiod,[405] Asteria was the wife of Perses, or
Persaios, and bore him Hekate, who is especially close to
Artemis. According to one tale,[406] Zeus, when he had coupled
with Leto, sought also to seduce her sister. Asteria fled from
him[407] in the same manner as Nemesis or Metis. She turned
herself into a quail (*ortyx*). Zeus overtook her in the form of an
eagle.[408] She turned herself into a stone, fell into the sea and
remained hidden beneath the waves. Thus she became the
island crag on which Leto was able to bear her son, having
just emerged from the waves so that the sun had not yet shone
upon her. The island was called Ortygia, "Quail Island"; or
it was called Delos, because it became visible (*delos*) when it
arose from the depths: Delos, the island birthplace of Apollon.

It was also told[409] that Leto turned herself into a mother-
quail—this is the name of the female leader of these migrant
birds—and Zeus coupled with her in the shape of a quail.[410]
In this tale[411] Delos had previously been a floating island,
drifting hither and thither upon our sea and not at all conspi-
cuous. It became Delos, a "widely visible star of the dark
earth", only when Leto chose it for her place of parturition and
the gods anchored it to the sea-bottom with four pillars.

It was further told[412] that Artemis was born first, and was
brought into the world without travail. The Moirai at once
appointed her to be midwife to her mother. Her birthday was

celebrated on the sixth day of the month, Apollon's on the seventh. A distinction is sometimes drawn between Delos and a separate island named Ortygia, the birthplace of Artemis. She had as her special realms an Ortygia off Syracuse in Sicily, and another Ortygia off Ephesus in Asia Minor. This latter Ortygia had a story of its own concerning Apollon. It was told[413] that the Kouretes assisted at Leto's travail—as they had assisted at Rhea's—and that on this occasion, too, they had made a din so that the jealous Hera should not heed the birth.

3

THE BIRTH OF APOLLON

I shall now relate our story[414] of the birth of Apollon. It was told that in her wanderings the pregnant goddess Leto visited all the mountains and islands of Greece, from Crete to Rheneia, which lies over against Delos. They all feared to receive the mighty god who was about to be born. They were all richer than the little, unfruitful island crag of Delos, to which Leto now appealed. The goddess promised the island wealth, which would come to it with worshippers of Apollon from all over the world.

Delos rejoiced and replied in friendly fashion, although not without fear. It had heard that Apollon was to be an unforgiving god, a great lord over mortals and immortals. Delos was therefore sorely afraid that as soon as the god saw the light of day he would despise the desolate island crag and would thrust it with a single stamp of his foot down into the depths of the sea. It would be peopled with polyps and black seals, not by men, and Apollon would depart to another country. At this Leto is said to have sworn that the god would build his first temple on Delos. She took the oath by the Styx, and yielded herself to the birth-pangs. For nine days and nine nights she suffered an anguish beyond her expectation. All the goddesses were assembled, of whom the most glorious may be mentioned here by name: Dione, Rhea, Themis and the sea-goddess Amphitrite, together with all the others, excepting only Hera. The latter even detained at her side the divine midwife, the goddess Eileithyia, hidden on Olympus behind golden clouds, so that she should see nothing of what was happening on Delos. The goddesses on the island sent the messenger Iris to fetch Eileithyia. They promised in reward for her services a golden necklet nine ells long. With this promise the one goddess persuaded the other, and they both came flying to Delos, in the form of two turtle-doves. Just as Eileithyia arrived on the island, Leto gave birth. She gripped with both hands the palm-trees that grew there, and with both feet she kneaded the soft meadow-land. The soil laughed beneath her, the god sprang forth and the goddesses cried aloud. They bathed the child clean with fair water and swaddled it in white cloth. The braided band around the swaddling-clothes was of gold. Yet the mother did not suckle the child. Themis gave him nectar and ambrosia. When he had tasted the immortal food, no swaddling-bands could any longer restrain him. Phoibos Apollon said to the goddesses: "Dear to me shall be lyre and bow, and in my oracles I shall reveal to men the inexorable will of Zeus." The goddesses were amazed, Delos shone golden and the island blossomed.

Descriptions are given[415] of how at this time the whole of Delos was fragrant; or of how swans circled singing seven times about the island,[416] while Leto still lay in the birth-pangs. As they circled an eighth time they no longer sang: the god sprang forth and the Delian Nymphs sang the sacred song of Eileithyia. The brazen welkin echoed, and not even Hera was unaffected, for Zeus took anger away from her. The foundations of Delos turned to gold, and all day long the round pool on the island shone golden. The leaves of the olive turned to gold—for this tree also grew on Delos, as well as the palm, and it was told of the olive, too, that Leto had supported herself upon it. The river Inopus overflowed with gold. It was further told[417] that a cock was present at the birth of the god—that fowl of which it was also stated that at moonrise it falls into an ecstasy and dances, although chiefly it is a witness of sunrise. Since that time the cock is thought to have been Leto's favourite bird.

4

APOLLON AND HIS ENEMIES

There were also tales of enemies whom Apollon vanquished immediately after his birth. Leto had previously been threatened by enemies in the course of her wanderings. As I have already said, the stories differed as to whether the goddess still had her children in her womb or carried them on her shoulders. One of Leto's assailants, and therefore also an enemy of Apollon and Artemis, was the giant Tityos (to judge by his name, a phallic being), son of Zeus and Elara.[418] While yet in his mother's womb he grew so great that his mother perished of him, and he was therefore finally born by Earth, in whom his father had hidden him. Tityos attacked Leto as she was approaching Delphi, and carried her off by force. According to one tale,[419] Artemis laid the giant low with her arrows; according to another,[420] it was the child Apollon who did this. It was also said[421] that Tityos was struck by Zeus's lightning. He lay in the Underworld,[422] struck down at his full length of nine hundred feet, and two vultures tore at his liver. Or else it was a serpent that did this, whilst—according to this story[423]—the liver always grew again with the moon.

It was further told[424] that the dragon Python, who appears in most stories as Apollon's real enemy, had previously pursued Leto, seeking to prevent the birth of her children. For this Apollon took vengeance[425] as soon as he was born, and slew the dragon. Or, if he did not do this immediately, he did so four days later. For the first place Apollon visited was Delphi, where the dragon—who was a son of Gaia—had his lair. This lair was a cave by a spring.[426] In another story, Python coiled around a laurel-tree. All tales agree that Apollon slew him with his arrows.

The older tales mentioned two dragons. But not both of them were slain. Apollon's real enemy was a female creature, a dragoness (*drakaina*) named Delphyne.[427] The name is connected with an old word for the womb, as also is the place-name *Delphoi*, which nowadays is called by its Latin name of Delphi. With the female serpent Delphyne dwelt a male serpent named Typhon, of whom it was said[428] that Hera bore him without her husband, in anger. She gave the one evil thing into the charge of the other, the dragon to the dragoness. It is not said that Apollon also slew the dragon who was Hera's son. The narrators seem to have confused the dragon of Delphi, Python, with Typhon or Typhoeus, the adversary of Zeus: in any case the two stories—the Delphic and that of Asia Minor, which I have already told—were very closely allied. The enemy dragoness, besides being called Delphyne, is also given the masculine form of the name,[429] as Delphynes, or is even called Python. This actually became an Apollonian serpent, and Pythia, the priestess who gave oracles at Delphi, was named after him. Many pictures show the serpent Python living in amity with Apollon and guarding the Omphalos, the sacred navel-stone and mid-point of the Earth, which stood in Apollon's temple.

In any case, Apollon's other enemy—in addition to Tityos, the phallic giant—was not Python but Delphyne, the womb-like giant serpent. It was told,[430] both in stories and in those songs that are known as paeans and were sung in honour of Apollon, how the god came to Delphi in his mother's arms as a little, naked boy with unshorn hair. He held his bow drawn and had an arrow in his hand. Here he was met by the monster, the enormous serpent. He shot arrow after arrow at the monster, and slew it. The song rang out: *"Hie, hie, paieon!"* For his mother bore him to be her champion as soon as he was born. Narrators who confused Delphyne with Python—and this confusion was thorough, perhaps even intentional—ended their story of the slaying of the dragon[431] by saying that its body was dissolved

LETO, APOLLON, ARTEMIS AND THE DRAGON

by the sacred power of the Sun, and that after the putrefaction (*puthein*) the place itself was called Pytho, and Apollon himself was from then on called Pythios.

It was further told[432] how the god, after capturing this rocky place of Delphi, obtained his first priests. Certain men from Crete were on a ship bound for Greece. Apollon leapt into the ship in the shape of a dolphin, sprawled upon it with a huge body and steered it to Krisa, the port of Delphi. Here he sprang, as a gleaming star, straight from the ship into his temple, from which he appeared as a long-haired stripling before the terrified Cretans and initiated them as his priests. There are many stories[433] of how he built the famous temple at Delphi, and of the various forms that he first gave it. One temple was said to have been built for him by bees, of wax and feathers. But afterwards, it was thought, Apollon sent this temple to the land of the Hyperboreans. Thither he came yearly, in a chariot drawn by swans.[434] I have already said that Leto came from the same region, in the shape of a she-wolf. It was told[435] that Apollon, too, could turn himself into a wolf, to destroy his enemies or to couple in love with his paramour Kyrene, of whom I shall have more to say later.

A Delphic temple built by men was set afire by human enemies of Apollon: by the sacrilegious Phlegyas, of whom I shall also speak, and his people the Phlegyans. He was struck by the arrows of the god,[436] and made atonement in the Under‚ world. Another being who often appeared as an enemy of Apollon was his half‚brother Herakles, son of Zeus and Alk‚ mene. It was told[437] of Herakles that, bloodstained and sick he entered the undefiled temple in Delphi. When he had asked how he could heal himself, and had received no answer, he stole the sacred tripod from which Pythia used to proclaim oracles. Apollon fought with him, and Zeus settled the dispute: Herakles gave back the tripod and was given counsel by the oracle. On another occasion the half‚brothers fought over a stag or a hind—these were beasts sacred to Apollon and Artemis. All this again takes us into heroic saga.

I must, however, go on to tell how Apollon had to atone for the killing of Delphyne, which he had perpetrated immediately after his birth.[438] This was the story[439] of his wandering from Delphi to the Vale of Tempe, in Thessaly, and of his servitude to King Admetos, whose name means "the untameable". This atonement lasted a "great year"—that is to say, eight years, which we used to call an *ennaeteris*, a nine‚year period. Only after this did he return to Delphi, as "the Undefiled", *Phoibos*, with a wreath and a branch of the sacred laurel‚tree of the Vale of Tempe. (A boy of Delphi later used to carry these from there in imitation of the god.) These years were Apollon's famous "pastoral time" by the river Amphrysos. Whilst he served Admetos,[440] the King's cows dropped twin calves. Apollon yoked a lion and a boar together for the King's chariot,[441] and thus Admetos won Alkestis to wife. When the time came for the King to die, Apollon saved him by making the Moirai drunk.[442] When death came for Admetos a second time, Alkestis went with him in place of her husband, but was brought back by Herakles. (This story, too, begins to take us away from mythology.) Another reason given for Apollon's servitude to Admetos was that he had slain the Kyklopes—or, at least, their sons. He did this to take vengeance on Zeus, because Zeus had smitten with his lightning Apollon's son Asklepios. I shall tell this story presently.

5

APOLLON AND HIS PARAMOURS

In a later version[443] of the story of Apollon's servitude to Admetos, the two were bound together by love. There were many love-stories concerning Apollon, the greater number and the most famous of which ended tragically—whether the object of the god's love was a boy or a girl. The reason why boys were numbered amongst the god's reputed lovers was that he himself was the god of just that age at which boys used to leave their mother's tutelage and live together. Their younger year-groups were subordinate to the older ones. They also attached them-selves to individual older men. For boys as well as for girls this was the age of fugitive bloom. The tales represent Apollon's love, for a person of either sex, as having been very dangerous.

Hyakinthos was a divine boy resembling Adonis.[444] Aphro-dite took vengeance on a Muse—so the story went—because the latter had scolded her for her love of Adonis. The Muse, Kleio, bore Hyakinthos to Pieros, the Muses' father, just as Myrrha had born Adonis to *her* father. The Muse Erato[445] and the singer Thamyris were rivals for the handsome boy, and this is how pederasty was believed to have started.[446] Another tale[447] reveals the resemblance between Hyakinthos and the boy Apol-lon. Like Apollon, Hyakinthos had a sister who was closely associated with him: her name was Polyboia. Together with her, he was conducted up to Olympus. His cult-image at Amyklai in Sparta is reported[448] to have portrayed a double being with four ears and four arms. In later legend Hyakinthos is always a tender youth, sometimes depicted as riding on a swan. It was told[449] that Apollon loved him and played with him at discus-throwing. One noon the god hit his beloved with the stone slab. From the blood of the accidental victim arose the hyacinth, which was a wild flower with dark blue blossom. Hyakinthos was, of course, no more "dead" than Adonis was: he was a god, and was, indeed, worshipped also as a dead hero. And it was claimed that the bulb of his flower could be used to postpone boys' puberty.

Amongst the boys whom Apollon loved, mention is made of a boy named Kyparissos, "Cypress".[450] In all these tales the beautiful boys are doubles of Apollon himself. Kyparissos was one such in that he unintentionally killed a creature beloved by him, just as Apollon had killed Hyakinthos. The beloved creature was a stag, one of those beasts which, as I have already said, were sacred to Apollon and Artemis. It had mighty, gilded antlers and on its brow it bore silver ornaments. It was tame, and Kyparissos loved it. He put wreaths on the stag and rode on it. One hot noon, as the beast lay in the shade, the young hunter Kyparissos mistook it for an ordinary stag. He threw his spear at it, and was inconsolable when he found that he had killed his pet. He wished either to die or to mourn eternally for his beloved. The only remedy that Apollon could offer the sorrowing boy was to turn him into a sorrowing tree, the cypress, an evergreen tree in which Kyparissos lives for ever.

Whoever wishes to tell of the maidens whom Apollon loved must, in most cases, tell also of a rival, who was often more fortunate than the god. Mention of such rivals is made by that blind poet, author of a great hymn to Apollon,[451] who was thought to have been Homer. The love-stories themselves were not told at length until later. Apollon's first love was Daphne, which is the name of the laurel. It was told[452] that Daphne was a daughter of the river-god Ladon and of Earth. Other story-tellers[453] said that her father was the river-god Peneios, lord of the Vale of Tempe in Thessaly. She was a wild virgin like Artemis, who herself, as Daphnaia or Daphnia, had her own sacred laurel-trees. Daphne was loved not only by Apollon but also by a youth named Leukippos,[454] "he of the white steed", or "the white stallion". Leukippos disguised himself as a girl in order to be allowed to accompany Daphne. Whilst bathing, however, he was discovered by her girl companions. The result was that he either died or disappeared. Daphne, pursued by Apollon, begged Mother Earth to save her, and was turned into a laurel, which thereafter was the god's favourite tree, a branch of which he wore as a wreath. A tree which, like most trees, is naturally bisexual, affords, of course, the most perfect example of the uniting of the two sexes.

Another story[455] is that involving Dryope, the daughter of Dryops, "the Oak-Man". She was a playmate of the Hama-dryades, the oak-nymphs. To win her, Apollon first of all turned himself into a tortoise. The nymphs played with the strange creature, and Dryope laid it in her bosom. Thereupon the tortoise turned itself into a serpent. The nymphs fled in terror. Apollon begat a son on Dryope. The girl spoke of this to nobody. She took to herself a husband and bore her son in wedlock with this man. Afterwards the Hamadryades stole the girl and made her one of themselves. In another of Apollon's reported metamorphoses, he turned himself into a wolf,[456] in the form of which he coupled with the nymph Kyrene. There were many stories concerning Apollon's love-affairs with girls, but I shall conclude my account of them with the tale of Kyrene, which I shall tell in its best-known form.[457]

She was a virgin huntress, a figure resembling Artemis. She was the daughter of the Thessalian King Hypseus—a name that refers to the heavenly heights and therefore means that he was a sky-king—and her mother was a water-nymph. It was also told[458] that Artemis gave her two-hunting dogs. Kyrene lived in the woods of Mount Pelion, and with spear and sword protected her father's herds against beasts of prey. Apollon espied the girl as she wrestled unarmed with a lion. In astonish-ment he summoned the wise Centaur Chiron from his cave, which was close by. Chiron advised him to take Kyrene secretly to wife. So Apollon carried off the wild virgin, in his golden chariot drawn by swans, to North Africa, where later the town of Cyrene was to be founded. On Libya's golden bridal couch they consummated the marriage. Chiron prophe-sied that Kyrene would bear a divine son. Hermes would take charge of him and bring him to the Horai and the goddess Gaia. They, marvelling at the child laid on their laps by Hermes, would drop nectar and ambrosia between his lips, and thus would make him immortal. They would make of him a Zeus, a holy, undefiled Apollon, to be a joy unto men, who would love him; to be the most faithful guardian of herds; to be the Agreus and Nomios, the hunter and herdsman, as Apollon also was; to be the Aristaios, "the best god of all".

Of this second Apollon and second child-Zeus it was told[459] that his father took him to the cave of Chiron, to be brought up by the wise Centaurs. When he was fully grown, the Muses prepared his wedding (I shall presently mention his son Aktaion, born to him by Autonoe, the daughter of Kadmos), and the Muses taught him the arts of healing and soothsaying. They appointed him guardian of their herds in the Thessalian country of Phthia. When Sirius, the star of summer's heat, blazed over the Cyclades and the people found no salvation from the plague, then, at Apollon's bidding, they invoked Aristaios. Thereupon, and likewise at his father's bidding, he left Phthia and settled in the island of Ceos, where he made sacrifices to Zeus and to Sirius. In his honour the Etesiai, the trade-winds, blow for forty days on end. He invented[460] the beehive and bee-keeping, the oilpress and the making of cheese. He is said to have been the first to lay snares for wolves and bears, and to have freed the island of Sardinia from wild birds.

6

THE BIRTH AND DEATH OF ASKLEPIOS

One of the love-stories of Apollon is the tale of the birth of the divine physician and healing god, Asklepios. Apollon himself was also a physician, and his healing art failed only on those whom he had slain. Homer[461] mentions Paieon as the physician of the gods, him who healed the immortals when they were wounded. "Paieon" was a surname of Apollon. Asklepios, who healed mortals and even brought them back from death to life, was, like Aristaios, a second Apollon who besides being regarded as a son of Apollon was also called "Zeus"— despite the fact that, according to a legend which I shall presently recount, it was Zeus who killed him.

An ancient story[462] is told of the love-affair of a goddess of Lake Boibeis in northern Greece. In the local dialect this name meant "the lake of Phoibe". The goddess herself was also called Brimo, "the strong one". According to this story, the details of which were kept secret, her lover was Hermes, a phallic god who in ancient times was simply a phallus. Also in ancient times, but already in the style of heroic saga, was told another story of the love-affair on Lake Boibeis.[463] A maiden washed her feet in the lake. She was the daughter of King Phlegyas, "the fiery red", whom I have already mentioned as one of the enemies of Apollon. Her name was Koronis, "the Crow-Maiden". Apollon had a son by her, but she took as her husband Ischys, the son of Elatos, "the Pine-Man". The name Ischys has to do with "strength". The Latins[464] were not wrong in translating it as *Valens*. It was reserved also for the father of Koronis's divine child. The story[465] in which Apollon was the father went on to tell that the raven—a favourite bird of Apollon, which at that time was not black, but white—brought the god the news of Koronis's marriage to Ischys. Apollon's first anger fell upon the raven, which since then has been black. The punishment of Koronis and the birth of Asklepios are described in my next tale, which is of later date.[466]

The maiden already had within her the pure semen of the god. Then came a guest from Arcadia, by name Ischys the son of Elatos. Koronis could not resist him, and gave herself to him secretly, without the knowledge of her father. Apollon did not fail to observe her unfaithfulness. He sent his sister to Lakereia (whose name means that it is a city of chattering rooks) on

Lake Boibeis, where Koronis's home was. She was slain by Artemis's arrows, and many women of the Phlegyans with her. There was a devastating pestilence and funeral pyres burnt in great number. When the fire was already blazing around Koronis, Apollon said: "I can no longer endure it that my son should perish with the mother!" He took Asklepios from the corpse on the pyre, and brought him to the Centaur Chiron, who taught him the art of healing.

Other tales circulated in Epidaurus, the famous cult-place of Asklepios, where so many sick people were healed by sleeping in the temple. These tales said nothing of Koronis's infidelity and death. Instead, they told[467] that the mother of the god had a second name, "Aigle", "the luminous". Her father was Phlegyas, her mother was a daughter of Erato the Muse. At the birth of the divine child, which took place in the sanctuary, the attendants were Artemis and the Moirai.[468] It was also told that Phlegyas, that man of war, came with evil intent to the Peloponnese, to spy it out and later to conquer it. With him came Koronis, who already at that time, and without her father's knowledge, was pregnant by Apollon. She bore Asklepios on Epidaurian soil and exposed him on the mountain that was formerly called the Mount of Myrtles, but was later called Mount Nipple. Asklepios was suckled by a goat and guarded by a sheepdog. Aresthanas, the herdsman, noticed the absence of the two animals and sought for them. Thus he found the child, and he thought to take it home with him. But as he came nearer he saw that a radiance like lightning shone from the suckling. He realised that there was something divine about it, and he withdrew. The news was at once put about that this child would in future find remedies for the sick and would even bring the dead back to life. The dog became a beast sacred to Asklepios, like the Apollonian serpent.

It is never said that Asklepios brought the dead back to life in Epidaurus itself. Various tales mention heroes whom he resurrected, amongst them Hippolytos,[469] the favourite of the

PLATE VII

a HEPHAISTOS ESCORTED TO OLYMPUS BY DIONYSOS,
A MAENAD AND SILENOS

b PELEUS STRUGGLING WITH THETIS IN THE PRESENCE
OF CHIRON AND THE NEREID PONTOMEDA

PLATE VIII

a HELIOS, THE STARS AS LEAPING
BOYS, ENDYMION, EOS, KEPHALOS AND SELENE

b EOS MOURNING FOR MEMNON

virgin goddess Artemis. The tales inform us that the resurrection of a dead person provoked the wrath of Zeus. He slew
the divine physician with his lightning. Apollon avenged his
son by killing a number of Kyklopes. All this is merely a later
explanation of the god's servitude to Admetos, which he had
to suffer for the slaying of Delphyne.

7

TALES OF ARTEMIS

It will be remembered that one of the names of the Great Mother
of the Gods in Asia Minor (a goddess who besides being a
mother also had strong hermaphroditic characteristics) was
Great Artemis. Our Artemis was never called "mother", although she was just as close to her mother Leto as to her
brother Apollon. She appeared always as a maiden, but also
resembled a boy in her strength and wildness, as do girls of
that especial age which was under her protection. It was told[470]
that she besought her father to give her only nine-year-olds as
companions. This was the age at which girls left their mothers
and entered the service of Artemis: in earlier times all girls did
this, but later only certain chosen ones. They remained in the
goddess's service until they were nubile. At Athens the little
handmaidens of Artemis were called *arktoi*, "she-bears". Artemis herself must at one time have been supposed to be a bear
—or, in more ancient times, when the fauna of Greece was
more southern, a lioness.

On the other hand, she was always described as a virgin
huntress, and her companions were also virgins. Woe upon the
man who espied her bathing in the wild brooks and pools! For
this offence the Cretan Siproites[471] was turned into a woman.
Many know the story[472] of Aktaion, son of Aristaios and
Autonoe and nephew of Semele, the mother of Dionysos. It is
a tragic story, and was told in various forms. According to the
best-known version, Aktaion, whom Chiron had brought up

to be a hunter, surprised Artemis while she was bathing. The goddess punished him by turning him into a stag, which as a rule was her favourite beast but on this occasion was her victim. Aktaion's fifty hounds tore to pieces their metamorphosed master, and Autonoe had the grievous task of assembling the bones of her son. It must have been an older tale in which Aktaion clothed himself in a stag's pelt and approached Artemis in this disguise. In a later version of it, the wild hunter sought to rape Artemis; or else it was Semele, the beloved of Zeus, whom he coveted, and it was Artemis who cast the stag's pelt over his shoulders. All the tales agree that he was torn to pieces.

Another story concerning Artemis had as its tragic heroine a companion of the goddess, a certain Kallisto. This is the proper name formed from the adjective *kalliste*, "the most beautiful", and it was a name of Artemis herself. It was told[473] that Kallisto had been a nymph of Artemis's retinue, a huntress who wore the same garments as the goddess. In different tales she had different fathers: Nykteus, "the man of Night"; Keteus, "the man of the sea-monster"; or Lykaon, "the wolfish". Indeed, Kallisto herself also had various names, such as Megisto,[474] "the greatest", or Themisto,[475] a form of the name Themis. Zeus had seduced her, according to a comic writer, after assuming the shape of Artemis herself.[476] In the ancient stories Artemis still, of course, had the shape of a she-bear, and Zeus coupled with Kallisto as a bear. The original story was of a wedding of animals, and was described as such:[477] in the shape of a beast Kallisto mounted the couch of Zeus. In later stories Artemis discovered while bathing that her companion was pregnant, and in wrath turned her into a she-bear. The goddess is thought also to have killed the culprit. Nevertheless Kallisto finally appeared in the sky as the Great Bear,[478] after having borne to Zeus a son who was the first ancestor of the inhabitants of Arcadia. His name, Arkas, is connected with *arktos*, a bear. It was also said[479] that Kallisto bore twins: Arkas and Pan, the goat-footed god of the same country. The

ARTEMIS KILLS AKTAION

wildness of Arcadia and the antique character of its inhabitants were well suited to such gods and to such ancestors.

8

THE STORY OF BRITOMARTIS

The story of Britomartis is also a tale concerning Artemis. By this name, Britomartis, the Cretans invoked a divine maiden whom Artemis especially loved. Translated from the Cretic, the name means "sweet virgin".[480] In other parts of the great island she was called Diktynna, the goddess of Mount Dikte. This name also contains an echo of our word for a net, *diktys*. A net actually plays a part in the story.

It was told[481] that Britomartis was a daughter born to Zeus in Crete, and that she was a nymph and huntress. Minos, son of Zeus, fell in love with her. He pursued the wild maiden through the mountains of Crete. The nymph hid herself now in the oak-woods, now in the low regions. For nine months Minos was on her traces. He almost caught her on a steep crag of Mount Dikte. Her dress became caught on a bough of myrtle; but she herself leapt from the height into the sea, into the nets of fishermen, who saved her. Artemis raised her to the rank of goddess.

In the tales[482] told by the dwellers on the island of Aegina, Britomartis came there in a fisherman's boat. The fisherman, whose name was Andromedes, sought to violate her. But the goddess disappeared into the forest that already at this time covered the mountain where she has her shrine. On Aegina, however, she was not called Britomartis, but Aphaia, because she suddenly became invisible (*aphanes*). This explanation is certainly incorrect, since the two words are unrelated. But Aphaia's temple, on a southern mountain-spur of Aegina, can still be visited.

9

SURNAMES OF APOLLON AND ARTEMIS

Many surnames and appellations of Apollon and Artemis have already been woven into the stories I have been telling. Some of the names that I have not yet mentioned, such as Delphinios, which connects Apollon with dolphins, are self-explanatory. Only a few of the names—which are numerous —refer to known tales or descriptions.

It was described to us[483] how Apollon, who first came to Delphi with a drawn bow, later strode into the city in a long, fragrant robe, with the lyre in his hand, and thence, in a moment, appeared on Olympus in the assembly of the gods, who were at once seized with a longing for music and song. The Muses sang antiphonally of the immortal gifts of the gods and of the sorrows of ignorant and feeble men. The Charites, the Horai, Harmonia, Hebe and Aphrodite—a group of nine goddesses—danced in a circle, each holding her neighbour's wrist. Artemis, too, entered into the dance, and Ares and Hermes sported with the dancers. In their midst Apollon smote the lyre, beautiful and tall as he strode amongst them, alight with radiance. Brightly shone his feet and his raiment. Thus he appeared as *Musagetes* and *kitharodos*, as "Leader of the Muses" and "Singer to the Lyre". For our ancient story/tellers and poets it was as if the sunlight had been turned into music. "He brings all Nature into harmony", sang one of these poets of ours,[484] "the splendid Apollo of Zeus, he unites Beginning and End, and the plectrum of his lyre is the bright ray of the sun."

Artemis, similarly, was not always the Huntress, sending her gently slaying arrows upon mortal women and wild beasts. She was worshipped also under surnames that reveal the pleasure she took in the dancing of strange dancers both male and female. As Karyatis she rejoiced in the dances of the girls of the nut/tree village of Karyai, those Karyatides who in their ecstatic round/ dance carried on their heads baskets of live reeds, as if they were dancing plants. In honour of Artemis as Kordaka men per/ formed the dance *kordax*, with female movements. Another practice in her honour was that of girls wearing phalluses, as actors in comedies used also to do. At one of her festivals the men wore stags' antlers on their heads. Phallic masqueraders worshipped the goddess as Korythalia, a surname which means the same as Daphnaia, "Laurel/Maiden". She also had sur/ names referring to the moon, such as Hegemone and *keladeine* (I have already explained their meanings): these names she shared with the Charites. When the moon shone, Artemis was present, and beasts and plants would dance.

CHAPTER IX

Hera, Ares and Hephaistos

IT is time to speak of Hera's sons, Ares and Hephaistos. According to Homer both were also sons of Zeus but, according to Hesiod, Ares only. Yet Homer quotes Zeus[485] as saying that he hated Ares because he took his pleasure only in strife, war and battles (a remark, by the way, that could also be applied to Pallas Athene) and because he resembled his mother Hera, so that his proper place was amongst the Titans, in the deepest depths of Tartaros. Nevertheless Ares, in Homer's own description of him,[486] was untrue even to his mother. He knew no Themis and helped the enemy. He was a gigantic figure which, when it fell down[487] (as once when hit by a stone hurled by Athene), sprawled at a length of seven hundred feet. This figure was in all respects lacking in dignity. When "the brazen Ares" was wounded[488] he screamed like nine or ten thousand men.

Homer did not think that Hephaistos, either, was especially dignified. It is known that he limped and was more a dwarf than a giant. Yet at least he was a skilled master-craftsman and a peace-maker between his parents. The laughter he provoked amongst the gods on Olympus put an end to their strife.[489] From the description Homer gives of the two brothers, it is easy to tell how much our greatest poet hated war and strife. It is he whom we probably have to thank for the fact that so little is known about Ares: almost nothing, in fact, except that he was a son of Hera and an ally of the savage land of Thrace. His name sounded like *ara*, "curse"—although, indeed, this word also means "prayer"—and was almost another word for war; and the tales that had once given a more personal account of the god, perhaps as a child, were almost completely forgotten.

He is, however, shown as a child in the portrayals of him by the Etruscans, who must have got the prototypes for these from

our ancient artists. The story of his being conceived without
a father was preserved only amongst the Romans; who certainly
did not themselves invent the story, for such tales are characteristic of our goddess Hera. Typhaon, too, was borne by Hera
without a father: he is a figure who should not be overlooked
in this context. I shall proceed to say more of Typhaon, by way
of beginning my account of Hera as a mother. Hera is the link
between all the stories immediately following.

I

HERA'S MATERNITIES

It will be remembered that the dragoness of Delphi, whom
Apollo later slew, received from Hera a dragon, Typhaon,
whom the great goddess brought into the world in wrath
against her husband when he, Zeus, bore Pallas Athene. In
anger spoke Hera—so the tale went[490]—to the assembled
immortals:

> "Hear me, all of you, gods and goddesses, how Zeus
> undertakes to bring shame upon me—how he is the first
> to do so, after having taken me to wife. Without me he has
> born Athene, who is glorious amongst all the immortals,
> whilst my own son, whom I bore, Hephaistos, is the least
> of us all. I myself threw him into the sea; but Thetis, the
> daughter of Nereus, caught him up and cared for him with
> her sisters: she might well have done us another service!
> Thou deceitful monster! How hast thou dared to bear
> Athene? Could *I* not have borne thee a child? Was I not
> thy wife? Now I shall see to it that I may have a son who
> shall be glorious amongst the gods! I shall do it without
> dishonouring thy bed and my bed, yet without coming to
> thee. I shall stay apart from thee and remain with the
> other gods!"

Thereupon Hera went apart also from the other gods. She

prayed and smote the earth with her palm: "Hear me, Gaia and Ouranos, thou who art on high, and you Titans who dwell beneath the earth in Tartaros, you who are the ancestors of gods and men: hear me, all of you, and give me a son who shall not be weaker than Zeus himself! As Zeus was mightier than Kronos, so let my son be mightier than he!" She struck the earth with powerful hand. Gaia, the source of life, quivered; and Hera rejoiced, for she guessed that she had had her will. Thenceforward for a full year she did not lie with Zeus, nor did she sit by him in the place where they formerly took counsel together. She abode in her temples and enjoyed the sacrifices. When a year later the time came, she gave birth to something that resembled neither gods nor men: Typhaon, that terrible disaster for mortals. Hera brought him to Delphi and the dragoness took charge of him.

The story of Hera's conception of Ares, as told by a Latin poet,[491] is similar yet different. Here the goddess Gaia appears in the form in which she was the mother of the plants, especially of the flowers, and was invoked by the Romans as Flora, "the flower-goddess". She herself speaks, and tells almost the same story as the one I have just related. The wife of the king of the gods felt insulted for the reason I have explained, and proposed to make every effort to become pregnant without the aid of her husband. She was on her way to Okeanos, to ask for comfort and advice, but had broken her journey at the palace of the great goddess Flora, who gave her the herb—according to this story, a flower, but, in another story, a species of grass[492]—the magic simple whose touch could make the most sterile being fruitful. Hera was touched by the simple, and conceived the war-god. Pregnant she went back to Thrace, where she bore her son.

Hephaistos—according to the tale as here told by Hera herself—was not a fatherless birth, but simply misbegotten, and, as I shall shortly explain, a premature birth. This story sounds no less ancient and no less appropriate to very old times than that of the husbandless conception. Hesiod preferred to use the latter story,[493] in which Hera sought to compete with her husband by giving birth to the most gifted master-craftsman of all the descendants of Ouranos. I might at once proceed to tell these stories concerning Hephaistos; but I must first relate an ancient tale concerning Ares of which at least a trace has been preserved. It introduces another very ancient theme, which is common both to our mythology and to those of other peoples: the theme of twins.

2

ARES AND THE ALOADAI

The Dioskouroi Kastor and Polydeukes, the sons of Leda, were not the only twins in our mythology. The statement that this pair was, in respect of one half of it, subject to death—that is to say, associated with the Underworld—does not conflict with the statement that they were both divine beings. Nevertheless their deeds belong much more to heroic saga than to mythology. Other pairs of twins who were originally divine —such as the Apharides Idas and Lynkeus, the adversaries of the Dioskouroi—have passed completely into heroic saga. A very ancient pair of twins were the Aktorione Molione, "the two sons of Aktor and Molione", heroic boys who were hatched from a silver egg and whose bodies were fastened together.[494] Herakles could slay them only by a trick, and their mother avenged them. On the other hand, the Theban Dioskouroi, Amphion and Zethos, sons of Zeus and Antiope, were themselves the avengers of their mother. They took vengeance on another woman, who had usurped their mother's position. Amongst these ancient and originally divine pairs of twins were the Aloadai, or Aloeidai, who almost succeeded in slaying Ares and were betrayed by their mother.

It was told:[495] Otos and Ephialtes were twin boys who did not live long. Their father was Aloeus, whose name is derived from *aloe* and *halos*, "round place" and "round disk". Their mother Iphimedeia said that she had been made pregnant by

Poseidon. She was in love with the god,[496] and she repeatedly went to the sea and scooped water into her bosom with her hands until Poseidon begat the twins by her. In beauty these boys were second only to the famous hunter Orion, of whom I shall have more to say. Life-giving Earth had nurtured them to be giants. At the age of nine they were already nine ells broad and nine fathoms tall. It was more precisely said[497] that every month they grew by nine "fingers". They declared war on the gods of Olympus and planned to heap Mount Ossa on Mount Olympus, and Pelion on Ossa, and thus climb up into Heaven. Indeed, they would have carried out this plan if they had grown up to be youths. But Apollon killed them first. According to another story,[498] they could not be slain except one by the other. As they were trying to carry off Hera and Artemis, a doe sprang between them: it either was sent by Artemis or was Artemis herself in beast's form.[499] The twins hurled their spears at the doe, and each hit the other. Thus they came to the Underworld, where they were bound, each separately, to a pillar: on the pillar sat the dreadful owl "Styx".

One of the daring deeds[500] of the Aloadai was to capture Ares and shut him up in a brazen jar—one of those big jars, usually made of clay, which we have to this day. Here the god remained for thirteen months, and he would have perished had not the twins' stepmother, Eriboia, revealed the lostling's whereabouts to Hermes. Hermes stole the prisoner, who was already nearly dead of torment. It may be assumed that at this time Ares was still a boy, of the same age as the Aloadai themselves. In the Etruscan pictures I have mentioned, the boys are shown standing on the rim of a jar in which a fire is blazing: this is clearly the preliminary to an initiation ceremony. The further tale[501] that Ares, on the island of Naxos, hid himself in "an iron-eating stone" is reminiscent of the Dactyl boy Kelmis, whom his two brothers tormented and purified like iron on the anvil. Of Ares's upbringing, and of his tutor Priapos, who taught him dancing first and war only afterwards, I shall have more to tell later.

3

THE FALL AND UPBRINGING OF HEPHAISTOS

Other tales about Ares concern his relations with Hephaistos.
The story in which they both appear together with Aphrodite
is a famous one. Still another story, in which they appear with
their mother Hera—once again, a woman between the two of
them—will follow later. Hephaistos's premature and otherwise
unhappy birth—which forms the background to what followed
—has already been mentioned. But I must explain its significance more closely. The tale described the birth of a child who
limped on both feet, since the soles and heels were turned back
to front and were not fitted for walking, but only for a forwardrolling motion of the whole body. This disfigurement is clearly
shown on ancient vasepaintings; and I shall presently come to
the account of how Hephaistos, when cast forth from Olympus,
took a whole day in falling, like a sort of Catherinewheel in
the sky, before he reached the earth. His birth was premature
because it occurred during the three hundred years in which
Hera's relationship with Zeus was secret. The misbegetting was
the result of this prematureness, and the story of the husbandless
conception was only an excuse for it: so it was said,[502] and it
was also said[503] that Hephaistos was born from Hera's thigh.

Homer let Hephaistos himself tell the tale[504]—in words that
made no attempt to conceal the son's anguish at the fact that
Hera had sought to keep the misbegetting secret. The goddess
herself had declared what she did. She threw the child into the
sea, and it would have gone ill with him had not Eurynome
and Thetis caught him as he fell and taken him into their
bosom. For nine years Hephaistos remained with the two goddesses, and he fashioned for them, in a grotto by Okeanos,
clasps and buckles, earrings and necklets. No one knew of
this, neither god nor man, except the two seagoddesses who
had saved him. Homer puts into the mouth of Hephaistos
another story[505] of his fall. Perhaps it was the same story, but

giving another explanation for the fall: Hephaistos sought to aid his mother against Zeus, but his father seized him by the heel and hurled him down from the sacred threshold of the palace of the gods. All day Hephaistos fell through the air. As the sun was setting he fell on Lemnos, almost unbreathing. He was discovered and taken care of by the Sintians, a barbarian people who were said to have worshipped him on the island. This happened at a time when Zeus had set his wife to hang on a golden cord between Heaven and Earth in punishment for her persecution of Herakles.[506] Hera was strung up by both hands, with two anvils on her feet.

I shall shortly mention another occasion on which Hera was bound—this time by Hephaistos, in revenge for his mother's having cast him out. Not all stories, by the way, agree that it was his mother who did this. According to one tale,[507] Hera brought her son after his birth to the island of Naxos, to Kedalion, who was to be his tutor and to teach him smithcraft. Kedalion was a figure resembling the Kabeiroi. His name was as much as to say "the phallic one". He was also numbered with the Kyklopes,[508] from amongst whom Hephaistos took his fellow-craftsmen: but Hephaistos did this only later, when the tales had begun to connect the god with the great Vulcans or volcanoes of the west, with Etna and Vesuvius. At a place where fire springs from the earth in Lemnos, on the small mountain of Mosychlos, Hephaistos's companions were certain Kabeiroi called the Karkinoi, "the Crabs". He himself was thought to be the god of subterranean fire. In our language *hephaistos* also meant, in a general sense, "fire". I shall speak of Kedalion again, in the stories concerning the constellation Orion.

4

THE BINDING OF HERA

That was an ancient story which told of the binding of Hera by Hephaistos—a story of the same sort as that of the binding of Ares and Aphrodite, or those of the first thefts of Hermes, which I shall tell shortly. All these are tales of guileful deeds performed by cunning gods, mostly at a time when they had not yet joined the family on Olympus, although Zeus and Hera were already ruling there. These last had been joined by their brothers and sisters. Zeus's daughter Pallas Athene and his son Apollon both shared his power. Leto was there with her son, Artemis with her brother. The great goddess Aphrodite was also of the company; so were Ares and Dionysos. Hephaistos, however, held aloof, as I shall tell. Of Hermes this tale makes no mention. The order of time in which these last-named and younger gods were received upon Olympus was never certainly established, and is in any case unimportant.

It was told,[509] as I have said, that Hera was ashamed of her misbegotten son, that she cast him from her and sought to conceal her motherhood, and that her son resented this. He was alleged to have been given the task, as the famous master-craftsman, of fashioning thrones for the Olympians. At any rate, he sent a beautiful throne for Hera. She was pleased with the gift, sat on the throne and was suddenly bound with invisible chains. Nay more, the throne soared into the air with the enchained goddess. None could release her, and there was great consternation amongst the gods. They perceived the stratagem of Hephaistos, and sent a message to him that he should come and set free his mother. The cunning master-craftsman replied stubbornly that he had no mother. At the council of the gods all were silent and did not know how Hephaistos could be brought to Olympus. Ares undertook the task. But he had to retreat before Hephaistos's flames, and came back ignominiously defeated. An old vase-painting shows how the fight between the two brothers concerning their enthroned and enchained mother was enacted on the comic stage. They are fighting with lances, Ares being given the name Enyalios, which is another of his names, and Hephaistos being given the name Daidalos, which reveals the original identity of the divine master-craftsman with Daidalos of Athens.

How the story continued after the defeat of Ares was not only told in words but also depicted in magnificent paintings, with which our ancient artists decorated many vases. It was Dionysos, the son of Zeus and Semele, who succeeded in fetching the author of the stratagem. He gave him wine, with whose effects Hephaistos was clearly not yet familiar, set the intoxicated god on a mule and escorted him to Olympus as if in a triumphal procession. The gods must have laughed when they beheld the drunken master-craftsman. But he was not so drunk as to set free his mother for nothing. The price he demanded was Aphro-dite, or marriage with another goddess equally well known to us, Pallas Athene. We know that he never had much luck with goddesses. Anyhow, Hera was set free.

5

HERA, IXION AND THE CENTAURS

It will have been noticed that when Hera wished to bear a child without Zeus, she nevertheless was scrupulous not to dishonour her husband's bed. She laid especial emphasis on this. The form of marriage that she protected as our marriage-goddess was monogamy, or—as seen from the woman's point of view—the fulfilment of herself through a single husband, to whom she should be the single wife. Hence Hera's jealousy and hatred of sons born to Zeus by others. Zeus, on the other hand, not only was the marriage-god in our religion, but also represented the principle of the other, non-maternal origin of life: the principle of paternal origin as being the higher, the father not being associated with a single woman nor standing in a relation of servitude to womanhood generally—like the relation of the Daktyloi to the Great Mother—and still less so to a single woman, but instead bestowing progeny as a divine gift upon all women. Hera seems to have preserved from earlier, pre-Olympian times an association with beings of a Dactylic nature. It was told[510] that in her pre-matrimonial days she was raped by a Giant named Eurymedon, and conceived a son of him. This son was not Hephaistos, but Prometheus, who is very close to Hephaistos. And there were tales also of how Zeus's wife—presumably in the dark days of her separation from her husband, when she was visiting primordial gods such as Okeanos or the Titans in the Underworld—was attacked by phallic beings called Satyrs, as one sees in pictures of the scene that are to be found in her famous temple near Paestum, or in vase-paintings.

Another, similar story[511] had its setting in Heaven. It was told of Ixion, king of the Lapithai, who in primitive times were the inhabitants of Thessaly. Ixion's father is said to have been Ares, or else Phlegyas, the notorious evildoer; but other persons are also named as having begotten him. His earthly wife was called Dia, which is only another name for Hebe, the daughter of Hera, and indeed was probably the name for Hera herself, as "she who belongs to Zeus" or "the Heavenly one" —for this is the meaning of the word. Ixion had promised to pay his father-in-law Deioneus, "the destroyer", a rich bride-price. When Deioneus came for payment, the son-in-law dug for him a fiery pit covered over with thin wood and dust, and devised that he should fall into it. Ixion was thus the first to introduce parenticide amongst mortals. He thereupon went mad, and no one, neither god nor man, would purify him of the murder, until Zeus himself took pity on him and not only gave him absolution but raised him up to Heaven, where he made him his guest and bestowed immortality upon him. In the palace where he was a guest, Ixion beheld Hera and coveted her. Hera reported this to Zeus. To discover the truth, Zeus fashioned an image of his wife from cloud. Ixion embraced the cloud and begat on it a child that was half man, half horse. Zeus, enraged at Ixion's twofold sin, had the evildoer bound to a winged, fiery wheel, which everlastingly spins through the air whilst the penitent repeats the words: "Thou shalt requite thy benefactor with thankfulness!" The scene of the punish-ment was later transferred to the Underworld. One can easily recognise in the whole story the punishment of an older, savage sun-god who had to be tamed beneath the rule of Zeus.

Ixion begat on the cloud without Charites—that is to say, without Aphrodite: the same thing was said[512] of the conception of Hephaistos. Of Ixion's son, a being of twofold shape named Kentauros, it was told[513] that he mated with the mares on Mount Pelion. This was the origin of the Centaurs, those wild forest-dwellers on whose four-legged body of a horse was set the upper body of a man. They were the dangerous neighbours of the Lapithai, who had to fight hard against the Centaurs when the latter sought to carry off their women—a famous event that took place at the marriage of Peirithoos and Hippodameia: it belongs properly to heroic saga. Another being named[514] as Ixion's son was Chiron, of whom I have already spoken. He was the most righteous of the Centaurs.[515] In a cave beneath the summit of Pelion he brought up the heroes and sons of gods. Outstanding amongst these was the divine physician Asklepios; for Chiron himself was the first physician and the first to understand the uses of herbs. It was also told[516] of Chiron that Kronos, in the shape of a horse, begat him by Philyra, "Lime-tree", a daughter of Okeanos. In an old vase-painting he appears in a robe covered with stars, with an uprooted tree over his shoulder carrying his spoils of the chase, and with his dog beside him: a savage hunter and dark god. His sorrows and his goodness will be described in the story of Prometheus.

CHAPTER X

Maia, Hermes, Pan and the Nymphs

OF Maia, who gave Zeus his cleverest son, Hermes the messenger of the gods, it is not easy to say what sort of goddess she was originally. Was she merely a nymph, as she appears in the Hymn ascribed to the age of Homer? We used to employ "Maia" as a term of address to a wise and good old woman. The word also meant "midwife", and in one dialect it meant "grandmother". As I have said, it was by this name that Zeus addressed the goddess Night when he sought an oracle of her.[517]

The mother of Hermes dwelt, at the time when she conceived and bore her son, in a dark cave of Mount Kyllene in Arcadia. But she was not the goddess of this mountain: if she had been, Sophocles would not, in a play of his based on the tale told in the Hymn, have specially introduced the nymph Kyllene as the child's nurse. Kyllene belonged to the mountain from her origin: Maia, on the other hand, was connected with the night sky in her character as one of the Pleiades. All these stars were retired maiden goddesses. They were thought[518] to be daughters of Atlas, of whom we know that he stood in the west supporting the arch of the heavens. The mother of the Pleiades is said to have been Pleione, or else Aithra, "the bright", both of whom were Okeaninai. Of the daughters it was said that they formed a maidenly band of Artemis and were pursued by the wild hunter Orion until Zeus turned them into doves (*peleiades*), after which he turned both the pursued and the pursuer into stars. Especially close to Maia was Kallisto, a companion of Artemis: I have already spoken of her at some length. When the bear-shaped Kallisto had borne Zeus their son Arkas, and had herself disappeared from the earth, the son was cared for by Maia.[519]

Was Maia never, even in the oldest times, anything more

than a Pleiad? Her association with Heaven and Night suggests
that she was of greater importance. There is, however, not a
single surviving story in which she appears in a principal rôle
—unless we count the famous tale told in the Homeric Hymn,
in which she appears as the mother of Hermes. This tale I shall
now relate, for the most part in the original words.

I

THE BIRTH AND FIRST DEEDS OF HERMES

Maia, the modest nymph—so the tale[520] begins—never entered
the assembly of the blessed gods. She dwelt in a deeply
shadowed cave, where Zeus played the love-game with her, in
impenetrable night, whilst Hera slept. None knew of this,
neither god nor man. The desire of Zeus found its fulfilment.
The tenth month came to the nymph and brought the matter
to light, the thing was revealed: she bore a son, of great cunning,
a deceitful flatterer, a robber and cattle-reaver, a bringer of
dreams and a nightly prowler, as are those who lurk in the
street before the gates. He was soon to achieve fame amongst
the gods by his deeds. In the early morning he was born, at
noon he played on the lyre, at evening he stole the cows of
Apollon—all on that same fourth day of the month in which
Maia brought him into the world.

Scarcely yet sprung from his mother's immortal body, he
remained not long in the sacred cradle, but rose up and strode
over the threshold of the tall cave, to seek for the kine of
Apollon. He found a tortoise and made thereof an inestimable
boon. Hermes it was who first from the shell of the tortoise
made a sounding instrument. The tortoise met him by the gate
of the cave, grazing and dragging its feet, as tortoises do. The
son of Zeus, the swift Hermes, saw it and laughed: "Already
a happy token! I am not displeased to see thee. Welcome,
beautiful dancer, companion to the banquet! Thou comest at the
right moment. Whence, tortoise, didst thou take so delightful

a toy, the protecting shell on thy back, thou who dwellest in the mountains? I shall take thee into my house; be thou of service to me! It is better to be indoors, outside it is dangerous. Even in thy life thou art a protection against harmful magic. When thou diest, thou shalt beautifully sing!"

Thus Hermes began by inventing the lyre. With both hands he took the tortoise into the cave, where he cut it up: his words and his actions were as swift as thought. He fastened into the shell two reed-pipes with a link at the top, and everything else that one sees on such an instrument in the old pictures of it. He strung on it the seven strings of sheep-gut. Then, when he had made ready the lovely toy, he tried its notes with the plectrum: the lyre rang out mightily in his hand. Beautifully sang the god, finding the words and music as he sang, in the musical mode in which youths at banquets exchange pert raillery. He sang of Zeus and Maia, how they played their love-game, and he lauded his own birth that resulted from it. He also commemorated the riches that the nymph received. Yet his thoughts were elsewhere. He laid the lyre in the sacred cradle; he yearned for meat. So he sprang forth from the fragrant cave, to prowl and lurk stealthily, as thieves do in the darkness of night.

Helios was going down with his team and chariot when Hermes arrived in Pieria, on the shady mountain of the gods, where also was their immortal herd of cattle, grazing on the fresh grass or sheltered in their stalls. The son of Maia, the prowler, he who was soon afterwards to slay the many-eyed Argos, cut off fifty cows from the herd. He drove them backwards, so that their hind-hooves were in front and their fore-hooves behind. They came to sandy soil. Hermes made for himself sandals such as no one else could devise, of branches of tamarisk and myrtle, and bound them beneath his feet. He was in haste, and he still had far to go. He was observed by an old man who tilled a vineyard in Boeotia near Onchestos, about half-way on the god's journey. Hermes said to him: "Old man, thou shalt have grapes in plenty; but thou hast not seen what thou hast seen, and thou hast not heard what thou hast heard! And thou shalt be silent, else it will be the worse for thee!"

So he drove the cows swiftly over mountains and valleys and blossoming meadows. Dark Night, his divine helper, had already passed by, and it was almost morning. Selene, daughter of Pallas, appeared in the sky just as the son of Zeus arrived with Apollon's cattle at the river Alpheios. Unwearied, the cows entered the cave-farmyard and ate the dove-soft, fine grass. Hermes meanwhile gathered wood and set about lighting a fire. Of laurel he made a tinder easy to handle. The warmth expanded to a conflagration. Hermes was the first to light a fire. In a pit arose a great blaze of dry wood. The flames shot up high, and the heat spread far around. Whilst the power of Hephaistos set the fire burning, Hermes, with mighty strength, brought two cows from the farmyard to the fire. He threw them down on their backs, turned them over and broke their spines. This he did first to one and then to the other. He cut off meat and fat and roasted the whole on wooden spits. The hides he set to dry on a rock, where, so the story goes, they could still be seen at the time of its telling. Thereafter followed the exact division of the meat into twelve parts, for the twelve gods of Olympus, with a share for Hermes himself. And howsoever he yearned for the sacrificial meat, howsoever the savoury fragrance tormented him, he resisted it and took not a morsel into his mouth—for the gods, to whom sacrifices are made, do not really consume the flesh of the victim. He heaped up the meat in the cave-farmyard, as a memorial to his first theft. The rest was burnt in the fire.

When the god was finished he threw the sandals in the river, put out the fire and scattered the black ashes. Thus the whole night passed—the second night, and Hermes was not yet home. Selene was already shining from the sky. Early in the morning he came to divine Mount Kyllene; nobody met him on the long journey, neither god nor man, no dog barked at him. Swift Hermes, son of Zeus, slipped into the hall of the cave through the keyhole, like a breath of autumn, like mist.

Straightway he strode light-footed through the cave into the rich innermost shrine, with noiseless tread. Swiftly Hermes laid himself in the cradle, drew the swaddling clothes around his shoulders and played like a little child with the sheets around his loins. Thus he lay, with his lyre beneath his left arm. But the goddess his mother had observed everything, and she spoke to the god her son: "Whence comest thou, thou sly one, whence comest thou by night, thou shameless boy? I fear that soon the son of Leto will drag thee through the door with chains upon thy body! Or else thou shalt pass thy life as thieves do, in the ravines. Go back whence thou camest! Thy father begat thee to be a sore vexation to gods and men."

Cunningly Hermes answered her: "Wherefore these words, mother, spoken as if to a baby that still knows little of evil, but is easily frightened and awed when its mother scolds it? For my part I choose that masterly skill which will best provide for me and thee for all time. Nay, we do not wish to sit amongst the gods without gifts or prayers, as is thy plan! Surely it is better to sport for all eternity amongst the immortals, in inexhaustible wealth, rather than to cower here in this gloomy cave! I mean to win the same sacred reverence as is paid to Apollon! Unless my father grants me this, I shall pluck up the courage—and I can do it!—to become a prince of thieves. If the son of Leto tracks me down, then something still worse may befall him: I shall go to Pytho and burgle his house. There I shall have enough tripods and basins, gold, gleaming iron and many robes to plunder. That thou shalt see, if thou so desirest!"

Thus they spake together, the son of Zeus and Lady Maia. Morning came from Okeanos and brought light to men. Apollon was already come to Onchestos, to the sacred grove of Poseidon. There he met the strange old man in his vineyard by the wayside. He spoke to him and told of the cattle that he sought: all of them cows with crumpled horns. Only the bull and the dogs had been left behind; the cows had gone, just as the sun was setting. Had not the old man seen a man pass by with cows? The old man answered: "My friend, it is difficult to tell of all that one sees. Many wayfarers pass by this place, both good and evil. How could one examine them all? Furthermore, I was digging all day long until sunset, here in the vineyard. Yet it seems to me that I saw a boy, but I am not sure of it, and I do not know who the little boy was, who came by with cattle, with a staff in his hand. He walked backwards behind the cows, continually looking over his shoulder: their heads were turned towards him." Thus spake the old man. Hastening his steps, Apollon observed a bird with outspread wings, and at once knew by this sign that it was a son of Zeus who had turned thief. In a single bound he was in Pylos, wrapped in darkly gleaming mist; he observed the tracks and said to himself: "How strange a thing! Those are certainly the tracks of cattle, yet they are leading in the opposite direction, towards the meadow of asphodel! But the footprints are neither those of a man, nor of a woman, nor of wolves, bears or lions. I cannot believe that even a Centaur would leave such huge footprints. That is still more perplexing."

Apollon had scarcely spoken when he was already on wooded Mount Kyllene, by the deeply shadowed hiding-place in the rock where the immortal nymph had brought forth the son of Zeus. All around was a sweet fragrance. Many sheep were grazing on the mountain. Apollon stepped over the stone threshold into the cave. When the son of Zeus and of Maia perceived the angry newcomer, he disappeared entirely into his sweet-smelling swaddling-clothes. As burnt wood is hidden beneath its ash, so did Hermes cover himself from Apollon. He huddled together his head and hands and feet, like one who is freshly bathed and woos sweet sleep. But in truth he lay there awake, with his lyre under his arm. The son of Zeus and of Leto recognised them, and well he knew them, the lovely nymph of the mountain and her beloved son, the little one curling himself up there so prudently and deceitfully. Apollon looked into every corner of the cave, with the metal key he opened three hidden chambers all filled with nectar and ambrosia. Much gold and silver lay there, many crimson-purple and gleaming white robes, such as are stored in the sacred houses of the blessed gods. When he had explored all corners of the house, the son of Leto addressed himself to Hermes: "Thou child there, thou in the cradle! Tell me, where are the cows? And the quicker the better! Else we shall scarcely part in peace! I shall hurl thee into black Tartaros, into the deadly darkness from which there is no salvation. Neither thy mother nor thy father shall restore thee thence to the light. Henceforward thou shalt be of the Underworld, and shalt have thy dominion amongst tiny people!" (By these, Apollon meant the dead.)

Guilefully answered him Hermes: "What unfriendly words dost thou speak there, son of Leto? What are these cows that thou seekest? Nothing have I seen or heard of them, or learned from others. Nothing can I declare unto thee, nor even win the reward of an informer. Do I seem like unto a strong man who reaves cows? Not thus am I employed, but far otherwise —in sleeping and drinking mother's milk, lying in my swad-dling-clothes or in my warm bath. Only beware, therefore, lest anyone should learn the reason for thy scolding! It would indeed be astonishing news, that a newborn child should go out yonder in search of cows. Yesterday was I born, my feet are tender and the ground is hard! Yet, if thou wilt, I shall swear to thee on the head of my father that neither am I guilty nor have I seen anyone else steal thy cows—whatever cows these may have been! This is the first time I have heard of them!" As he said this he blinked earnestly, raised his eyebrows and emitted a long whistle to cover the emptiness of his words.

Smiling, said Apollon: "Ah, thou, my pet! Thou cunning deceiver! Thou speakest like a trained thief! Many herdsmen shall suffer at thy hands in the mountains, when, lusting after meat, thou shalt come upon their herds! But if it is thy wish that this slumber of thine shall not be thy last, then leap up from thy cradle, thou companion of black night! For this shall be thy especial glory amongst the immortal gods: thou shalt be the Prince of Thieves for all eternity!" Thus spake Apollon, seized up the child and sought to carry it off in his arms. But Hermes had expected this: he let fall a token in his half-brother's hand, an evil messenger of the stomach, and thereupon at once sneezed. Apollon immediately dropped him and, despite his haste, sat down on the ground beside the child and scolded him. But soon he said: "Nay, forward, then, cheerily, thou swaddled babe, son of Zeus and of Maia! With such bird's tokens I shall find my cows! Thou shalt be my guide!"

Hermes leapt up and ran before Apollon, with his swaddling-clothes around his shoulders, making signs with his hands beside his ears, bemoaning his lot and cursing all the cows in the world, insisting on his innocence and even threatening Apollon with the wrath of Zeus. But it would be superfluous to quote his words exactly, for you will certainly have realised that these gods were playing a game. Why did Apollon sit down on the ground beside Hermes, if not in sheer laughter? Yet the tale went on to describe in detail how the game was continued on Olympus, at the very knees of the father: Zeus behaved as if Hermes were a stranger to him, and asked Apollon where he had found this lovable captive, this newborn boy who so much resembled a messenger. Was it fitting, he asked, to bring such an object into the assembly of the gods? At this Apollon described the doings of the little robber. He reported how his cows had been stolen, how Hermes had played the trick with the huge sandals, and how Apollon had finally discovered him in the darkest corner of the gloomy cave, where no eagle could have seen him. What was more, Hermes had tried to conceal the brilliance of his eyes by covering them with his hands! Apollon then proceeded to give an account of the lies that Hermes had told.

Thereupon Hermes pointed a finger at Zeus and said: "Father Zeus, to thee I shall tell the truth. For I am truthful and cannot lie. He came into our house early this morning in search of his cows. He brought with him no witness, such as might have seen what had happened and could give evidence before the gods. He sought forcibly to compel me to make a confession, and he threatened to throw me into Tartaros—since, indeed, he is a young man in his prime, whereas I was born only yesterday, as he himself knows. . . ." And so on: Hermes's own father would surely believe him, and might it go worse with Hermes if he were not telling the truth! He, Hermes, felt ashamed before Helios and the other gods! Now again Hermes forswore himself, but this time, in Zeus's presence, not on the head of his father but on the splendid entrance to the palace of the gods; and he threatened Apollon with retribution. Zeus, he said, ought to help the younger! At this the father burst into huge merriment, bade the brothers be reconciled, and commanded Hermes to lead his brother to the place where he had hidden the cows. Having spoken, Zeus made with his head that sign which even Hermes had to obey, like all gods and men.

So the two splendid sons of Zeus hastened to Pylos. Hermes drove the cows out of the pen that lay there hidden in a cave by the river Alpheios; he drove them forth into the light. Apollon had already seen from afar the cows' hides on the mighty rocks, and he marvelled at the strength of the boy, that he had been able to slaughter two head of cattle. Hermes performed yet another wonder: when Apollon sought to tie him and the cows with withies, Hermes caused the withies to take root again in the ground and grow up over the cows, so that they could not get away. Then he appeased his brother's anger with the sound of the lyre. Apollon laughed aloud for joy. The wondrous tone pierced his heart, and he was seized by sweet yearning as he listened with all his soul. The son of Maia stood there, at his left-hand side, fearing not, playing on the lyre and singing with a lovely voice in honour of the immortal gods and dark Earth, telling how they came to be and how each received his portion. In his song he praised above all gods Mnemosyne, since he himself, the son of Maia, was of her portion. Of the other gods he sang, all in the fairest and most fitting order, in accordance with their dignities and the order of time in which they came to be.

Apollon's yearning for the lyre was unquenchable. He reckoned that the instrument was well worth the fifty cows, and he admired his brother for having invented it. He praised the lyre, whose sound has a threefold effect: joyfulness, love and sweet sleep. He, too, said Apollon, was a constant com-panion of the Olympian Muses, but hitherto only as a flute-player. From now on the fame of Hermes and his mother would be secure amongst the gods; and he, Apollon, would promise anything in exchange for the lyre. Crafty Hermes behaved graciously: he gave Apollon the lyre, and received for it, as a first reward, Apollon's herdsman's crook and herdsman's status. He had, of course, to swear to his brother that he would not steal from him the lyre or the bow. Thereupon Apollon presented Hermes with a further gift, a golden three-leaved staff, which bestows wealth. (The tale does not here specially refer to the well-known staff of Hermes, with its entwined double serpent—the staff of the Messenger.) The only thing that Apollon might not cede to his brother was the power of high soothsaying; for Apollon alone was entrusted with the knowledge of the decisions of Zeus. But he gave Hermes the soothsaying of three swarming virgins—three sister bees on Parnassus—and also his own former dominion over the beasts, together with the office of initiated Messenger on the path leading to the House of Hades in the Underworld: the office of Psychopompos, the escort of souls. Such a liking had Apollon taken to the son of Maia, who furthermore received from Zeus the right to traffic with immortals and mortals: the office of Messenger of the Gods. Human beings, too, benefit by Hermes—but not greatly: for sometimes he wilfully leads them astray in the dark Night.

2

HERMES, APHRODITE AND HERMAPHRODITOS

Either the story of the first deeds of Hermes was at one time told in greater detail, or else it was later amplified with the tale[521] of how the cattle-thief seized his opportunity, whilst wrathful Apollon was threatening him, to steal also his quiver and arrows: whereat his brother burst out laughing. All this happened in Apollon's "pastoral time", which was spent in Thessaly. In this country his younger brother could feel as much at home as in Arcadia. The religious images erected to him were either in the "Cyllenian" style, in which the image was a phallus of wood or stone, or else in that related style in which the image was a rectangular pillar with a head and an erect phallus—an image which in our language is called a *herma*. This form of image is said[522] to have come from the Mysteries of the Kabeiroi—that is to say, from northern Greece, where Thessaly lies. Lake Boibeis in Thessaly was the scene of that love-story of Hermes which I related when speaking of the birth of Asklepios. It was told[523] that when the god beheld the goddess—sometimes called Persephone, sometimes Brimo[524] —his natural impulses were shamelessly excited. In that region this same goddess must also have been thought to be the god's mother; for sometimes Hermes is mentioned[525] as the fruit of the love-affair on Lake Boibeis. When it is also stated[526] that Hermes begat Eros by Artemis, this is again the same story. We are always confronted with the same Great Goddess, to whom Hermes—in that form of his ancient religious images which was connected with the Daktyloi—was both husband and son.

In a more widely known tale, the goddess thus closely associated with Hermes was Aphrodite. The two were regarded as brother and sister, both of them being, in one genealogy,[527] children of Ouranos, the night-sky, and Hemera, the brightness of day. Indeed, Hermes and Aphrodite must

clearly have been twins, for they had the same brithday.[528]
on the fourth day of the lunar month. Their son was Eros:[529]
or else, indeed, he was that other being of whom I shall now
tell. This last had, as a child, been entrusted by Aphrodite to
the nymphs of Mount Ida,[530] where he was reared to manhood
in a cave. In the features of the lovely boy could be discerned
those of both his father and his mother. When he was fifteen
years old he left his mountain home and swept across the whole
of Asia Minor, everywhere admiring the rivers, springs and
fountains of the region. Thus he came to Caria, to the magnificent fountain of the nymph Salmakis. She was not a companion of Artemis, she never hunted, but simply combed her
hair and admired herself in the mirror of the water. When she
saw the boy—whose name might equally well have been Eros
—she fell in love with him; but she could not seduce him.
He repulsed the nymph; but he could not resist the water,
and plunged into the fountain. Salmakis embraced the boy,
and the gods fulfilled her wish: she became one with the son
of Hermes and Aphrodite, that son who was called Hermaphroditos and since then was indeed a hermaphrodite, a
female boy—yet not like Attis, who entirely lost his manhood.

In this form the story was certainly not ancient. It will be
remembered, however, that, in Amathus on Cyprus, Aphrodite was herself worshipped as Aphroditos. So in that country
we find, too, in a single being that union of female and male
which was also achieved by Salmakis: a union that even in
these days finds expression in our language, when we speak
of a married couple as being an *androgyno*, a "man-woman".
The opposing counterpart to such mutual fulfilment is presented in the tale of Narkissos, a tragic boy-figure who so much
resembled Hyakinthos that the two were often confused together. It was told[531] of the beautiful Narkissos that in his
sixteenth year he for the first time saw his reflection, in one of
the many fountains on Helicon, in the region of Thespiai in
Boeotia, a region where Eros was especially worshipped.
Narkissos fell in love with his own reflection and pined away,

or else killed himself.[532] From his body arose the flower that is today still called the narcissus: a name derived from our ancient word *narke*, "stupor".

Another figure that could equally well be confused with Hyakinthos, and was therefore also supposed[533] to be a boy beloved by Apollon, was Hymenaios, so named after the cry of "Hymen", a melodic refrain in our marriage-songs. The word also meant a girl's maidenhead—her "flower", as it is metaphorically called.[534] There was more than one story[535] of how at his marriage the fair youth Hymenaios died in the bridal chamber; and there was also a tale[536] that he wore girl's clothes in order to follow the beloved maiden whom he was to marry. He can be seen in a Pompeian wall-painting, where he is depicted as a second Hermaphroditos. This quality of the young god seems to refer to the condition that led up to marriage, and was ended by marriage, both for boys and for girls: a condition that connects Hymenaios not only with Hyakinthos but also with Adonis.

3

THE BIRTH AND LOVE-AFFAIRS OF PAN

Reckoned amongst the sons of Hermes was the great phallic god of the inhabitants of the Peloponnese, especially of Arcadia —a goat-horned, goat-legged god named Pan. A story resembling that of Apollon's servitude to King Admetos in Thessaly was told also of Hermes.[537] Furthermore, the love-story linked with it introduces Dryops, the "Oak-Man"; just as Dryope, of whom I have already spoken, occurs in the story of Apollon. The story concerning Hermes, on the other hand, was set in Arcadia. Hermes pastured sheep for a mortal master, and whilst so doing fell in love with a nymph, the "Nymph of Dryops". It is not stated that Dryops was Hermes's mortal master, but he seems to have been so. Hermes's desire found fulfilment, and a magic child was born, with goat's feet and goat's horns, crowing and laughing. When his mother had borne him, she sprang up and fled, leaving none to suckle the child: so terrified was she when she saw its wild and bearded face. Hermes picked up his son, wrapped him in a hare's pelt and hastily brought him to Olympus. He sat down beside Zeus and the other gods, and introduced his son to them. The immortals were delighted with the child—Dionysos most of all. They named him Pan because "all" had been pleased by him.

In our language *pan* means "All", and the god was later identified with the physical Universe—although his name, except for its sound, has nothing to do with this. The story I have just told suggests that Pan was one of the youngest generation of gods. It will be remembered, however, that each generation of gods must have had its own Pan: seeing that there was already a Pan in Zeus's cave, who helped Zeus against the Titans, or against Typhon; and seeing, also, that a Pan was—together with Arkas—a son of Zeus and Kallisto. Our great poet and mythologian Aeschylus[538] distinguished between two Pans: a son of Zeus, a twin brother of Arkas; and a son of Kronos. The distinction between various Pans was also expressed in composite names such as Titanopan, Diopan, Hermopan—referring in each case to his father—or Aigipan, which was used by those who did not wish to assign any particular parentage to the god. In the retinue of Dionysos, or in depictions of wild landscapes, there appeared not only a great Pan, but also little Pans, Paniskoi, who played the same part as the Satyrs, of whom I shall speak presently. This resemblance to the Satyrs, of whom there must at first have been more than one, led to a dispersion and multiplication of the god Pan, who perhaps, when he originally came into being, had only a single twin brother and represented the darker half of a divine male couple.

Everyone knows the characteristics that were ascribed to Pan in numerous lesser tales: dark, terror-awakening, phallic, but not always malignant. He could, of course, sometimes be malignant, especially at noon, if he were awakened from his sleep.[539] At night he led the dance of the nymphs, and he also ushered in the morning and kept watch from the mountain summits.[540] Many love-stories were told of him,[541] in which he pursued nymphs. These chases often had the same result as Apollon's pursuit of Daphne: the nymph Pitys turned herself into a pine; Syrinx turned herself into a reed-pipe, from which Pan fashioned the *syrinx*, a herdsman's flute with a row of holes; Echo, chased by Pan, became a mere voice, mere refracted sound. But Pan's greatest passion was for Selene. Of this affair it was told[542] that the moon-goddess refused to company with the dark god. Whereupon Pan, to please her, dressed himself in white sheep-skins, and thus seduced Selene. He even carried her on his back. It is, of course, uncertain whether even in the earliest time it was necessary for him thus to change his shape in order to play the rôle of successful lover with a goddess who repeatedly lets herself be embraced by darkness.

4

THE STORIES CONCERNING PRIAPOS

What was the name of that god of whom it was publicly said that he was both father and son to Hermes?[543] He cannot be named with complete certainty, for of the lines of the inscription that gave the necessary information only a fragment has been preserved. I have already said that Hermes himself appeared, in his quality of phallic god, as both husband and son of one and the same goddess. It follows that another phallic god could fill both rôles: when Hermes was regarded as the father, then this other was the son, and vice versa. This relation between the two exactly corresponded to the relation between the Great Mother and her male partner, whom she bore, took to husband and bore again.

In the aforementioned dedicatory inscription this other god

was in all probability Priapos, the phallic god of the cities of Priapos and Lampsakos on the Hellespont, which is the modern Dardanelles. Priapos, too, was numbered amongst the sons of Hermes,[544] and it was claimed[545] for him that he was none other than the Hermaphroditos. His mother was said to be Aphrodite, and his father was usually supposed to be Dionysos, or sometimes Adonis,[546] or even Zeus himself.[547] The tale of Priapos's birth is obviously modelled on those of the births of Hephaistos and Pan. It was the story[548] of a misbegetting. Aphrodite had born a child so monstrous—with a huge tongue and a mighty belly, a creature excessively phallic, and indeed phallic to the rear (a thing that was said also of Phanes)—that she cast him from her, forsook him and denied him. The alleged cause of the misbegetting was the envy or jealousy of Hera (a cheap theme, and certainly not an ancient one). Hera, it was said, had applied to the body of the pregnant Aphrodite an evil, magic touch. A herdsman had found the monster, and had realised that the peculiar position of his phallic organ—in other words, that characteristic which was not merely phallic, but hermaphroditic—was useful to the fertility of plants and animals.

We had other divinities of excessively—indeed, of purely— phallic character, whose sphere was begetting and fertility: such as Orthanes, "the erect" (he, too, was said[549] to be a son of Hermes); Konisalos, "the dust whirler"; or Tychon, "he who hits his mark". Amongst us the sphere of the Hellespontine Priapos was so restricted that he played the part only of a grotesque garden-god, a sort of scarecrow. Writers invented obscene and comic situations for him. They told[550] how he tried to assault the sleeping Hestia—or Roman Vesta—and was given away by the braying of an ass. In fact, the ass-sacrifices made to him in his own country were famous. In Bithynia in Asia Minor it was told[551] of him that he was a warlike god, one of the Titans or of the Idaioi Daktyloi. Hera made him tutor to the child Ares, but he first of all trained the boy to be a perfect dancer, and only later to be a warrior.

This puts Priapos into the group of phallic or half-animal tutors of the gods, a group that includes Kedalion, Chiron and Silenos, but also includes Pallas, the tutor of Athene.

5

NYMPHS AND SATYRS

Nymphs appeared in many stories told of greater deities. There could be no better place in which to speak of them than in this account of Hermes. Of all the gods Hermes was the only nymph's son who had a permanent place on Olympus; and this fact was clearly reflected in his close and steady association with those goddesses who were called *Numphai*. This associa-tion must have been the reason why the great goddess who was addressed, under *one* of her names, as Maia, was compelled, as mother of Hermes, to set aside or to conceal her original status. The word *numphe* meant a female being through whom a man became the *numphios*, i.e. the happy bridegroom who had fulfilled the purpose of his manhood. The term could be applied to a great goddess as well as to a mortal maiden. If, however, some being were described simply as a nymph, even if she were also described expressly as "goddess" and "daughter of Zeus", this did not mean that she had the eternal character of the great gods.

Amongst eternal beings could be numbered, for example, the Nereides (who were closest to the nymphs)—as eternal as their element, the sea. On the other hand, those water-nymphs (Naiades or Naides) who belonged to fountains, and not to greater waters, were no more everlasting than the fountains themselves. Still less so were the nymphs associated with field and forest, especially with single trees, as were the Dryades or Hamadryades, the "Oak-Nymphs". They died with their oaks. There was[552] an ancient method of calculating a nymph's span of life: "Nine human spans lives the chattering rook; a stag as long as four rooks; a raven as long as three stags; a

palm as long as nine ravens; and as long as ten palms live the
beautiful-haired nymphs, the daughters of Zeus."

There was a statement to much the same effect[553] in the tale
of Aphrodite and Anchises, in which the great goddess
entrusted her mortal son to the nymphs of Mount Ida—deep-
breasted goddesses. For the nymphs were more often nurses
of gods and heroes, deputies and manifold images of their
mothers, than they were mothers themselves.

> "They are neither human beings nor immortals," so it
> is stated in this tale, "they live long, they feed on ambrosia
> and dance their round-dances with the gods. Silene and
> Hermes play the love-game with them in the corners of
> their pleasant grottoes. Pines and oaks began growing
> when they were born, and thrive together with them.
> Mightily stand such trees, their name is 'Grove of the
> Gods', and mortals never lay iron to them. Yet if, by the
> will of Fate, death comes to them, the beautiful trees first
> of all wither up, then they loose their barks, their branches
> break off, and at this the souls of their nymphs also depart
> from the light of the sun."

These words make it plain that nymphs were at first associated
with the trees of a Grove of the Gods: especially with trees
that were dear to one or other of the greater goddesses, and
whose griefs—so it was told[554]—caused the great goddess,
too, to grieve.

Both at earlier and later times the nymphs also appeared as
themselves: with beautiful countenances, clad in long gowns,
led by Hermes, usually three of them at a time. Three appears
to have been their basic number, the number of the Graces
and of the other well-known Trinities, all of which imaged the
dispersed form of a great Threefold Goddess. The nymphs can
also certainly be said to do this. Hermes, their constant companion—often in the presence of Pan—represented the male
fourth beside the female Trinity. The Silenoi, whom I have
just mentioned, formed part of a corresponding relationship in

which the male element was represented in the plural. Such beings—doubtless originally men who in dances and proces-sions presented the phallic escorts of the great goddess—were called, in an ancient Peloponnesian dialect, Satyroi, "the full ones": a term descriptive of their "abundant", and therefore sexually excited, condition. This was the more general name for them. "He-goats" who played the same rôle—men in goat-skins; or, in the tales, goat-like divine playthings of the nymphs —were also called Satyrs. The word *silenos* was also connected with such dancers, who in this rôle appended horses' tails to their persons. Silenoi, creatures with pointed ears, hooves and horses' tails, but in other respects in human-phallic shape, with snub-nosed faces and unruly manners, had the same privilege, of presenting themselves in the guise of a troop of male deities, as was possessed by the Satyrs. There were even tales of a single Satyros,[555] who oppressed the people of Arcadia and was slain by all-seeing Argos; or of a single Silenos, the tutor of Dionysos. For all these figures—Satyrs and Silenoi, whether human or divine—were associated with this god. They were all mortal, however, even those of them who were divine.[556] In Asia Minor there were tales of a Silenos who, when made drunk and taken captive, revealed deep truths; and of another figure, named Marsyas, who was so foolish as to compete with Apollon in music, and was defeated and stripped of his shaggy hide: a penalty which will not seem especially cruel if one assumes that Marsyas's animal guise was merely a masquerade.

It would be superfluous to speak further of the "good-for-nothing, mischief-making Satyrs", as they have at all times been described.[557] They suffered no penalty for loving nymphs, who for ordinary mortals could be highly dangerous: as, for example, when the beautiful boy Hylas disappeared whilst drawing water—a disaster brought about by the nymph of the well and by moonlight,[558] or, indeed, by a trinity of nymphs[559] "goddesses terrible unto men who live in the open air". In our language *numpholeptos*, "one seized by the nymphs", was the word for what the Latins called a *lymphaticus*—a term in which *lympha* is a rendering of "nymph", but in the sense of "water"—or *lunaticus*, "moon-sick", which was a later word for a person who became crazy from time to time, or only slightly, and was regarded as a victim of the nymphs. There was a special relationship between humanity as a whole and the Meliai, the "Ash-Nymphs": but these had a special ancestry, being children of Ouranos and Gaia, born of the blood of their maimed father. I shall describe this relationship when I come to tell of the manner in which human beings came into existence.

CHAPTER XI

Poseidon and his Wives

AFTER the stories of Zeus and his spouses, and of his daughters and sons—of which I have not told all: the stories concerning Dionysos are still to come, and those concerning Herakles have their proper place in heroic saga—I shall now speak of Zeus's brother Poseidon and the marriages that he celebrated.

Only one of these marriages, it should be said, has the significance of those marriages of Zeus that led to the establish-ment and confirmation of his rule, and thereby to the final ordering of the world. This was Poseidon's marriage with Amphitrite, whereby Poseidon espoused the sea and became its ruler. In the story involving Halia he was not yet the recog-nised ruler of the sea. His alliance with Demeter—which is probably reflected also in the name Poseidon, or Poteidan, "Husband of the goddess Da"—presupposes an earlier and close alliance with terra-firma and the soil. Even if it is not accepted that the component "Da" in the god's name is the shortest form of "Demeter", in its meaning of "Earth", never-theless Poseidon's surname of Gaiaochos means the same thing, "Husband of Earth". The tales concerning him depict a turbulent god who neither served the female, like the purely phallic beings, nor held supreme dominion over all, as Zeus did. In his quality of father—for he could also be called simply Pater,[560] "Father"—he came somewhere between the two sorts of male god: those, on the one hand, who served the Great Mother; and, on the other hand, the Olympian Father—who nevertheless, in the times of struggle and while the new rule was being established, still resembled Poseidon. Poseidon con-tinued to be a darker father beside his heavenly brother; he continued, longer and more closely than Zeus, to be associated with animal shapes; and the sea was indeed his most fitting dominion. Yet he was not as dark as Hades, King of the Underworld, the third brother and also Zeus's sinister counter-part, since the latter ruled only above.

Well-known portrayals of Poseidon show him majestically holding the emblem of his power, the trident. His suppressed savagery and menacing wrath were equally classical.

I

POSEIDON'S BIRTH AND RAM-MARRIAGE

The story of Poseidon's birth connects the god with two land-creatures, the sheep and the horse. Deities in Greece, and indeed throughout the Mediterranean, had ram-shapes long before they had horse-shapes. Of the two animals the horse was the later to be introduced from the north. In earlier times Hermes and Apollon likewise appeared in the shape of a ram: the former, however, only in his quality of a begetting god, the latter also as sun-god. Traces of these manifestations have been preserved in our religion, but there is no tale expressly concerning them. As regards Poseidon, who made the horse more closely his own sacred animal than did any other of our gods, we have two stories involving the sheep and the ram.

It was told[561] that when Rhea had borne Poseidon she hid the child amongst a flock of sheep, by a spring named Arne, "the spring of sheep". To Kronos, who sought to devour the newly born, she gave a foal—as she gave him a stone in place of the child Zeus. In another version[562] of the story, the nymph of the spring to whom Rhea entrusted the child had at that time a different name. It was only when Kronos de-manded his child of the nymph, and she denied that she had it, that she and the spring acquired the name Arne, as if the word had to do, not with "sheep", but with the similarly sounding verb meaning "to deny". This version is certainly late and incorrect. Another story concerning Poseidon, in which he married in the shape of a ram, was as follows:

Poseidon's bride, of whom the story was told in the style of heroic saga,[563] was named Theophane, which means either "she who appears as a goddess" or "she who causes a god to appear". Her father, King Bisaltes in Macedonia, was[564] a son of Helios and Gaia. The beautiful Theophane was contended for by suitors, but Poseidon carried her off and brought her to an island whose name perhaps meant "the island of the Ram". In any case, the tale goes on to relate that Poseidon turned his bride into a sheep and himself into a ram—indeed, that he also turned all the inhabitants of the island into sheep. The result was that when the suitors came in pursuit, the couple could not be discovered, and Poseidon consummated his ram-marriage, of which was born the ram with the golden fleece that Phrixos was later to carry to Colchis, thus causing the voyage of the Argonauts. All this, however, belongs completely to heroic saga.

2

POSEIDON AMONGST THE TELCHINES

According to a tale[565] that I have already touched upon when giving an account of the Telchines, Rhea carried the newly born Poseidon into safety with this people of skilled crafts-men, the Underworldly inhabitants of the island of Rhodes. Kapheira, a daughter of Okeanos, was Poseidon's nurse. It was the Telchines who forged his trident for him.[566] But it was never suggested that this jealous people could have taught him their crafts. Mention was also made of a sister of the Telchines, a sister whose name was Halia, "the sea-goddess".

When Poseidon had ripened into manhood—so the tale continues—he fell in love with Halia and begat by her six sons, also a daughter named Rhodos, from whom the island got its name. This was a time when Giants had sprung up in the eastern part of the island, and when Zeus had already defeated the Titans. Aphrodite had just been born of the sea, near Cythera, and was already on her way to Cyprus. The insolent and high-handed sons of Poseidon prevented her from landing on Rhodes. For this the goddess punished them with madness, so that they sought to lie with their own mother. This they did, and they also oppressed the islanders with their deeds of violence. When Poseidon observed this, he avenged the disgrace that his sons had brought upon their mother by causing them to sink beneath the earth; since when they have been called Gods, or Spirits, of the East. Halia threw herself into the sea, and since then has borne the name Leukothea, "the white goddess", and is worshipped by the islanders as an immortal.

Of the goddess named Leukothea I shall later have a quite different story to tell. Halia's daughter Rhodos is the same person as Rhode, who was also said to have been a daughter of Aphrodite or of Amphitrite. All three names—Halia, Aphrodite, Amphitrite, and furthermore also Kapheira—must have been applied to one and the same great goddess. On the more northerly islands of the Mediterranean she was also called Hekate, Kabeiro or Demeter Kabeiria, and was thought to be the mother of the Kabeiroi.

3

DEMETER, AND POSEIDON'S STALLION-MARRIAGES

Da was a primitively ancient name for Ga or Gaia. De-meter or Da-mater was probably so named in her quality of "Earth-Mother", and it was in this quality that she married Poseidon. Both deities had it in common that they were particularly closely associated with farm-life and its products. The same statement can, of course, be put another way round: that they were associated with the factors that governed, and therefore to some extent produced, a certain agricultural form of exis-tence: the goddess with corn—concerning this association there were sacred stories, which I shall tell presently—and the god with the steed since the introduction of horse-breeding. In her marital alliance with Zeus, Demeter was predominantly the *alter ego* of Mother Rhea, who bore Persephone to her own son, and in so doing bore her own self anew—a mystery of which little was publicly told. In her alliance with Poseidon, on the other hand, she was Earth, who bears plants and beasts, and could therefore assume the shape of an ear of corn or a mare.

It was told[567] that when Poseidon began to pursue Demeter with amorous importunities, the goddess was already engaged in seeking her abducted daughter Persephone. Demeter turned herself into a mare and mingled with the grazing steeds of King Onkios. Poseidon perceived the trick, and coupled with Demeter in the shape of a stallion. The wrathful goddess turned into Erinys, the goddess of anger, and was actually called Demeter Erinys until she washed away her anger in the river Ladon, and after this bathe acquired the surname Lousia. She bore to Poseidon a daughter, whose name might not be spoken outside the Mysteries, and at the same time she bore the famous steed Arion, the horse with a black mane. Arion inherited its black mane from Poseidon—so the story was conceived even in times of great antiquity. In the tale[568] of the marriage of Medousa and Poseidon this mane became "the dark locks" of the god. When Perseus had cut off the Gorgon's head of Medousa—a head which had the countenance of an Erinys—forth from the neck of that bride of Poseidon sprang the magic horse Pegasos. Another tale[569] declared that the bride of Poseidon, she who bore Arion, was a Harpy. As I have already said, appellations such as Erinys, Gorgo and Harpyia all mean much the same thing.

Demeter reproduced herself in an unnameable daughter—here, too, we recognise a trace of the tales of the Mysteries—and Poseidon reproduced himself in a steed. Well known is the story[570] of how the first horse was created by Poseidon in competition with Pallas Athene: at a stroke of his trident the horse sprang forth from the rocky soil of Attica. There was also a version[571] of this story in which Poseidon fell asleep on a rock in Attic Colonus, and his semen fell on the rock, which bore the first steed, whose name was either Skyphios, "the crooked", or Skironites, "the child of limestone".

4

POSEIDON AND AMPHITRITE

None of the gods who ruled our sea before Poseidon, had anything at all to do with the horse: neither the hundred-armed Briareos, whose second name, Aigaion, is connected with *aix*, "goat"; nor "the Old One of the Sea" under any of his various names or metamorphoses—in none of which did he have a horse's shape. Before there was any such thing as a sea-horse, a god shaped like a bull used to tow a goddess through the sea. Poseidon himself assumed this bull's shape,[572] and in his quality of sea-god he had bulls sacrificed to him. For the bull, too, appeared on the shores of the Mediterranean much earlier than the horse. Hippokampoi—"horse-monsters"—half horse and half serpent-like fish; sea-Centaurs, whose animal lower bodies were a combination of horse and fish; Okeaninai and Nereides, with names revealing their female equine nature—such names as Hippo, Hipponoe, Hippothoe and Menippe: all these first appeared in the Greek sea only when Poseidon had taken possession of it. This he did by means of his marriage with Amphitrite.

Hesiod numbered Amphitrite amongst the fifty daughters of Nereus.[573] She could, however, easily have been taken for an Okeanine,[574] a daughter of Tethys. For each of these two, Amphitrite and Tethys, was, beyond comparison with all other goddesses, and in however particular a sense, *the* mistress and proprietress of the sea, to whom belonged all foaming waves and sea-monsters. Of Amphitrite this is expressly stated.[575] It was told[576] that Poseidon espied the goddess as she danced with the Nereides on the island of Naxos, and

ravished her. The story went on to say[577] that Amphitrite
fled from Poseidon to the western extremity of the sea, to Atlas
or to the palace of Okeanos, which lay in the same quarter.
Her hiding-place was revealed to the pursuer by dolphins.
Indeed, it was a dolphin who persuaded the goddess and led
her to her bridegroom. It was rewarded by being set amongst
the stars.

After his marriage with Amphitrite, Poseidon was the ruler
of our sea. The ruling couple resembled in many respects Zeus
and Hera. Just as Zeus could be invoked simply as "Husband
of Hera",[578] so could Poseidon be addressed as "Husband of
Amphitrite of the golden spindle".[579] Their nuptial procession
was modelled on that of Dionysos and Ariadne: not only
horses, bulls and rams, but also stags, panthers, lions and tigers
appeared as marine monsters ridden by Nereids. Of the Tritons,
the male participants in these oft-depicted processions of
divinities, I shall have something further to say.

5

AMPHITRITE'S CHILDREN

Poseidon, the turbulent husband not only of Amphitrite, but
also of many Nereids, Naiads, nymphs and heroines, was the
father of numerous sons who played their parts in heroic saga.
Amongst these were not only heroes, but also savage, violent
beings who were defeated by the heroes—such beings as
Polyphemos the Kyklops, whose punishment by Odysseus
called forth the vengeance of Poseidon. These stories of the
gods which I am now relating afford no occasion for further
description of these beings. But I can speak of the children
born to Poseidon by Amphitrite—or, at least, of those two of
them who are the most famous, and whom I have already
mentioned: Triton and the island-goddess Rhodos.

Hesiod[580] called Triton "him of wide force", and described
him as a great god who dwelt at the bottom of the sea, in the

golden palace of his beloved mother Amphitrite and his lord
and father Poseidon. The poet declared that he was a terrible
deity. I have mentioned his love-affair with Hekate, and also
that Herakles overcame him by force in the presence of the
threefold "Old One of the Sea"—whose art of metamorphosis
this younger god apparently did not possess. Triton was half
fish, half human in shape, and can best be compared with the
Silenoi and Satyroi. His only difference from them lay in the
fact that they developed from disguised human beings into
land-creatures, whereas Triton's prototypes were men who
decked themselves with the tails of fishes or dolphins. An
ancient vase-painting from Italy shows a trio of such dancers.

The tales concerning Triton can be summarised as follows:
he was the Silenos or Satyros of the sea, a raper of women—
indeed, a raper of boys, too, and from of old these rapes were
performed by several Tritons at once—a being who could
awaken terror and lead men astray with his conch-horn. The
Tritons were sometimes accompanied by Tritonesses. But
usually it was Nereids who accompanied them as they swam
in nuptial processions through the sea, celebrating the marriage
of Poseidon and Aphrodite, or the birth of Aphrodite, or
those mysteries that were said to have been revealed by the
Nereids to mankind.

The story of the goddess Rhodos, daughter of Amphitrite,
is set entirely amidst the foaming waves of her mother; yet it
introduces us also to the family of the sun-god. The name
Rhodos is inseparably connected with *rhodon*, "a rose", just as
the goddess is inseparably connected with the island. It was
told[581] that when Zeus and the other gods were apportioning
the earth amongst themselves, the island of Rhodes was not
yet visible: it lay hidden in the depths of the sea. Helios, the
sun-god, had not yet presented himself at the apportionment;
so that the others left him, the undefiled god, without posses-
sions. When they suddenly remembered him, Zeus proposed
that they should cancel the apportionment and begin again.
But Helios would not permit this. He said that he could see

TRITON

a fertile piece of ground rising up from the sea. He called on
Lachesis, the goddess of apportionment, to hold up her hands
and vow, together with the other gods and the son of Kronos,
that whatever was now appearing should fall to his portion.
And so it came about: the island sprouted up from the salt
waters, and it belongs to the begetting father of the sun's rays,
the charioteer of the fire-darting steeds. On the island the god
took to wife the goddess Rhodos, and begat sons by her.
Originally the island and the goddess were as much a single
person as were Delos and the star-goddess Asteria; or Lemnos,
island of the Kabeiroi and of Hephaistos, and its Great
Goddess, who was also called Lemnos.[582]

CHAPTER XII

The Sun, the Moon and their Family

THE Sun and the Moon—considered solely as themselves and under the names Helios and Selene, which were the Greek words for these heavenly bodies—played no great part in our mythology. Instead, they lent their golden and silvery rays to other divinities, who were at least as much human as they were celestial and astral. However sunlike or moonlike these other divinities might appear—Zeus and Hera, Apollon and Artemis, to name no others—for us they ranked *above* the celestial bodies. These gods taught men secrets of life in the form of images—a thing that the Sun, Moon and other stars could never do by themselves.

Yet even the god Helios, the god "Sun", had a more closely interwoven connection with human existence than was possessed, outside mythology, by the celestial body, "the sun". This was not only because we instinctively measured him by human standards and saw him in human image. Considering him in this fashion, we thought of him as indefatigable[583]— an unwearying charioteer, originally drawn by bulls[584] and only later by "fire-darting steeds".[585] He was interwoven with our existence as the source of vision: outwardly as the begetting father of the sun's rays,[586] but also inwardly, and for a deeper reason, as if our eyes were themselves children of the sun, that "unwearying eye".[587] "Thou ray of the Sun, much-seeing mother of the eyes",[588] were the opening words of a paean by our great poet Pindar—a paean being a song that was sung in honour of Apollon. It was not *a priori* impossible to regard the sun as a maternal divinity. Our language even had a feminine name, "Helia",[589] that means "sun": it was the name of one of the daughters of the Sun, a sister of Phaethon—for the family of Helios contains many divine maidens and women.

For us Helios was above all a father, and as a father was interwoven with our whole existence: as all-seeing and all-hearing witness[590] of our doings—a sort of higher conscience that hovered over us and could be called upon to testify to the truth[591]—and as begetting father, from whom continually originate all the days of our lives. Every morning he bestows upon us a day of life, unless he chooses to withhold one or all of these. For example, he withheld for a long time from Odysseus, and for ever from Odysseus's companions, the day of their return home.[592] A begetting and conscious god, he was in our mythology not merely a blind productive force. When he went down each evening, our ancestors took this to mean simply that Helios had another dominion: either on the other side of the earth, over the men, whether living or dead, who dwelt there (this idea was expressed[593] even by quite ancient poets and philosophers); or in the depths of the sacred darkness of Night,[594] where he dwelt with his mother, his wife and his dear children. When the Greeks say, to this day: "Helios is king", this only sometimes means that it is noon; the phrase is commonly used to describe the sunset.

It was told[595] that at the hour of his setting the sun-god climbs into a great golden beaker—that same beaker which he once lent to Herakles, when the hero journeyed to the western isles of Okeanos to fetch the cattle of Geryoneus. This beaker carries the god—so we were told[596]—over the foaming waves. It is a hollow resting-place full of delights, a vessel that Hephaistos wrought of precious gold and equipped with wings. Over the surface of the water it carries him, the sleeping god, at furious speed from the abode of the Hesperides to the land of the Ethiops, where the swift chariot and steeds halt for him until the approach of the Goddess of Morning, the early-born Eos. The manner in which Helios, over there in the east, mounts his chariot and appears again in Heaven was often described and portrayed for us. As one poet says:[597] "Terribly glance his eyes from the golden helmet, dazzlingly pours forth the brilliance of the rays. On his temples gleam

the cheek-pieces of his helmet, embracing a delightful, far-
shining countenance. In the rushing wind the god's thin
robe flashes like lightning around him. Beneath him his
stallions are snorting." In most pictures of him, Helios wears
no helmet, only the crown of rays on his head, and is a beautiful
youth. His horses are winged, and before his chariot boys are
leaping far and wide, or making ready to leap: they are the
stars. The two goddesses Eos and Selene, the sisters of Helios,
go before him—the moon-goddess often in a chariot that is
plunging downwards.

The genealogy of Helios has already been described in the
tales of the Titans. Indeed, under the rule of Zeus he alone
retained the appellation of Titan. The Titaness Theia bore
him, with his two sisters, to the Titan Hyperion. She was a
many-named goddess, for whose sake men esteem gold: so, at
least, it was said[598]—perhaps because she was entitled to
golden gifts, as also and especially was Persephone. Besides
being called Theia—"the Divine", a word for precisely that
quality by virtue of which the gods were gods—the mother of
the Sun was also called Euryphaessa, "the widely shining",[599]
and was adorned with the surname "The Cow-Eyed". These
names recall such names as Europa and Pasiphae, or Pasiphaessa—names of moon-goddesses who were associated with
bulls. In the mother of Helios we can recognise the moon-
goddess, just as in his father Hyperion we can recognise the
sun-god himself. This last name means "he above", "the one
overhead"—in other words, the Sun, to whom Homer gives
the same name, calling him not only Helios, but in other
passages Hyperion,[600] or by the double name of Hyperion
Helios.[601] Our ancestors seem to have regarded him as a self-
begotten divinity, similar to the many-named husband and
son of the Great Mother, a Daktylos or a Kabeiros. The wife
of Helios was, admittedly, called by a different name from that
of his mother; but her name, Perse[602] or Perseis,[603] was also
one of the names of the moon-goddess Hekate, and doubtless
represented the Underworldly aspect of the "widely shining"

PLATE IX

ATHENE AND HEPHAISTOS
CREATE ANESIDORA, *i.e.* PANDORA

PLATE X

ZEUS, HERMES, EPIMETHEUS AND PANDORA

goddess. The name of the queen of the Underworld, Perse-phone, can be taken to be a longer, perhaps simply a more ceremonious, form of Perse. Another name of the wife of the sun-god,[604] Neaira, "the New One"—which is to say, the new moon, the moon in its darkest phase—gave a more accur-ate idea of the occasion on which the moon-goddess became the mother of Helios's children: the occasion of the seeming encounter of Sun and Moon at the time of the new moon.

Named as daughters of Helios and Neaira were Lampetia, "the illuminating", and Phaethousa, "the shining". According to the tale contained in the Odyssey,[605] these two guarded the three hundred and fifty cattle of Helios on the island of Thrinakia. The number is that of the days of the year,[606] in which twelve lunar months together constitute an incomplete year of the sun. It was natural that Helios, when Odysseus's companions had devoured his cattle, should retaliate[607] by taking away from all of them the day of their return home. Nor is it surprising that in the story of Helios's son Phaethon—a story that I shall tell in a moment—the number of the daughters of the sun was increased to three. The third sister was called[608] Aigle, "Light"—that is to say, "moonlight"—or Phoibe, which is also a well-known name of the moon-goddess. Still later, Phaethon was said to have seven sisters,[609] who were supposed to be recognisable in the seven stars of the Hyades—amongst them being Helia, the female Sun. It is known that the three Charites were also supposed[610] to be daughters of the sun. They should, however, be distinguished from the famous Heliades: Kirke, daughter of Helios and Perse, the seductive enchantress of the Odyssey[611] who used to turn her visitors into animals; Pasiphae, who appears in Cretan tales; and Medeia, who, according to surviving stories, was a cruel sorceress who tore her victims to pieces, and to whom the sagas concerning Jason and the Argonauts gave lasting renown as the murderess of her brother, of her father-in-law and lastly of her own children. She was closely connected with the moon: but, as I have indicated, her proper place is in heroic saga.

Two of the sons of Helios became famous. Aietes, the father of Medeia, has certain dark characteristics. In heroic saga he is a king of Colchis, a country on the Caucasus; but originally he was scarcely distinguishable from Hades, the invisible and invisibility-giving king of the Underworld, the opposite and counterpart of Helios. The other son, Phaethon, "the brilliant", was called by this surname of his father, who was also called Helios Phaethon,[612] just as *his* father was called Hyperion Helios.

I

THE STORY OF PHAETHON

Even in antiquity there were scholars who, if they could not recognise the common story behind the various tales of a given single and singly named mythological figure, would get out of their difficulty by asserting that there were several figures bearing this name. This assertion was almost always over-hasty; and it would be equally over-hasty for us now to seek to distinguish between two divine youths named Phaethon. We already know that this appellation was given to a son of Helios, a sort of younger or smaller sun. It may be added that other heavenly bodies could be given this name, but only if they resembled "a little sun". In later times the planet Jupiter[613]— or the planet Saturn,[614] which amongst ourselves and also in the east bore the same name as the Sun[615]—was held to be Phaethon. Originally, however, this name was given to the star closest to the goddess Aphrodite. In the east this star was the planet of the love-goddess, and is therefore to this day called Venus. In our nation it was held in esteem as being the star of evening and the star of morning, as Hesperos and as Phos-phoros or Heosphoros; as if there were two different stars. Phosphoros was said to be the child of Eos and Kephalos,[616] as also was Phaethon in the story that I shall now tell. In this story the star's relationship with Aphrodite is of such a nature as to remind one of Adonis. The story of Phaethon should by rights be numbered amongst those concerning the great love-goddess's paramours.

It was told[617] that Aphrodite took a fancy to the godlike Phaethon, the son of Eos and Kephalos. He was still in the tender bloom of youth, almost a little boy, when the love-goddess snatched him away. He thereupon became the guardian of her all-holiest shrine, having been appointed to this office by Aphrodite, who raised him to the rank of a god or a divine spirit, or Daimon, a rank carrying with it the same sort of immortality as was possessed by Adonis. Even in those other tales in which Phaethon's father was not just the half-divine Kephalos, but Helios himself, Phaethon had, at least, a mother and a stepfather who connected him with the world of mortals and the dead. In one tale[618] his mother was called Klymene. Her husband—that is to say, her son's stepfather— was supposed[619] to be Merops, who was king of a country especially loved by the sun-god: of Ethiopia, or the island of Cos. Quite possibly "Merops" meant the sun itself. Klymene was a name of the Queen of the Dead, Persephone; and in one tale[620] Merops's wife came prematurely into the realm of the dead, as Persephone had also done.

The story of Phaethon, son of Helios and Klymene, related[621] that the boy, as a young sun-god, one morning climbed upon his father's chariot. He journeyed too high, and fell. One can recognise here the early-rising and soon-disappearing star of the morning. In the same story it is added that Zeus hurled his lightning at the over-audacious charioteer, but did not hit him until Phaethon had already plunged into the river Eridanos. There arose a great conflagration, which could be extinguished only by the Flood. This conflagration certainly did not originally enter into this tale, according to which the youth was merely thwarted in his lofty flight. In later tales[622] Phaethon drove the Sun's chariot too near the earth, destroying everything by fire, and this was why Zeus had to strike him down. In antiquity the river Eridanos was identified with the Po. The daughters of the Sun mourned for their brother on its banks. From their tears arose amber, and they themselves turned into poplars. Finally all of them, together with Eridanos,[623] were raised up into the sky as constellations. The story's original ending, however, can be discovered from a Cretan tale. In Crete[624] the wrecked charioteer was called Adymnos, or Atymnios. He was a brother of Europa,[625] and could be seen to reappear every evening. It is a fact that the fallen star of morning appears again as the star of eve, and in the evening sky he is certainly Aphrodite's acolyte.

2

SELENE AND ENDYMION

The moon, with its visible changes and almost visible move‑ ment, its changeable relation to sun and earth and its partici‑ pation in both light and darkness, provided the material for many stories: for tales whose heroines were great goddesses, or perhaps only one goddess, the greatest of all, a goddess whose many‑sidedness makes it *a priori* impossible for us completely to identify her with a celestial body. With the visible goddess Selene were associated many heroines: huntresses and female runners, pursuing and pursued virgins of heroic saga. Even in antiquity it was known that the swift alternations of moon and sun[626] in the sky correspond to such images. Of the old stories of the gods in which a cow‑shaped Moon‑Goddess consummated her marriage with the bull of the sun, there finally remained, in later reliefs, only Selene's cattle‑drawn chariot. She had possessed a two‑horse equipage in contrast to the four‑horse chariot of Helios, and can also be seen riding alone on an ox or a horse, a mule or a stag. She was invoked as a winged, celestial being,[627] but she could be carried off by a goat—on one occasion actually by Pan himself, who, as I have already told, seduced her by wrapping himself in a sheep‑skin.

Besides being called Selene—a word connected with *selas,*

SELENE

"light"—the goddess as she appeared in the sky was also called Mene. This was the feminine form of *Men*, a word that meant the moon, the lunar month, and in Asia Minor also meant a moon-god. There was a story[628] of a marriage of Selene with Zeus: the moon-goddess bore to the heavenly ruler a daughter named Pandia, "the entirely shining" or "the entirely bright"—doubtless the brightness of nights of full moon. The two love-stories concerning her—those of her affairs with Pan and Zeus—entered into our mythology: not so, however, a later story[629] of a marriage between Selene and Helios as the moon-goddess and moon-god in the shapes in which they can be seen in the sky. Our Selene was the sister of Helios, as purely sisterly a being as Artemis was to Apollon. Any marriage between them had had to be confined entirely to the invisible, Underworldly regions, where they both had quite other names and other forms of manifestation than those they had in the sky. The only famous love-story that was told of our moon-goddess originated from Asia Minor, and was set in a cave.

It was told[630] that when Selene disappeared behind the mountain-crest of Latmos in Asia Minor, she was visiting her lover Endymion, who slept in a cave in that region. Endymion, who in all portrayals of him is shown as a beautiful youth, a herdsman or hunter, received the gift of everlasting sleep— doubtless, in the original story, from the moon-goddess herself,[631] so that she could always find him and kiss him in his cave. The name Endymion means one who "finds himself *within*", encompassed by his beloved as if in a common garment. According to a poet of a later period,[632] the god Hypnos, the winged god of sleep, fell in love with Endymion. He gave the youth the ability to sleep with open eyes. In our tales[633] Endymion was a king of Elis, the country of the Olympic Games, which are known to have been founded by an Idaean Daktylos (Endymion is closer to a Daktylos than to Adonis). He begat by Selene fifty daughters, the same number as that of the months of an Olympiad. His everlasting sleep was a gift from Zeus, who had permitted him to choose his own manner of death:[634] with the result that Endymion had chosen perpetual sleep instead of death. According to other story-tellers, this condition was inflicted on him as a punishment because, after being raised by Zeus to Heaven, he had behaved like Ixion in seeking to make love to Hera. It is plain that the moon-goddess, besides appearing under the name Selene, could also actually support the dignity of the Queen of the Gods.

3

EOS AND HER PARAMOURS

The children of the Titan couple Hyperion and Theia constituted a trinity: besides Selene, Helios had another sister, the

Goddess of Morning, Eos.[635] She can be seen, just like the moon-goddess, running before the rising sun-god, or riding, as a winged figure, in a four-horse equipage, a proper sun-chariot. It would not be entirely correct to translate Eos as "red of morning". Her arms and fingers were doubtless rosy, and her robe was saffron-yellow, but she herself was something more than simply a coloured phenomenon in the sky. She was the new day, and was also thus named,[636] as Hemera, "Day", or by an ancient name, Tito,[637] a feminine form of Titan which likewise meant "day".[638] As in the name Helia, so, too, in Eos we find the female counterpart to the sun, and also a wilder, more turbulent sister of Selene: a sister whose love-stories were more passionate than those of the moon-goddess herself.

Of all her loves, that which became most famous was the love she had for Tithonos. She had carried him off in a golden chariot,[639] and Homer tells us[640] that whenever she brings light to men she rises from her bed by Tithonos's side. Tithonos is a masculine form of Tito, and belonged, as did this name for Eos, to an older, non-Greek language. As a god and as a mortal youth he was native to Asia Minor, and was doubtless close to Adonis and Phaethon. The last-named appears[641]— under this name, and as Phosphoros,[642] Heosphoros[643] or Heöos[644]—together with the Cyprian Paphos[645] in the list of the sons of Eos, or as her grandson by her son Tithonos, whom she bore in Syria. It was told[646] that Eos, the goddess with the golden throne, had carried off the godlike Tithonos, a youth of the family of the kings of Troy. Thereupon she went to Zeus and besought him to bestow eternal life upon her beloved. Zeus granted her request. But it had not occurred to her that it would have been better to ask for Tithonos the boon of youth and protection against increasing age. As long, therefore, as Tithonos was young, he lived joyfully with Eos, by Okeanos, on the eastern edge of the world. When white strands had appeared on his handsome head and in his beard, the goddess no longer shared her bed with him. Instead, she tended him like a little child, gave him the food of the gods and beautiful raiment. And

when hoary old age took away from him all power of move/
ment, the goddess set him in a room and locked the doors.
Only the voice of Tithonos emerged from this room: he had
no more strength in his limbs. Certain details of the story not
contained in the foregoing tale are given by other narrators:[647]
Tithonos turned himself into a cicada. Eos bore him sons.
The most famous of these was Memnon,[648] who came to
Troy from the eastern land of the Sun, Ethiopia, to aid his
father's family, and who fell by the hand of Achilleus: a tragic
episode of heroic saga, which is said to have plunged the
goddess into deep grief. A magnificent vase/painting shows
her weeping for her dead son.

Eos's great love for handsome youths, whom she used to
carry off by force, so greatly dominated the tales concerning
her that it was even asserted[649] that her continual passions were
a punishment inflicted on her by Aphrodite because she had
caused Ares to desert the love/goddess. Indeed, Eos appears
in our mythology as a second implacable Aphrodite. Of the
youths whom she loved often only the names are known—the
name, for example, of Kleitos,[650] "the renowned". His beauty
had caused the goddess to carry him off so that he might be
amongst the immortals. A curious name was that of the fair
Kephalos, whom I have already mentioned as a son of Hermes
and Herse, and as the father of Phaethon. *Kephale*, the word
from which the name is derived, means "head". For this
beautiful head there was a dispute in Attica between Eos and
Prokris, Kephalos's wife. The story of Kephalos and Prokris
takes us again into heroic saga. This female rival of Eos was
one of those heroines who had more moon/like characteristics
than any goddess. On the island of Kephallenia there was a
tale[651] of a Kephalos who coupled there with a she/bear. We
know that this animal is one form of manifestation of Artemis,
or, in the story of Kallisto, of an otherwise/named double of
the same goddess. Finally Eos carried off Kephalos.[652] She
did the same to many unnamed lovely boys, as we see in
ancient illustrations. It may well be that Kephalos, the "Head",

can now be seen in the sky. Perhaps he is the "Head" in the constellation Orion, another astralised favourite of Artemis and Eos, of whom I shall now tell.

4

STORIES OF ORION

A whole wreath of stories is gathered around the constellation Orion. In our skies it shines with especial splendour, and it was said to have formerly been the wild hunter Orion, a gigantic figure who towers up into our mythology as if out of a barbarous and primitive age. His name was rightly asso-ciated[653] with those of the boy-giants Otos and Ephialtes, the Aloadai. These, it was said, were second in beauty to Orion only. I have mentioned in my account of the goddess Maia how a troop of divine maidens fled from Orion and were finally turned into the seven-star constellation of the Pleiades. Orion pursued them—in one tale[654] his quarry was a single maiden only, named Pleione, but in other tales[655] he pursued Pleione and her daughters—through Boeotia for either five or seven years. Perhaps already in the ancient tales they were wild doves (*peleiades*) whom the wild hunter was in fact seeking to slay, but at the same time they were goddesses, as also was the she-bear who entered the heavens in their and Orion's com-pany.[656] I shall presently explain the close relationship between this particular hunter and Artemis. It is doubtless the reason why the Pleiades whom Orion pursued were said[657] to have been hunting companions of the goddess. I shall now tell the stories concerning the hunter.

In one tale[658] Orion was thought to be the son of Poseidon and of Euryale, a daughter of Minos. This story of his parentage reveals how close he was at one time to the wild hunter of Crete, who, too, was known as Zagreus, and to Minos himself, the pursuer of Britomartis. In Boeotia, however, a different story[659] was told of the giant hunter's parentage. In Tanagra dwelt the hospitable Hyrieus, whose name means "the Bee-Man". I have told, in the story of Kronos, how the gods in primordial times got drunk upon honey. According to other narrators, it was not Hyrieus, but a king named Oineus,[660] or Oinopion,[661] who played an important part in Orion's story. These names are connected with *oinos*, "wine", just as the name Hyrieus and that of the town Hyria, which belonged to Tanagra, were connected with *byron*, "a beehive". It was told that Hyrieus, or Oinopion, was visited by three gods. (Usually the gods mentioned were Zeus, Poseidon and Hermes.) These three gods allowed their semen to flow into the hide of a sacrificed bull, and commanded their host to bury the leathern sack that had been filled in this manner. From it, after ten months, arose Orion, an Earth-born giant.[662] Thus the gods bestowed a son upon their host, who had previously been childless.

In the continuation of the story[663]—especially as it is told on the island of Chios—the effects of wine played an important part. Orion, while drunk, raped Merope, the wife of his step-father Oinopion. In another tale[664] the Merope who fell victim to the intoxicated giant was one of Oinopion's daughters. It was told[665] that Orion paid suit to Merope, and to win her freed the island of Chios from wild beasts; but Oinopion sought to break faith with him, and for this reason Orion got drunk and forced his way into Merope's chamber. Or else Oinopion himself made the wild hunter drunk, blinded him while he slept and cast the blind giant out upon the shore. The kernel of all these tales seems to be that the drunken giant laid violent hands upon his stepfather's wife, and that Oinopion blinded him in punishment. His deed must have been especially dreadful, to merit such dreadful suffering. If it were not for the story of the three gods—which could, in any case, have been invented for the sake of a pun: one of the words for "to shed semen" is *ourein*, and in the story the name Orion is derived from this—the penalty suggests that the giant must have violated his own mother. A similar tale of the effects of wine is told⁶⁶⁶ of Lykourgos, the enemy of Dionysos. The punishment of this sin by blindness is found in other tales beside that of Oidipous.⁶⁶⁷

Merope could have been Orion's mother, just as Semele was the mother of Dionysos, and Elara was the mother of the phallic giant Tityos; although the god and the giant were not actually born of these mothers, but in other fashions. There was also a tale⁶⁶⁸ of a wife of Orion, named Side, "Pome׳ granate", whom he thrust down into the Underworld because she compared herself in beauty with Hera. Such a name was an appropriate one for the Queen of the Underworld, as also was the name Merope. Concealed in these names is a mother׳ wife with whom Orion sinned, and this is why the sin was punished by blindness. A soothsayer told Orion⁶⁶⁹ that he could cure himself only by exposing his eye׳sockets to the rays of the sun. The blind giant heard the din of a smithy, and went in the direction of the sound. He crossed the sea—either by walking upon it,⁶⁷⁰ or more probably, since he was a giant, by wading through it—and came to Lemnos, where the smithy of Hephaistos was working with a great din.⁶⁷¹ Although the tales expressly mention this god, nevertheless it was Kedalion, Hephaistos's tutor, whom Orion seized and set on his shoulders, so that the dwarf could lead the giant towards the sun. Blind Orion met the rising Helios, and was cured. It was also told⁶⁷² that he went back to punish Oino׳ pion. But the latter had hidden himself beneath the earth, in a brazen chamber. Thus began Orion's wanderings, which ended in his being transported into the heavens. As a hunter he threatened⁶⁷³ to exterminate all creatures on earth. Artemis and Leto were in Crete when he was hunting there. But Earth brought forth against him the scorpion, which stung the wild hunter and afterwards accompanied him into the heavens as a constellation. Or else⁶⁷⁴ it was Artemis who sent the scorpion against the aggressor, when he had already seized hold of her robe. She was also, of course, capable of killing her assailant with her arrows,⁶⁷⁵ and actually did so in another story, which is unique of its kind.

It was told[676] that Eos had already taken Orion to be her husband when Artemis slew him with her arrows on the island of Ortygia. This island was the spot at which the sun rose: it was the birthplace of Apollon, the island also called Delos. Here Orion had challenged Artemis to a discus-throwing contest.[677] The goddess was angry at this—or else, in the majority of tales, at the fact that the giant had attacked the Hyperborean maiden Opis (another name for Artemis herself). According to this unique story,[678] however, Artemis was in love with the hunter. Apollon observed this and took it hardly. He scolded her, but his words were unavailing. Then he suddenly saw Orion's head, far away in the sea, appearing as a dark speck, and challenged his sister to compete with him in shooting at this target. Artemis hit the head, which she had not recognised, and afterwards transported her beloved to a place amongst the stars. Orion's constellation, too, often shows only its head above the horizon. Those people, however, who refused to accept the story of his metamorphosis into a constellation claimed[679] that Orion is still hunting in the asphodel-meadows of the Underworld, with his brazen club in his hand, still pursuing the beasts that he slew on earth.

5

TALES OF THE GODS OF THE WINDS

There was also a tale[680] of a husband of Eos who achieved a higher rank than was assigned to any husband of hers of whom I have yet told. This was Astraios, "the Starry One", whose name I mentioned as that of a son of the strong goddess Eurybia and of the Titan Krios.[681] It is expressly said[682] of him that he was "the ancient father of the stars". To him, the god of the night sky, the goddess of morning bore not only the Morning Star, Heosphoros, but also the gods of the winds: gods, that is to say, only of the principal winds, those deserving

BOREAS ABDUCTS OREITHYIA

of worship. Of these, however, she bore all four, although Hesiod mentions only three of them by name: Zephyros, the west wind, Boreas, the north wind, and Notos, the south wind. To the fourth—Apheliotes, the east wind, or Euros, the south-east wind—Hesiod refers only by the surname Argestes, "the bringer of brightness". These winds, so he tells us,[683] are of divine origin, and bring great benefits to mortals. There are, however, also the gales, children of Typhoeus, which descend upon the sea to the great hurt of mankind. They blow in turn from several directions, wrecking ships, destroying sailors, whilst others of them lay waste the blossoming earth, the lovely works of men, and cover everything with dust and confusion.

The whole rose of the winds, which amongst us, too, consisted of at least eight winds, had, of course, no place in our mythology. Not even of pleasant Zephyros, the harbinger of spring, can I tell any ancient story; unless it be the story[684] of how he coupled with the Harpy Podarge, the swift-footed mare, on the meadow by Okeanos, and begat by her the soothsaying steed of Achilleus. Boreas, the north wind, is the only wind that our mythology presents as a major figure: winged, with two faces, looking forward and back—in which respect Boreas resembles only the all-seeing Argos. In quite

ancient portrayals of him, Boreas actually had serpent-feet.[685]
He not only coupled with blood-mares,[686] but was the male
counterpart of Eos—a raper of maidens. He was thought to be
a savage Thracian, since he blew from the north, from Thrace;
and it was told[687] of him that he carried off an Attic maiden,
a daughter of King Erechtheus named Oreithyia, which means
"she who swarms in the mountains". She was playing with her
companion Pharmakeia, "the sorceress", by the cool stream of
Ilissos, near Athens, when Boreas snatched her away. Of this
marriage were born in Thrace the winged twins Kalais and
Zetes, of whom I have already said that they alone could
defeat the Harpies.

According to another tale, the winds were subject to a king
named Aiolos, and were completely his instruments, having no
personality of their own. The name Aiolos means both "the
mobile" and "the many coloured": doubtless he was originally
a god of the starry heavens, like Astraios. The story about him
has been preserved in the account of the adventures of Odysseus.[688] It was told of King Aiolos, in the manner of sailors'
yarns, that he was a friend of the gods and ruled over the
floating island of Aeolia. The steep, craggy island was surrounded by brazen walls. In his palace Aiolos had twelve
children, six daughters and six youths. The daughters were
married to the sons, and the couples revelled all day long with
their father and mother. At night they slept together. Odysseus
came to this island with his shipmates, and for a month Aiolos
entertained them in his palace. When they wished to start their
voyage home, he gave them a bag made of the hide of a nine-
year-old bull. In this he had shut up the winds, so that he could
still them or let them loose as he chose. He bound them fast
with a silver cord in Odysseus's ship, so that none of them
could drive it off its course, and left only the west wind blowing
into the sails. Everyone knows the story in the Odyssey: it was
all in vain. Odysseus's shipmates supposed that he was hiding
gold or silver in the bag, and they let out the winds. Thus even
mythology itself deviates into fable.

CHAPTER XIII

Prometheus and the Human Race

I HAVE already mentioned all the progeny of the Titans and Titanesses, with the exception of the line of Iapetos. This line is closely connected with the human race. Mankind, considered as a great family, is the counterpart of the race of gods—that is to say, the family of the Olympian gods—and had as much a place in our mythology as did the Sun and Moon and all the starry heavens. The race of gods was composed of immortals, the human race of mortals. The latter, however, was particularly closely connected with certain deities who did not arrive on Olympus, but were apparently as much subject to death, and especially to suffering, as mortals are. Many of our philosophers held the view that the human race was eternal. In our mythology it was considered to be at least long-lived. For although it was doomed to annihilation, it was not confined to a single age, any more than were, for example, the nymphs. Indeed, nymphs often appear also as wives of the first men, at a time before the creation of Pandora, when human beings were only men, a purely male species.

This male species, that of the first men, was connected with the Titan race of Iapetos, especially with two of his sons, Prometheus and Epimetheus. I shall presently tell the stories in which these two acted as representatives of mankind. According to the followers of Orpheus, the Titans were men's sinful ancestors. Hesiod[689] told us that Father Ouranos had given them the name "Titans" as a term of abuse and as a pun, as if the word were derived from *titainein*, "to overreach oneself", and from *tisis*, "punishment": the Titans had "overreached" themselves, in their foolhardiness, by attempting to perform a great work, and for this were later punished. This work was not performed in the ancestral line Ouranos-Kronos-Zeus; for the Titans were always hostile to Zeus, the finally victorious scion of this line, and took no part in the mutilation and overthrow of the fathers. Their especial quality of foolhardiness (*atasthalia*) was one that they shared with men,[690] who for this very reason were repeatedly threatened by the gods with destruction. Hesiod describes the race of Iapetos as consisting entirely of punished evildoers. The story of the Titans, those enemies of Zeus and of the gods, is a preliminary to the story of the human race.

The name Iapetos has for us a foreign sound. Apart from the fact[691] that he was finally thrust down into Tartaros, together with the other Titans, all we know of him is the genealogical tale[692] of his marriage with Klymene (which is elsewhere a name of the Queen of the Underworld), instead of whom we sometimes find Asia[693] or Asopis.[694] Iapetos led Klymene, the Okeanine with the beautiful ankles, back to his home, and with her mounted their common couch. She bore him sturdy Atlas and overweening Menoitios, and also Prometheus and Epimetheus. Of Menoitios it was said[695] that he was an evil-doer whom Zeus struck with lightning, for his foolhardiness and lust of aggression, and cast him down into Erebos. Atlas supported the wide heavens,[696] standing and propping up the burden on his head and hands, at the edge of the earth, beside the Garden of the Hesperides. He was mightily compelled to do so, for this was the fate decreed for him by Zeus. He is known to have been the father of many goddesses—the Hesperides, Maia and the Pleiades. In ancient, now lost tales,[697] he was a god of dangerous wisdom, well acquainted with the depths of the sea. Even in earlier times he owned the pillars that held earth and sky asunder. Under the dominion of Zeus he presented the picture of a giant condemned to eternal toil, at the western edge of the earth, whilst Prometheus suffered his punishment at the eastern edge. Of Prometheus and Epimetheus I shall tell more in the course of what immediately follows.

PLATE XI

a ATLAS AND PROMETHEUS

b THE UNBINDING OF PROMETHEUS

PLATE XII

THE MASK OF DIONYSOS IN THE LIKNON

I

THE ORIGIN OF MANKIND

Gods and men are of common origin, says Hesiod,[698] who based this statement on the most ancient tales. One of these tales I have already told:[699] how Gaia, Mother of Earth, conceived of the blood shed by maimed Father Ouranos, and brought forth upon the mighty earth the Erinyes, the huge Giants and those nymphs who are called Meliai, "Ashes". In the great tale[700] of the various successive human races—"the ages of antiquity", as they were later called—the "Ashes" produced the race of bronze. In his story of the theft of fire Hesiod[701] preserved for us the word *melioi*, the masculine form of *meliai*, as meaning the human beings—or, more accurately, the men—who belonged to the Ash-Nymphs. These men, the Melioi, were later described[702] as lying beneath the ash-trees like fallen fruit. In many other tales—and almost every country of Greece or Asia Minor had such a tale—the first male being, Primordial Man, sprang directly from Earth, who in this manner, too, was the common mother of gods and of mortals.

Concerning the first peoples of the various countries—from whom the later inhabitants of these countries invariably traced the descent of the entire human race—the tale told to us[703] was something as follows: "It was Earth who first brought forth men, bearing a lovely fruit, since she wished to be the mother not only of unfeeling plants and unreasoning animals, but also of creatures orderly and devout. it is difficult, however, to make out whether the first man to spring up was Alalkomeneus, by Lake Kopais in Boeotia; or whether the first men were the Idaean Kouretes, a divine race, or the Phrygian Korybantes, who were the first men seen by the sun-god when they shot up like trees; or whether the birthplace of the first man, or the first men, was Arcadia, which bore Pelasgos, a man who existed before the moon—or Eleusis, which bore Dysaules, dweller in the Rharian Fields—or Lemnos, which bore Kabeiros,

amidst ineffable Mysteries—or Pallene, which bore Phlegraean
Alkyoneus, the oldest of the Giants". Another tale[704]—or,
more correctly, an utterance, which in Athens was said to
have been made by a certain wise woman—gave the credit to
the soil of Attica: "In the days when the whole earth sent forth
and blossomed with living things of all kinds, both beasts and
plants, our Attic earth proved itself, as regards wild beasts, to
be sterile and pure; of all living creatures it preferred man,
and bore a being who surpasses all others in reason and alone
worships justice and gods."

One can detect in these words a certain purposiveness that is
out of place in mythology, in which everything is spontaneous
and self-evident, and nothing is polemically directed against
others. The speaker intended not only to draw a flattering
distinction between the Athenians, as *gegeneis*, "earth-born", or
autochthones, "autochthonous" (which originally meant the same
thing), and the inhabitants of all other regions, but also to mark
a difference between the soil of Attica and all the rest of the
earth—although she herself recognises the divinity of Earth as
a whole when she goes on to say[705] that it is not Earth who
imitates womankind in conceiving and bearing, but womankind that imitates Earth. Moreover, it was not the Athenians
but the inhabitants of the island of Aigina who were said to
have crawled out of the earth as an entire people—which they
did, in any case, not as human beings, but as ants. It was
told[706] that after the goddess Aigina had borne Aiakos to
Zeus, her son was left entirely alone on the island. When he
had grown up to be a youth, he found this solitude wearisome.
Thereupon Zeus turned the ants on the island into men and
women, and bestowed upon Aiakos the people of the Myrmi-
dons—a name that sounds like *murmekes*, "ants". It was this
people that built the first ship. In a later form of the tale, Zeus,
to please Aiakos, caused men to grow out of the earth. The
poetic name for human beings, *meropes*, doubtless referred to a
tale told by the inhabitants of the island of Cos. King Merops,
whose subjects were the first people to bear this name, was, as I

have already said, the stepfather of Phaethon, and his was probably only another name for the Sun itself. *Merops* was also our
name for the bee-hawk, a bird that lays its eggs in the ground
and is therefore a sort of husband of Earth. Thus the term
meropes for human beings expresses the fact that they were born
of Earth—and also, of course, the fact that they are the scions
of a begetting sun-god.

Whenever the story of the origin of mankind was set on a
particular island, the goddess of that island was said to be its
mother: in other words, our well-known Great Mother-God-
dess, under the name of the island itself. In Asia Minor the part
was played by Rhea, on our mainland by the same goddess in
her particular local manifestations. She bore the beings who
became the ancestors of the human race. It will be remembered
how she, the Great Mother, always had with her Daktyloi,
Kouretes, Korybantes or Kabeiroi, whom she had bred from
within herself and with whom she also bred further. In the
various tales these beings became entire primitive peoples, such
as the Telchines, the aboriginal inhabitants of the island of
Rhodes. All primordial gods of this kind were at the same time
primordial men. The difference between their two qualities
doubtless lay in the fact that as primordial men they ceased to
be husbands of the Great Mother, and received other wives.
On Lemnos there were tales[707] of three Cabirian nymphs,
Nymphai Kabeirides. They were the daughters of the Great
Goddess and the Kabeiros who bred from her, and they had
three brothers, with whom they formed three pairs, which can
be described as the first primordial human couples.

In most of the tales, the first male beings who were thought
of as primordial men had a quality in common with Kronos,
that son of Mother Earth with whom began the story of the
race of gods: the quality of cunning. It was told[708] of Alalkomeneus, the primordial man of Boeotia, that he had given
Zeus the crafty advice whereby the ruler of the gods regained
the offended Hera and enticed her back into matrimony. As
I have already said, Alalkomeneus was thought also to have

been the tutor of the goddess Athene, who must therefore have been born after him. Under the name of Athenais she probably became the wife of primordial man. In the story of Pelasgos, the primordial man of Arcadia, it will be remembered that not even the Moon—who in our mythology is female—had yet come into being. I shall shortly tell in greater detail of how the first men—a pair of brothers, in the story of Prometheus and Epimetheus—were joined by the first female being whom they might marry. Here I shall merely mention that Pandora, the first woman, was in one tale created as a statue, but in another tale emerged from the earth as a goddess.

The story of the creation of the first woman by master-craftsmen, of whom well-known examples were the Daktyloi and the Kabeiroi, formed the background to the later tales of the origin of mankind. As craftsmen capable of such work I have already mentioned Hephaistos, the greatest of the Kabeiroi of Lemnos, and Pygmalion, or Pygmaion, king of Cyprus. Another such craftsman was Prometheus, who was also a being "of crooked thoughts",[709] like Kronos. The tales that I shall presently tell distinguish him from Hephaistos. Yet it was told also of Prometheus that he was an illegitimate son of Hera—although not, indeed, by Zeus, but by the Giant Eurymedon;[710] that he helped at Athene's birth with his two-edged axe;[711] and that he pestered the goddess as Hephaistos did.[712] It should be added that he was regarded as the older god of the two. It has been stated[713] that he was originally called Ithas, or Ithax, and was the herald of the Titans. According to another story,[714] he belonged to a primitive tribe of Kabeiroi. He and his son Aitnaios—which may be taken to mean Hephaistos—were two Kabeiroi in the neigh-bourhood of Thebes, where they were visited by Demeter, who brought them her Mysteries, just as she brought these, in other tales, to the primordial man Dysaules or to the King of Eleusis. One difference remained, however, between Prometheus and the heavenly outcast and fire-god Hephaistos: namely, that the latter was a simple being, as simple as fire itself, whereas

Prometheus was a twofold being. He was usually accompanied by a partner less cunning than himself, his brother Epimetheus, who was a sort of left hand to him.

The tale went:[715] There was a time when the gods existed, but there were as yet no mortals. When the appointed time came for mortals to come into being, the gods fashioned them under the earth, of earth and fire and all that mixes with these. When the gods then sought to bring them into the light, they ordered Prometheus and Epimetheus to equip these crea- tures and to distribute amongst them such abilities as would be most fitting for each. Epimetheus besought Prometheus to let him carry out the distribution by himself. The heedless fellow distributed everything amongst the beasts, so that man was left utterly unprotected and bare. Thus the provident Prometheus was compelled to steal fire, as well as the arts of Hephaistos and Pallas Athene, from the temple that these two gods shared, and to bestow them upon mankind. Since then man has been able to survive, but Prometheus—although the fault was his brother's—was punished for what he had done. This tale comes down to us from a wise man—from Protagoras the Sophist, it is said, who gave his own twist to an ancient story. Somebody else told[716] that Prometheus created a First Man of marvellous beauty, and kept him hidden. Eros revealed the secret to Zeus, who sent Hermes to fetch the beautiful being. The figure was given to drink of the elixir of immortality, and now gleams in the heavens as Phainon, "the Shiner", which was our name for the planet Jupiter. As well as this being,[717] Prometheus also created other men, of water and earth.[718] According to these tales, which are not very ancient, he also created the beasts.[719] Certain late-period sarcophagi in Rome are adorned with reliefs showing how Prometheus fashioned man: in the form of a small statue, on which Athene is bestowing a soul, by bring- ing to it a butterfly—which in our language is called *psyche*, like the soul. In our country, in the region of Phocis, visitors used to be shown[720] great blocks of a stone that was said to smell like a human body, and to be left over from the clay of

which Prometheus made men. I shall later recount the tales of
how men could arise, or re-arise, from stones.

2

RIVALRY WITH ZEUS AND THE THEFT OF FIRE

It was not only in *our* mythology that mankind's ancestors were
divine beings who had to be subjected to deprivations and
limitations before a clear distinction could be drawn between
gods and men. In other mythologies, too, there were tales
in which the first men were highly defective creatures. To speak
only of our own ancestors: they were born of ash-trees; or they
were ants turned into men; or they sprouted from the earth—
like vegetables, a mocker might say;[721] or they were formed
from clods of earth; and always they needed the perfecting
touch, a sort of second creation, to enable them to live as men.
For example, a human race consisting only of males was incomplete in its very nature, even if it had as its mother the
Mother of the Gods. In our mythology the double task of
separating mankind from the immortals and of giving completion to mortals fell to Prometheus. He began by kindling a
spirit of rivalry with Zeus—a sort of rivalry between brothers
—and thus provoked a clear separation, as a result of which he
and his brother, together with mankind, were defeated after
a seeming victory, and Zeus and the gods were left as the true
victors. Thereupon Prometheus came to the help of vanquished
mankind with at least *one* divine gift, that of fire. A second
gift, woman—a gift which, according to the sequel to the first
story, was bestowed by the gods, but according to other tales[722]
was a work of Prometheus—proved to be a beautiful evil. The
raising of man to a full and complete being required—as I shall
presently relate—the further gifts of Demeter and Dionysos.
    The names Prometheus, "the foresighted" or "the provident",
and Epimetheus, "he who learns only from the event" or "the
heedless", contain a reference to the existence of beings who

need to be provident and are in danger of heedlessness—in other words, of men—inasmuch as the heedless and the provident character were inseparably yoked together. The tale went:[723] When gods and men met together in Mekone, the place which is called "the Field of Poppies", where they were to be separated one from the other, Prometheus divided up a mighty bull. He laid it in friendly fashion before the assembly, seeking to deceive the insight of Zeus. For himself and his people he filled the stomach of the animal with sliced meat and fat offal. For Zeus he wrapped the bones handsomely in gleaming fat. Thus the contents of neither portion could be perceived. Then spoke to him the father of gods and men: "Son of Iapetos, thou illustrious lord, how unequal hast thou made the portions!" Thus Zeus, full of eternal counsel, rebuked him. Prometheus of the crooked thoughts answered him with a soft smile, aware of his deceit: "Zeus, most famed and greatest of the eternal gods, choose thou the portion that thou desirest!" Zeus, full of eternal counsel, doubtless saw through the stratagem, but in his soul he had an ill intent against men—an intent that was to be accomplished. With both hands he took the white, fatty portion. Full of bitter wrath was his heart when he beheld the white bones so skilfully concealed. Since that time earthly mortals, when they make sacrifices to the gods, have burnt only the white bones upon their altars. On this occasion, however, Zeus said in sudden rage: "Son of Iapetos, thou who art wiser than us all, it seems that thou hast sought to betray us!" Thus spoke Zeus, full of eternal counsel, in his wrath. He never forgot the treachery, and withheld from men, the progeny of the ashtrees, the gift of fire. He hid it away—or so the later repetition of the same tale[724] goes on to explain. The great son of Iapetos stole it back from Zeus and brought it to men, in the hollow stalk of a narthex.

Thus ends this tale, which is immediately continued in the story of Pandora. The First Woman was welcomed by Epimetheus, and thus men were again weakened, as they had been by the concealment of fire. The question of where Prometheus found the hidden fire is answered in several tales, all of which have been lost, as also has the tragedy in which the Titan's quest of fire was told of by Aeschylus. Since the scene of this tragedy was the island of Lemnos, it was believed—and also pictorially recorded—that Prometheus took the flame from the workshop of Hephaistos. Yet there is a somewhat more detailed story[725] which tells us at least this much, that Prometheus secretly made his way to the fire of Zeus (which must mean the hearth-fire of the divine palace on Olympus), took fire from it and hid the flame in the hollowed-out stalk of a narthex—the same sort of plant as served in Dionysiac processions as the thyrsus, the long staff of male and female Bacchantes. Then, brandishing the stalk so that the flame should not go out, he ran joyfully, as if flying, back to mankind. It was also told[726] that Prometheus, like a second Kedalion, reached the sun itself and lit his torch at the Sun's wheel. In the later version in which this account was preserved, the Titan was helped by Pallas Athene. In the original stories this can scarcely have been the case, and only in these later tales was Prometheus's action a real theft.

3

THE STORY OF PANDORA

Let me now go on with the tale of the rivalry between gods and men—between Prometheus and Epimetheus, on the one side, and Zeus on the other. As I have said, its sequel is the story of Pandora. In Hesiod's well-known version of this story, the poet's prejudice against women is certainly noticeable, but not to such an extent as to lead one to suppose that he entirely invented the whole tale. He must have found it ready to his hand, and have enjoyed it so much that he told it twice, on both occasions linking it with the successful bringing-back of fire. One of his accounts runs as follows:[727] The Thunderer was pierced to the soul, and anger filled Zeus's heart, when he beheld the light, visible from afar, of the fires kindled by men.

He straightway prepared for men an evil thing that would weigh equal with the boon of fire. At Zeus's bidding the famed master-craftsman Hephaistos wrought the image of a bashful maiden. The goddess Athene adorned it with a girdle and whitely shimmering raiment. From the head of the maiden she caused to hang down a richly wrought veil, a marvellous thing; she caused wreaths of flowers to hang at her sides, and on her head she set a wreath of gold, fashioned by the master-craftsman with his own hand as a special favour to Zeus. In this wreath many beasts of the earth and sea were wonderfully portrayed, almost as if they were alive; the whole work shone with lovely charm. When the beautiful evil had been made ready, as a counterpoise to the good, Zeus led the maiden, so daintily adorned by the owl-eyed daughter of the mighty Father, to the place where gods and men were assembled. Both immortals and mortals were all amazed when they beheld that threatening wile against which men are defenceless: from her is descended the race of women.

Hesiod's other story[728] on the same subject runs as follows: "Son of Iapetos," quoth Zeus, "thou art wiser than all of us, thou rejoicest that thou hast stolen fire and hast deceived me. This shall work harm unto thyself and unto men yet to be. For they shall receive from me, in retaliation for the theft of fire, an evil thing in which they will all rejoice, surrounding with love their own pain." Thus spoke the Father of Gods and Men, and laughed aloud. He bade Hephaistos straightway to mix earth with water, to set in it a voice and strength, and to create a desire-awakening beautiful maiden, whose face should be like those of the immortal goddesses. Athene was ordered to teach her womanly crafts and weaving. Golden Aphrodite was ordered to encompass her head with the radiance of lovely charm and rending desires. Hermes had Zeus's command to fill the figure with bitchy shamelessness and treachery. They all did as the ruler had bidden. The famed master-craftsman fashioned from earth the likeness of a bashful maiden. Pallas Athene adorned it with girdle and raiment. The Charites and

Peitho set golden necklets upon it. The Horai wreathed the maiden with spring flowers. In her breast Hermes planted lies, flatteries and treachery. The Messenger of the Gods furthermore gave her a voice, and named the woman Pandora, since all the Olympians had created her as a gift, to the bane of men, eaters of bread.

When once the threatening wile, against which there is no defence, was made ready, the Father sent the glorious, swift Messenger, taking with him the gift of the gods, to Epimetheus. This latter paid no heed to what Prometheus had once told him, that he should accept no gift from Zeus, but should send it back again, so that no evil for mortals should grow out of it. He took the gift, and only later perceived the evil. Formerly mankind had lived on the earth without evil, without troubles or sicknesses such as bring death to men. Now the woman removed the lid from the great vessel, and caused it to overflow everywhere, to the sore grief of mankind. Only Elpis, "Hope", was left inside, in unbreakable captivity, beneath the rim of the vessel, and did not fly out. The woman clapped the lid down upon her—for such was the will of Zeus. The rest of the swarm, numberless and sorrow-bringing, roams everywhere amongst mankind, the earth is full of evil, full of evil is the sea. Sicknesses visit men by day, uninvited they come by night —doomful and soundless, for Zeus, full of wise counsel, with-held speech from them. And all this means that there is no way of deceiving the insight of Zeus.

Such was the sequel to the story of the creation of woman, the sequel telling how the young creature, newly arrived in the world, in sheer curiosity removed the lid of a receptacle similar to the great earthenware jars in which to this day we keep oil and grain, and how she thus let out the swarm of evils which—like Ares on a former occasion—had been shut up in it. With these evils—that is to say, with the sicknesses —death also came into the world of men. Thus was completed the separation between men and the immortal gods. The female figure, who is the ancestress of all mortal women, was

PANDORA RISING FROM THE EARTH

called Pandora, of which the correct interpretation is "the rich in gifts", "the all-giving": a name also of the Earth itself,[729] of which she was made. In an old portrayal of her, the name written beside her is actually Anesidora, "the sender-forth of gifts", which is one of the names of the earth-goddess. Yet the first wife of the first men, although she came from Earth and was associated with Earth by name as an *alter ego* (I have already quoted the saying that woman imitates Earth, and not the contrary), was nevertheless a creation of artifice. In the tales I have just quoted she was a work of Hephaistos; in other, lost tales she was a creation of Prometheus—or, indeed, of Epimetheus. In this latter version, which is preserved only in vase-paintings, Pandora rose from the earth—she often appears only as a mighty and beautiful head of a woman—but the earth had previously been worked upon with hammers. Epimetheus still holds his hammer in his hand as Pandora emerges in front of him. An Eros flits above her head, with his troop of joyful heralds of marriage. Hermes is hastily approaching with a flower: he has been sent by Zeus, by whose will all this has occurred. Yet primordial men—who in the vase-paintings are not Kabeiroi, but Silenoi or Satyrs—would never have received the gift of woman, rising like a full moon in their midst, beneath hammers and picks, had not Mother Earth been willing to bestow upon them her own image. She did not do this, of course, without the co-operation of her industrious sons themselves.

4

THE PUNISHMENT AND UNBINDING OF
PROMETHEUS

The story of the punishment of humanity by means of the First Woman was ancient enough, but our mythology told of still more ancient punishments, more cruel penalties and sufferings—or such as at least seemed more cruel. It should be borne in mind that our gods not only had human qualities but also had much in common with the Sun, with certain constellations, and above all with the Moon and her sufferings: manifest sufferings, which could be seen in the sky. Hera was punished, as I have already told, by being suspended between Heaven and Earth with anvils attached to her feet. There was an old tale[730] of how she was wounded: an arrow of Herakles hit her right breast, inflicting on the goddess a hurt that could never be healed. I have also already told the story of the punishment of Tityos: how his liver was gnawed away, but repeatedly grew again with the moon. All these sufferings—both those of Hera when she hung suspended or when she was wounded in the breast, and those of Tityos with his waning and waxing liver—correspond to sufferings visible in the heavens.

Prometheus underwent the same punishment as Tityos, and furthermore he was suspended in bonds at the highest point of the Caucasus, nailed there by Hephaistos.[731] It was told[732] that Zeus bound Prometheus, that cunning Titan, with special chains, and drove a pillar as a stake through him in the middle. An ancient vase-painting shows Prometheus with the "pillar through the middle": he is being attacked by an eagle, which, as usual, is attacking him from in front. Zeus—so it was said[733] —had sent the bird to devour the Titan's immortal liver. All that the eagle tore away during the daytime grew again in the night. The punishment was intended to be a lengthy one. Zeus must originally have meant that the enchainment should last for all eternity, so that men should never again have such a cunning ally against the gods. At the end of Aeschylus's lost tragedy, *Prometheus the Bringer of Fire*, it was stated[734] that the Titan was bound for thirty thousand years. In those days this meant the world's longest period. In the tragedy that has been preserved, *Prometheus Bound*, it was prophesied[735] that he would be set free in the thirteenth generation. And so it came about.

The liberator was Herakles, who shot the tormenting bird with his arrow. If this were all, the tales of rivalry between men and gods would merely end by going off into heroic saga. But the fact is that all Prometheus's sufferings for the sake of mankind were the sufferings of a god. In the view of Aeschylus, and of all who were well disposed towards humanity, these sufferings were unjust, and of such a nature as necessarily to bring about the end of Zeus himself. Hesiod's explanation[736] of the unbinding was that the Olympian wanted to bestow fame upon his son Herakles. Aeschylus reminded us of the possibility of Zeus's being succeeded by another ruler of the world, of whom I shall speak in a moment. Prometheus learnt this secret from his mother Themis—or Gaia, so we read in an interpolated text.[737] Zeus set him at liberty as the price of keeping the secret. Even so, however, Prometheus had to provide an heir to his torments,[738] an immortal who went down into the Underworld and suffered in his stead. This immortal was the wise Centaur Chiron,[739] whom Herakles had accidentally and incurably wounded with a poisoned arrow. The inventor of the art of healing took upon himself the suffering and death of the beneficent Titan. Nevertheless the unbound Prometheus—so ended the story in the stage version by Aeschylus—thenceforward wore a special wreath[740] as a sign of his subjection to the power of Zeus. As another emblem he bore an iron ring,[741] which was said[742] to have had a stone set in it to remind him of the crag on which he suffered. It is, of course, possible that the iron ring was a last survival from the time when Prometheus was an iron-working Kabeiros or Daktylos.

5

THE STORY OF NIOBE

I have already made it plain that the story of mankind did not begin in all parts of Greece with Prometheus, Epimetheus and Pandora. In Boeotia the primordial man Alalkomeneus arose by Lake Kopais, and there founded his family with Athenais —that is to say, with the goddess Athene, who in this story rose out of the water at the same place. In another tale[743] the wife of Alalkomeneus was called Niobe. As humanity's first mother she had the further distinction[744] of being honoured in Thebes as the mother of seven Meliai, the mortal Ash-Nymphs, who were doubtless the wives of the primordial men of that region. In Argos it was told of Phoroneus, the son of a Melia, that he was the First Man,[745] that he founded the first human community[746] and brought fire from Heaven.[747] He needed fire for smithying and for making sacrifices.[748] The goddess to whom he sacrificed and offered his forged weapons was Hera.[749] To oblige her Zeus made Phoroneus the first king: formerly Zeus himself had ruled over men; but Hermes created a confusion of human speech, which spoilt Zeus's pleasure in this rule. Associated with Phoroneus in this tale is Niobe,[750] who was the first mortal woman to be loved by Zeus.[751] It was also said[752] of her that she was the mother of Phoroneus, or sometimes that she was his daughter. It is more probable, however, that in Argos, too, she was the wife of the First Man, just as she was in Boeotia. She bore to Zeus the ancestors of the inhabitants of the country, Argos and Pelasgos.

None of the other tales said that Niobe was the First Woman

or the mother of the ancestors of the Greek peoples. Instead, they gave an account of the great number of her children, and of how she set herself up against the goddess Leto, who had borne only Apollon and Artemis. Leto and Niobe had once been very close friends—so we learn from our great woman poet Sappho.[753] At the time of this friendship there obviously can have been no absolute distinction between gods and human beings. Niobe herself is sometimes described as a goddess,[754] although in saga[755] she was supposed to have been only a haughty queen, a daughter of the Lydian King Tantalos. In all these tales she had to make heavy atonement. The story of this is told by Homer.[756] Her twelve children perished, six daughters and six stalwart youths. Apollon killed the sons with his silver bow, and Artemis killed the daughters, in anger against Niobe because the latter had entered into rivalry with Leto by boasting that this goddess had borne only two children, whereas she herself had borne many. For nine days the children lay in their blood, and there was nobody to bury them, for the son of Kronos turned all the neighbours into stones. On the tenth day the celestial gods themselves buried the dead. On this day Niobe, exhausted by weeping, first broke her fast. Finally she was turned into a rock, which now stands in the Sipylos range, and as a stone she continues to grieve; for such was the will of the gods.

Other narrators of the story believed that Niobe had fourteen, eighteen, nineteen or twenty children, who perished, through no fault of their own, so that the difference between gods and men should be clearly marked. Only one daughter, Chloris, was said[757] to have been spared, and to have become the wife of the long-lived hero Nestor, to whom Apollon gave the years that he took from the sons of Niobe. The unquenchable tears that flow from a rock on the Sipylos range in Asia Minor[758] are believed to this day to spring from Niobe's eyes. The petrified mother of sorrows is pointed out to travellers. It should never be forgotten that in our mythology she was an original mother of mankind.

6

THETIS AND THE FUTURE RULER OF THE WORLD

In speaking of Thetis I have continually indicated that, although she is described only as one of the Nereides,[759] she was in fact one of our greatest sea-goddesses, like Amphitrite, Eurynome or her grandmother Tethys herself. Together with the hundred-armed sea-god Briareos she had protected Zeus; and she and Eurynome had succoured the child Hephaistos. Had Thetis married a son of Kronos, as Eurynome married Zeus or as Amphitrite married Poseidon, the consequences for the future of the world would have been still greater than the consequences of these two unions.

It was told[760] that Zeus and Poseidon were rivals for Thetis. They yearned to take the lovely goddess to wife. Eros had entered into both of them. Nevertheless their divine insight prevented them from consummating the marriage. For they followed the advice of an oracle. Themis, giver of counsel, rose up between them and prophesied that it was the will of Fate that, if the sea-goddess were to bear a son to either Zeus or his brother, this son would possess a more powerful weapon than lightning or the trident. This prophecy was the secret that Prometheus, in the story of which he was the hero, had learnt from his mother Themis. In the play[761] the chained Titan proclaimed the coming of the new ruler of the world, for he foresaw that Zeus would soon go off to his marriage with Thetis. In other tales[762] the sea-goddess withstood Zeus, either from fear or from loyalty to Hera,[763] who had reared her. But Zeus would not have desisted from his suit had he not been warned, and had he not feared the same fate as befell Kronos. According to Aeschylus, he had extracted the warning from Prometheus, under torture of his sufferings inflicted by the eagle.

Themis advised[764] the quarrelling brothers, Zeus and Poseidon, to give Thetis to a mortal hero, the devout Peleus, on a night of full moon. The brothers consented. It was also said[765] that Zeus had sworn to marry her to a mortal because he was angered by the goddess's resistance to him. Peleus, who dwelt on Pelion, the mountain of Chiron, was aided by the wise Centaur.[766] In vain Thetis played all the tricks of meta-morphosis such as were used by the old sea-divinities against their assailants. She turned herself[767] into fire and water, into a lion and a serpent, and into various sea-creatures. It was a soundless struggle.[768] Dwellers by the sea reported[769] that she finally assumed the shape of a cuttlefish and was in this shape when Peleus took her. Destiny was fulfilled.[770] The gods brought her gifts, that they might worthily celebrate the mar-riage of which was to be born the greatest hero of the Trojan War, Achilleus, the all too short-lived son of Thetis. At this celebration the apple of Eris fell between the three goddesses, Aphrodite, Hera and Pallas Athene. Then followed the Judgment of Paris—an epoch-making event in the world's history, as our heroic saga tells of it. It was the beginning not only of the Trojan War, but also of the Age of the Heroes, which itself was a further attempt by the gods to weaken man-kind. This was expressly stated in an epic poem which described the events leading up to that great war:[771] Earth suffered under the burden of mankind, which had grown too numerous. Zeus took pity on the goddess Earth and resolved to ease her burden.

7

THE DESTINY OF MANKIND

The deeds and sufferings of the heroes had no place in our stories of the gods—although our story-tellers were all too fond of bringing the gods into the heroes' adventures and wars. On the other hand, the stories of the gods were certainly bound up with the destiny of the human race—or, more properly, of the human races; of which, according to a story that I shall now tell, there was a series. Such tales as this, or as the tale of how Earth suffered under the burden of mankind, or the story of the Flood, all came to us from the east; but in Greece they never obtained such acceptance as amongst the eastern peoples. The story-tellers only occasionally referred to a Flood, to which they attributed various causes, in order to explain phenomena such as the disappearance of the Telchines from Rhodes. Indeed, their references to the Flood are so much at variance that we must finally distinguish between at least three great Floods:[772] that of Ogygos, that of Deukalion and that of Dardanos, the three Floods being named after the three survivors and saviours of the human race. The story of Deuka-lion I shall tell presently; but first I must relate the tale of the series of races, or of ages.

Originally there were four distinct ages or races. Hesiod, however, described five of them, since he did not wish to identify our heroes either with the race of bronze or with his own race, that of iron. He attributed the origin even of the first race, that of gold, to the Olympian gods: which was not entirely correct, as he himself states that at this time Kronos still ruled, and not the later Olympians. As he told it,[773] the immortals who dwell upon Olympus first of all created man-kind's golden race. The men of this race lived under Kronos, who at that time ruled in Heaven. They lived like the gods, free from care, without trouble or woe. Pitiful old age hung not over them, with ageless limbs they revelled at their ban-quets, free of all evil. When they died, it was as men overcome by sleep. All good things were ready to their hand: the life-giving fields bore of themselves and brought forth fruits in plenty. Gladly men lived on these fruits, at peace together, a community wholly of good men. They were rich in cattle, and friends of the blessed gods. When this race had sunk into the sheltering depths of the earth, they became—in accordance with the will of Zeus—good spirits who walk upon the earth as watchers over men, who protect justice and guard against injustice, everywhere invisibly present. They bestow wealth: for this, too, is in accordance with their royal nature.

The second race created by the Olympians, the race of silver, was much inferior. It resembled the golden race neither in body nor in soul. For a hundred years a son would remain under his mother's tutelage, playing at home like a child. When these men had at length matured and were in the flower of youth, they continued to live only for a short while, being subject in their folly to all sorts of sufferings. They could not restrain their unbounded greed for power over one another. They refused to worship the gods or to bring sacrifices, as it is customary for men to do in accordance with their various ways and usages. Therefore Zeus in his wrath caused them to disappear, because they offered no worship to the Olympians. Now that this race, too, is sunk into the sheltering depths of the earth, men call them the subterranean blessed, and they occupy only a second position, although they, too, are accorded a certain veneration.

Father Zeus then created yet a third race of men, the race of bronze, which did not even resemble the silver one. He created them from the ash-trees. They were a terrible and mighty race, who took pleasure only in the woeful works and violent deeds of Ares. These men ate no food made of flour; of steel was the soul of these unapproachables. They had the strength of giants, and mighty hands on their mighty limbs. Of bronze were their weapons, of bronze were their habitations and in bronze they worked; for black iron had not yet come to be. Perishing by their own hands, in battles one against the other, they descended into the musty palace of dreadful Hades, men without names: no matter how fearful they were, black Death took them, they were compelled to leave the bright light of the sun.

When this race, too, had sunk into the sheltering depths of the earth—this was Hesiod's variation on the tale of the four ages—Zeus created the divine race of the heroes, those who fought the famous wars for Thebes and Troy. They were more righteous and better than the bronze race, and after death they came to the Isles of the Blest, girt by Okeanos: the islands where the life-giving fields bear sweet fruits thrice yearly, where Kronos rules, set free by Zeus from his chains. For the fifth race, that of iron, which followed thereafter, Hesiod had nothing but abuse: he would have preferred to live either earlier or later. His description of this race went off into gloomy prophecies, beginning with the prophecy that children would come into the world grey-haired, and ending with the prophecy that the goddesses Aidos and Nemesis, swathed in white raiment, would return home to the gods and leave mankind to perish undefended.

Hesiod's narrative makes no mention of a great Flood. Other story-tellers,[774] however, told that this was how Zeus sought to exterminate the race of bronze. In the simplest version of this story, Prometheus had a son named Deukalion, who ruled over the country of Phthia, in Thessaly, and took to wife Pyrrha, "the red-blonde", the daughter of Epimetheus and Pandora. When Zeus sought to destroy the race of bronze, Deukalion, on the advice of Prometheus, made a wooden box, stored in it all that was necessary, and climbed into it with Pyrrha. Zeus caused mighty rains to pour from Heaven, and thus flooded the greater part of Greece. All men perished, saving a few who had fled to the nearest high mountains. It happened also at this time that the mountains of Thessaly were split asunder, and the whole country as far as the Isthmus and the Peloponnese became a single sheet of water. Deukalion floated over this sea in his box for nine days and nine nights, and finally landed on Parnassus. There he disembarked, when the rains had ceased, and sacrificed to Zeus who had guided his escape. Zeus sent Hermes to him and gave him leave to ask for whatever he wished. He wished for human beings. Zeus bade him take stones and throw them over his shoulder. The stones that Deukalion threw became men, and those that Pyrrha threw became women. Hence the word *laoi* for people and peoples: in our tongue the word for "stone" is *laas* or *laos*.

The account of the second creation of mankind was not based solely on this very ancient pun. In another version[775] of the story, Deukalion and Pyrrha received instructions from the nearby oracle of Themis—which was later the oracle of Delphi—to throw behind them the bones of their "great mother". This they must have taken to mean Pandora, who was said[776] in other stories to have been the mother of Deukalion, too: the solution of the riddle lay in discovering who was meant. The couple threw behind them the bones of Mother Earth. The new human beings who sprang up from these bones—that is to say, from stones—were likewise descended from the oldest Mother of all. There was also a story[777] concerning the first human being to be created on this occasion. This was the girl Protogeneia, who was raped by Zeus. The name means exactly the same as Protogonos, "the first to be born", which is also a surname both of the goddess Earth herself[778] and of a more famous ravished daughter, Persephone.[779]

CHAPTER XIV

Hades and Persephone

THE third of the three world-ruling sons of Kronos was the
dark counterpart not only of Zeus but also of Helios. Hades
is the most recent form of his name, an older form was Aides,
or Aidoneus, and a still older form was Ais, which was
preserved only in connection with the word for "house" or
"palace". "The House of Hades" was the Underworld, which
indeed was later also called simply Hades, the place having
acquired the name of its master. The meaning of Ais, Aides
or Hades is most probably "the invisible" or "the invisibility-
giving", in contrast with Helios, the visible and visible-making.
It also expresses a still stronger contrast than the contrast
between Hades and the heavenly king Zeus, whose name once
meant "brightness of day". This meaning, however, was thrust
completely into the background by the human visage of the
ruler of the gods. Zeus exercised a function that in our mythology was never exercised by the sun-god: Helios never appears
in the rôle of a king of the Underworld and is never addressed
as "Sun of Night". Instead, as Zeus Katachthonios, or
Chthonios—I have already mentioned these surnames—Zeus
was a "subterranean Zeus"; and this again was only another
name for Aides or Hades.[780] When mention is made of
"another Zeus"[781] or "the hospitable Zeus of the departed",[782]
this always refers to Hades. It never means "another god of
the daylight heavens", but a ruler of the Underworld who
corresponds and is equal to the Zeus of the world above.

Our mythology divided the world, indeed, into three parts:
either because in earlier times it was ruled much more by a
threefold goddess than by a male divinity—the latter being
merely the husband of the former—or because the oldest goddess, the Mother of the Gods, has always had three sons, two
of them older, and more closely identified as brothers, than the

third, the youngest, who is destined to gain supremacy. We must here recognise a basic scheme in which either a female or a male trinity predominates. The female trinity is subordinate to a male fourth, and the male trinity to a female fourth. As soon, therefore, as the third brother appeared upon our shores and became the new master of our sea, our religion could find room for him. (I am speaking, of course, of Poseidon.) Records exist of the worship of a trinity in which he is not included, a cult of Zeus as "Heavenly God" (*Hypsistos*), as God of the Underworld (*Chthonios*), and, under a third aspect, without a name.[783] With the advent of Poseidon the trinity became all the more clearly defined. An ancient vase-painting shows the three brothers as three rulers of the world, with the emblems of their power: Zeus with his lightning, Poseidon with the trident, Hades with his head turned back to front. This last was he who might not be looked upon, the dreadful god of death, who caused all living things to disappear, who made them invisible. People who sacrificed to the beings of the Underworld had to do so with averted gaze.

The subterranean brother of Zeus—for this is what Hades became in our mythology, even if originally he was only the dark aspect of an otherwise bright god—had many names besides those I have already mentioned. He had not only names that expressed his quality of god of the dead—such as Polydegmon, "the receiver of many guests". He was also Plouton, "the wealthy one" or "the wealth-giving", and Eubouleus or Euboulos, "the good counseller". The same names—Ploutos, Euboulos, Eubouleus—were given also to that perplexing, mystic son whom he begat by a goddess who was likewise known under many names, and, furthermore, both as mother and daughter: as Gaia and Rhea, as Rhea and Demeter, and, especially in her relation to Hades, as Demeter and Persephone. In the public version of the tale, Hades did not cohabit with his sister Demeter. It was Zeus who did this, in the more secret tale which I have already told, or else it was Poseidon, in another tale with which my audience is also familiar. Hades did, however, ravish his niece Persephone, who was also called simply Kore, "the Maiden". Her name Persephone is con‑ nected with Perse, Perseis, Perses, Perseus and Persaios—names of Hekate and her associates—and was probably used from pre‑Greek times as a name of the queen of the Underworld. She acquired the name "the Maiden" when, as first and only daughter of her mother (a characteristic which she again shared with Hekate, but also with Pandora and Protogeneia), she fell victim to the god of death. This is the story of the founda‑ tion of the realm of the dead, which for us would be unthink‑ able without its queen, and it is also the story of the foundation of the Eleusinian Mysteries. I shall first of all tell it as it was told in a great hymn composed in the style of Homer.

I

THE RAPE OF PERSEPHONE

Hades ravished the daughter of Demeter,[784] the daughter whom Zeus had given to him without her mother's know‑ ledge. The maiden was playing with the daughters of Okeanos, picking flowers—roses and crocuses, violets, irises and hya‑ cinths—on the lush meadow. Almost she picked the narcissus, too, that flower which the goddess Gaia, to please the god of the Underworld, had caused to spring up, a radiant wonder, as a wile to seduce the maiden with the rosebud countenance. All who beheld the flower, both gods and men, were aston‑ ished. A hundred blossoms sprouted from its root, sweet fragrance spread around it, the heavens smiled and the earth and the salty flood of the sea. With both hands the astonished maiden reached out for this jewel. The earth opened, a chasm appeared in the Nysaean Fields, and from it sprang the Lord of the Underworld with his immortal steeds, the Son of Kronos, the god with many names. He set the struggling maiden on his golden chariot and carried her off despite her wails.

Shrilly she cried out to the Father, the Son of Kronos, the supreme ruler. Neither god nor man heard her voice, not an olive stirred. Only the tender daughter of Persaios, the goddess with the gleaming head-dress, the goddess Hekate heard the cry from her cave; and it was heard, too, by Helios, the splendid son of Hyperion. The Father sat remote from the gods, in his much-frequented temple, receiving the sacrifices. It was his doing that his daughter had been carried off by her uncle, by that commander of many souls, host to many guests, the Son of Kronos, the god with many names. As long as she still could see the earth and the starry sky, the sea and the sun, the goddess hoped to see again her mother and the eternal gods. The mountain-peaks and the depths of the sea echoed her immortal voice. The Lady her mother heard it. Sharp pain laid hold of her heart, she tore the head-dress from her immortal hair, cast her dark raiment from off her shoulders, and flew like a bird over land and water in search of her child.

Nobody was willing to tell her the truth—neither god nor man. Not even a bird flew to meet her as a sign. For nine days the Lady Demeter wandered upon the earth, with two burning torches in her hands. In her pain she tasted neither ambrosia nor nectar, nor did she moisten her body with water. It was not until the third morning that Hekate—she, too, carrying a torch—met her and brought her tidings: "Lady Demeter, bringer of ripeness and giver of rich gifts, who was it, then, who stole Persephone and so deeply troubled thy heart? I heard the cry, but I did not see who it was. Had I done so, I would tell you the truth." Without a word the daughter of Rhea sprang with her, carrying in her hands the two burning torches, up to Helios, the watcher over gods and men. They halted in front of his horses, and the great goddess inquired concerning her daughter and the ravisher. The son of Hyperion answered her: "Daughter of Rhea, Lady Demeter, thou shalt learn the truth. I have reverence for thee and pity at thy grief for the maiden with the beautiful ankles. None other of the immortals is responsible but Zeus, who gave her as a wife to his brother

Hades. Hades carried her off in his chariot, taking her by force to the realm of darkness and paying small heed to her loud weeping. But thou, goddess, cease lamenting! There is no need to scold so inconsolably. In thy brother Hades thou hast received no unworthy son-in-law amongst the gods. Since the apportionment he has been honoured with a third of the world, and where he dwells he is indeed king."

So Helios spoke, and drove onwards in his chariot. His steeds obeyed his voice and drew the car as swift as birds. The goddess was plunged in still more dreadful and more gnawing grief. In her anger against Zeus she left Olympus and the assembly of gods, she went amongst men and visited their cities and places of work. Long she neglected her outward appearance, nobody recognised her, neither man nor woman, until she came to the palace of the wise Keleos, who at that time was a king in Eleusis, that city fragrant with sacrifices. She sat down by the wayside, sunk in the grief of her heart, by the Well of the Virgin, whence the people of the city drew water. There she sat in the shade, under an olive. She seemed like an old woman who can no longer bear children and has no more share in the gifts of the goddess of love. Thus appear the nurses of royal children and the elder serving-women of echoing palaces. Here she was seen by the daughters of Keleos, son of Eleusis, when they came to draw water in brazen pitchers for their father's house. They were four in number, goddess-like, in the flower of maidenhood: Kallidike, Kleisi-dike, Demo and Kallithoe, the eldest. They did not recognise the goddess—indeed, it is not so easy for mortals to behold immortals—and they said to her: "Whence art thou, old woman, and whither goest thou? Why hast thou left thy home, and why comest thou not into the palace? Within its shady walls thou wouldst be at home, in thy old age, just as are the younger women, who would use thee well both in word and in deed."

The goddess made friendly answer: she called the maidens "dear children", stated her own name, but in a distorted form, and told an invented story. She said that pirates had brought her thither against her will from Crete. When they had landed near Thorikos and were preparing a carouse for themselves on the shores with the other women, she had escaped, and now she knew not where she was. She besought help and hospitality in the house of which the maidens were the daughters. Perhaps there was a child there for whom she could care as its nurse? She would prepare the bed for the master and mistress, and would teach handiwork to the other women of the household. Kallidike, the most beautiful of the maidens, told her the names of the lords of the land: Triptolemos, Diokles, Polyxeinos, Eumolpos, Dolichos and her own father. They all had wives, and none of these would turn away the suppliant for protection. Any of them would take her in at first sight, so great was her resemblance to the goddesses. But she should wait until they, the four maidens, had asked their mother Metaneira, so that she would invite the stranger into her house and the stranger would not need to go elsewhere. There was indeed a sweet and recently born son in the palace: whoever took care of him and reared him would be envied by the other women, and with good cause, for she would be richly rewarded.

Thus the goddess was invited, with the promise of a great wage, into the house of Keleos. The maidens came running back and led her home. Demeter followed them with a veil over her face, in a long, dark robe that flowed rustling down to her delicate feet. They entered Keleos's outer hall, where sat the Lady Metaneira before her chamber. In her lap she held the child, the new offspring. The maidens ran to their mother. The goddess stepped over the threshold, her head touched the roof, the doorway was filled with divine light. The Queen was stricken with awe, astonishment and terror; she rose from her seat and demanded that the goddess should sit there. Demeter would not do this, but stood in silence, with eyes cast down, until the wise handmaiden Iambe set a stool before her, and threw over it a silver-white sheep-skin. Thereupon

Demeter sat down and lowered the veil from her head over her face. Long she sat there making no sound, in deep grief; she spoke no word and made no sign. Without smiling, without touching food or drink, she sat there mourning for her daughter, until the wise Iambe with mockery and jests so cheered the divine lady that she first smiled and then laughed, and her soul grew merry again. Later, too, Iambe knew how to console the goddess when she was wroth. Metaneira offered her a goblet of sweet wine, but Demeter refused it, saying that she was not permitted to drink red wine. She bade that barley should be mixed with water, that she might drink it with delicate mint. The Queen made the potion, and the goddess took it, as ever since then those have done who are dedicated to sacred purity and may not drink wine.

Only now did Metaneira speak the words of greeting and bid the stranger welcome. She believed, she said, that she could read in the eyes of the goddess her royal rank even in misfortune, which comes from the gods as much as good fortune does. But henceforth the goddess would be used exactly as herself. She entrusted to her charge her late-born, no longer hoped-for son. If the goddess would care for him and rear him until he reached the age of youth, she would indeed be rightly envied by the other women, so rich would be her reward. Demeter, the goddess with the beautiful wreath, undertook to care for the child, and promised his mother that she would be no bad nurse, but one who knew the charms against all evil influences. In her immortal hands she took Demophoon, son of Keleos, to her fragrant breast. Metaneira rejoiced. Demeter cared for the boy within the palace. The child grew like a god, without eating or drinking. The goddess anointed him with ambrosia, breathed upon him with her sweet breath and held him in her lap. Every night, without the knowledge of his parents, she exposed the child to the full strength of the fire, like a billet of wood that is being made into a torch. To his parents it was a great marvel how their son throve: he was as fair as one of the gods. Demeter would even have made him into a never-ageing immortal, had not Metaneira, in her thoughtlessness, one night peeped out from her chamber and seen what was being done to the child. She screamed, in terror beat both hands upon her thighs, and burst into lamentation: "Demophoon, my son, the stranger lets thee waste away in the great fire, and me she plunges into bereavement!"

Thus she lamented. The goddess heard her, and was filled with anger against the Queen. With immortal hands she laid the child aside, upon the ground, having first wrathfully taken him from the fire, and at the same time she said to Metaneira: "Ignorant are ye human beings, and thoughtless, ye can foresee neither good nor evil. Thou, too, hast in thy thoughtlessness suffered an irremediable harm. I swear the great oath of the gods, by the water of the Styx, that I would have made thy dear son into an immortal, who would have remained eternally young, and I would have won for him imperishable renown. Now he no longer has any way of avoiding death. Imperishable renown he shall receive, because he sat in my lap and slept in my arms. Continually the sons of the Eleusinians will at appointed intervals wage wars in his honour. But I, for my part, am Demeter, the mistress of all worship, a divinity of the greatest beneficence, who bring the greatest joy both to immortals and to mortals. Now you and your whole people shall erect to me a great temple and an altar in front of it, beneath the city wall and above the well with the beautiful dancing-place, on the spur of the hill. I shall teach you the sacred rites, so that in future you may offer me the worship that comforts my soul."

Thus spoke the goddess, and resumed her original stature and her true shape. She was no longer an old woman: she was bathed in beauty, a desire-awakening fragrance was spread around from her sweet-smelling robe; far shone the radiance of her immortal body; golden fell her hair upon her shoulders; brightness filled the chamber, as if with a flash of lightning. Forth from the palace strode the goddess. The Queen fell down in a swoon. Long she lay there making no utterance, not thinking to pick up the child from the ground. Her daughters heard his weeping and leapt up from their bed. One of them picked up the child and took it in her lap. Another lit a fire. A third ran to their mother, helped her to her feet and brought her from her room. All busied themselves with the child, washing him while he struggled and surrounding him with love. But he would not be comforted, for now he had worse nurses. They spent the whole night in praying to the goddess, quaking with fear. At the grey of dawn they told all to the widely powerful Keleos, as they had been bidden to do by Demeter of the beautiful wreath. The King summoned the people together and called upon them to build a rich temple and an altar to Demeter, upon the spur of the hill. They at once obeyed, and built as he commanded. The temple arose by the will of the gods.

When they had finished and saw the fruit of their labours, they went home. In the temple sat Demeter, remote from the blessed gods, and mourned for her daughter. A dreadful year she sent upon the all-nourishing earth, a year of bitter misery for mankind. From no seed would the earth allow anything to sprout; Demeter caused everything to lie hidden in the ground. In vain the oxen drew the ploughs on the fields, in vain fell the white barley into the furrows. She would have destroyed all mankind with evil famine, and the Olympians would have received no more worship or sacrifices, had not Zeus thought better of it. He first of all sent Iris, the lovely goddess with golden wings, to fetch Demeter back. Iris obeyed and hastened to Eleusis. She found Demeter in the temple, swathed in dark raiment, and implored her, but in vain: the goddess would not consent. Then the Father sent all the blessed gods to her: they came, one after another, to fetch back Demeter, and they brought her splendid gifts. But none could move the angry goddess to alter her decision. She would not set foot within the fragrant palace on Olympus, nor would the earth again bear fruit, until she once more saw her daughter.

When Zeus had learnt of this, he sent Hermes, the god with

the golden staff, into the darkness of the Underworld, to persuade Hades with soft words and to bring Persephone back from the gloom and up to the gods and the light. Hermes obeyed and sprang from the Olympian abode down into the subterranean depths. There he found the lord of the palace at home. He sat leaning on the bed beside his shamefaced wife, who in great grief was yearning for her mother. Hermes stood before them and told Hades, that lord of the dead, that dark-haired god, of the reason for his arrival. The eyebrows of Hades were raised in a smile. He was obedient to King Zeus, and at once spoke to his wife: "Go thou, Persephone, to thy mother, the goddess with the dark raiment, go with a gracious heart and be no more so exceedingly sad. I shall be no unworthy husband of thee amongst the immortals—am I not own brother to Father Zeus? If perchance thou comest here at times, thou shalt rule over all living creatures and shalt have the greatest honour amongst the gods. Whoever insulteth thee, and bringeth no sacrifice of contribution, shall atone for it eternally."

Thus he spoke. Persephone sprang up rejoicing. Her husband, however, secretly went up behind her and put into her mouth the honey-sweet seed of a pomegranate, so that she should not remain for ever with Demeter. He harnessed the immortal steeds to the golden chariot. The goddess mounted it, and Hermes, with reins and whip in his hand, drove the team out of the palace. Willingly flew the steeds and swiftly they covered the great distance. Neither sea nor rivers nor ravines nor precipices hindered their onrush: they flew above them, through the air. Hermes halted the steeds at the place where Demeter sat before her fragrant temple. At sight of the chariot she sprang up like a Bacchante in the mountains. Persephone, leaving the chariot, flew to meet her. Whilst they embraced, Demeter was already asking her daughter whether she had taken food in the palace of Hades. For if she had, she must spend one-third of the year below the earth, and only for the other two-thirds could she remain with her mother and the rest of the immortals, returning to them with the spring.

Persephone told how, at the moment when she sprang up in joy to return to her mother, her husband had secretly slipped the seed of a pomegranate into her mouth, and had compelled her to eat it. She also told how she had been carried off while she had been playing and picking flowers with the daughters of Okeanos and with Athene and Artemis. Thus she and her mother passed the whole day, enveloping each other in love. Then came also Hekate of the gleaming head-dress, and she, too, lovingly welcomed the daughter of holy Demeter. Since then she has been their companion and servant. Zeus sent his mother Rhea, the dark-robed goddess, as a messenger to the pair of them, to Demeter and Persephone, that she might fetch them. He promised them whatever honour they might desire, and that the daughter should pass two-thirds of the year with her mother and the rest of the immortals. Rhea sprang down from Olympus to the Rharian Fields, which had formerly been fruitful but now lay there sterile, without a single green blade, keeping the white barley hidden within the soil, in accordance with the will of Demeter, the goddess with the beautiful ankles. But soon again, as the spring went forward, the fields were to be thickly covered with ears of grain. It was on these fields that the goddess, coming from Heaven, now first set foot. Gladly they beheld each other, the mother and daughter, Rhea and Demeter. Rhea told what Zeus had promised, and besought Demeter to permit the life-giving corn to grow again.

Demeter consented, and caused the fruit of the heavy-clodded fields to sprout forth. Thickly she covered the broad earth with blade and blossom. Meanwhile the goddess went to the kings of Eleusis, and taught them the sacred rites, and initiated them into the sacred worship, which may be neither revealed, nor heard, nor even spoken aloud, for sacred awe of the goddess chokes the utterance. Blessed is the man on earth who has seen such things. But he who remains uninitiated and has no

PLATE XIII

DIONYSOS THE HUNTER, *i.e.* ZAGREUS, WITH MAENADS,
A HUNTRESS WITH TORCH AND SILENOS

PLATE XIV

DIONYSOS AND TWO MAENADS OFFERING A HARE
AND A FAWN

share in them will when he is dead have no portion in the like blessings in the musty darkness down below.

When Demeter had given all these instructions, the goddesses went up to Olympus, into the gathering of the other immortals. There they dwell beside Zeus, enjoying great honour. Blessed is the man on earth whom they love. They will readily send him Ploutos, the god of wealth, into his palace, to be for him a guest who bestows riches upon mortal men.

2

OTHER STORIES OF RAPE, CONSOLATION AND
ASCENSION

In the foregoing story Hades carried off Persephone from the distant shore of Okeanos, from the Nysaean Fields, the meadows on Mount Nysa which will also appear in the story of the birth of Dionysos. The time of day at which the rape occurred can be reckoned from the fact that during the journey to the Underworld the abducted maiden saw both the starry sky and also the Sun. Helios, for his part, also saw her as she disappeared from the earth's surface in the chariot of the god of the Underworld—that is to say, early in the morning, presumably. Her playmates were, besides the Okeaninai, also Athene and Artemis. The three great virgin goddesses, amongst whom Persephone was then still numbered, constituted a trinity, of which a third part fell victim to the ravisher and remained for a third of the year beneath the earth. Demeter was absent when her daughter was abducted. According to one tale,[785] she chanced at that moment to be on her beloved isle of Sicily, where—according to another tale[786]—the rape itself occurred, by Lake Pergus, which is near the hilltown of Enna. In this latter tale the ravisher disappeared with his victim in the neighbourhood of Syracuse, at the spot where since then has risen the spring of Kyane, "the dark spring".

On our mainland, too, it was claimed for many localities

that Demeter had come to them on her search for her stolen daughter. On this search—so it was told[787]—she visited the home of a man of that time, one of our primordial men, and was hospitably received. In Argos her host was the primordial man Pelasgos, whose wife Chrysanthis, "Flower of Gold", informed the goddess of the fate of her abducted daughter. But the town most famed as the place where Demeter first had news of Persephone's fate has always been Eleusis. The disciples of Orpheus have preserved a story about this more ancient than that story in the style of Homer which I have already related. In that great hymn the only evidence of extreme antiquity was the name of King Keleos, "the Woodpecker". This is a suitable name for a king ruling over forest-dwellers, who had no knowledge of agriculture until Demeter visited them and gave them grain, in gratitude to those who had given her hospitality and news of her daughter. This theme of gratitude was missing from the story I have related, but that story preserved another ancient theme: that of consolation. The goddess was consoled by the jests of Iambe. This name is derived from *iambos*, which is our word for jesting verse and is certainly not so old as the theme of consolation itself. I shall now relate the story of the consolation of Demeter as it was told by the followers of Orpheus.

In the Rharian Fields,[788] between Athens and Eleusis, Demeter encountered mortals who had sprung from the earth: the woman Baubo, the man Dysaules, and their sons Triptolemos, Eumolpos and Eubouleus. The name Baubo means "Belly". *Dusaules* had his name from "house where it is not good to dwell". It was said of their sons—for all three of them were their sons, although this is expressly stated of only two of them[789]—that Triptolemos was a cowherd, Eumolpos a shepherd and Eubouleus the swineherd. To judge by his name, Triptolemos, "the threefold warrior", must originally have been —like Keleos's son Demophoon, a "slayer of the people"—a figure like the war-god Ares. Under the name Eumolpos, "the sweet singer", one can recognise the officiating priest of the

TRIPTOLEMOS BETWEEN DEMETER, PERSEPHONE AND
THE PRIESTESS OR QUEEN ELEUSIS

Eleusinian Mysteries; and the name Eubouleus means that he
was the god of the Underworld himself. In the original story
it was doubtless this last who played the principal part, and
he alone appeared in the quality of a herdsman. It was told[790]
that Eubouleus's swine were swallowed up in the same chasm
as Persephone. This was why he was able to tell Demeter
what had happened to her daughter. Most of the tales mention
Triptolemos, too, as having been Demeter's informant, or
sometimes Triptolemos alone. This latter was the man who
received the grateful goddess's gift of grain, and went out into
the world to share the gift with mankind. If in earlier times
he had been a warlike being, he now became, through
Demeter, the tamer of the savage ways of primordial men who
did not yet know bread. The vase-paintings show him mounted
on a chariot consisting only of two wheels and a throne: above
the wheels, on which are wings and serpents, sits Triptolemos
with ears of grain in his hand.

The consolation of Demeter was also described as follows:[791]
Baubo received the goddess hospitably and gave her the barley
drink of which I have already spoken. The goddess rejected

it and refused to break her fast. Thereupon Baubo did something else. (She must be thought of as sitting with legs wide
apart in front of the sorrowing goddess, like her statues in the
shrines later set up to her.) She lifted up her gown, revealing
her uncomely womb, and behold! there was the child Iakchos
laughing in Baubo's womb. At this the goddess laughed too,
and smilingly accepted the drink. Iakchos was a name for the
divine child of the Eleusinian Mysteries, that son of Persephone
whose birth was proclaimed by the officiating priest. The initiates publicly declared,[792] in commemoration of a similar
consolation that they themselves had received on the way of
initiation: "I fasted, I drank the barley-drink." What they had
seen they might not reveal. Nor would it be easy to describe
more exactly what it was that Demeter saw in the unbared
womb of Baubo. Here we already touch upon the ineffable
part of the Mysteries.

Perhaps this story once meant that Demeter herself went
down into the Underworld, and there found Baubo and
Dysaules—beings in whose house it was so ill to dwell.
According to the tale told by the followers of Orpheus,[793] she
certainly descended into the Underworld through the same
gaping chasm as had swallowed up Persephone and the swine
—which were the sacrificial animals of both goddesses. The
famous black steeds of Hades,[794] and also Demeter's serpent-
chariot[795] in which she hunted for the ravisher, are of later
origin than the tale of the maiden's disappearance through a
chasm in the earth. The stories of Persephone's ascension from
the Underworld were adapted correspondingly. In the later
tale[796] she drove up to Olympus behind white steeds. But it
was also told[797] that Persephone was led back into the light
by the Moirai, the Horai and the Charites, a band of nine
dancers. Another comforter of the sorrowing mother—that is
to say, of Rhea and Demeter in one person—was Aphrodite.[798]
It will be remembered that this goddess was attended by Horai
and Charites in all her comings and goings, both at her birth
and at her other epiphanies. The only difference between

Persephone's resurrection from the Underworld and Aphrodite's birth was that the former rose from an abyss in the earth.
Two divine handmaidens wrapped the goddess in a robe, she
having been clad only in a thin shift. The scene can be admired on the throne of the Ludovisi. Terra-cottas in the same
style and of the same period, taken from Greek shrines in
southern Italy, show the goddess being drawn in her chariot
by an Eros and by the figure of a winged maiden.

3

TALES OF THE UNDERWORLD

If the story of Demeter's wandering into the Underworld to
find her daughter had been preserved, we would have more
information concerning the Realm of the Dead itself. For in
our mythology, the tales of the Underworld were usually bound
up with the stories concerning the journeys made into the
Realm of the Dead by divinities or heroes, by initiates or even
by uninitiates. In these stories the gods or heroes succeeded in
returning, whereas the initiates and uninitiates fared otherwise,
and the fate of the initiates was different from that of the
uninitiates. The greatest evildoers, such as Tityos, Phlegyas
or Ixion, were subject to eternal punishments; and special
punishments were reserved also for those who had struck their
parents[799] or offended a guest (that is to say, a stranger begging
for shelter) and for temple-robbers and perjurers—not to mention those guilty of more uncommon sins. In the Underworld
such evildoers were furthermore tormented by the Erinyes, who
in many cases had already persecuted them during their
lifetimes. Mention was also made of special Demons of the
Underworld,[800] such as that Eurynomos who in Polygnotos's
painting of the scene was depicted in bluish-black colour,
licking his teeth and sitting on the hide of a lynx. The same
painting also showed[801] Oknos, "the procrastinator", plaiting
a cord from the reeds of the marshy river of the Underworld,

whilst behind him an ass continually ate the cord away. Uninitiates could expect the same punishment as befell the daughters of Danaos, who killed their bridegrooms on the wedding-night and remained unfulfilled: they fetched water in a sieve, or in bottomless pitchers.

These figures and many others were described in the tales of the heroes' journeys into the Underworld. Herakles's journey was undertaken with the purpose of bringing back Kerberos, that furious hound of Hades of which I have already spoken. Theseus and his comrade Peirithoos sought to rob Hades of his queen, Persephone. These tales have been lost, and in any case they properly belong to heroic saga, as does that still more famous story of Orpheus's visit to the Realm of the Dead. He went there to find Eurydike, his wife, and win her back with song. She was delivered up to him, but according to one tale he lost her again. The story of how he lost her has been preserved in greater detail than that of how he first came down into the Underworld. We have equally little information concerning the descent of Demeter, which it would be appropriate to tell at this point. It may be that when the goddess came to the river which bounds the Realm of the Dead she crossed it by Charon's ferry: Polygnotos depicts[802] her priestess Kleoboia as travelling in this fashion. Perhaps the goddess observed the practice, customary amongst those who travelled on Charon's barge only by special favour, of carrying in her hand a golden bough—that famous golden bough which appeased the rough ferryman. This seems to be suggested by the Latin poet Virgil[803]—who can still teach us one or two things concerning the Underworld. According to southern Italian vase-paintings, the initiate wears a wreath of corn—the wreath of Demeter— and carries a bough in his hand when he appears before Hades and Persephone, who sit enthroned amidst the dead in a small, palace-like building as if in an open shrine. If he follows the instructions of the disciples of Orpheus,[804] he will have drunk of the spring that flows at his right hand, Mnemosyne, "Memory", and will have avoided the spring on his left with the white cypress beside it—Lethe, the water of forgetfulness.

As for the question of how uninitiates, and all who died after an unsanctified life, arrived in the Beyond, this is to some extent answered in the tale that describes to us the function of Hermes as Psychopompos, "Escort of Souls". It was told in the Odyssey[805] how he treated the souls of the slain suitors who had oppressed the faithful Penelope. Hermes, god of Kyllene, assembled the souls of the dead as they lay around. In his hand he held the beautiful golden staff with which, if he wishes, he can close the eyes of men as if by a magic spell. Or, if he chooses, he can use it to awaken sleepers. With this staff he marshalled the souls. They followed him whirring, like bats in the corner of a sacred cave when one of them falls from the chain in which they hang together. Whirring flew the souls, led by Hermes, the god who assuages all evil. They flew, by dark ways, past the stream of Okeanos and the white cliffs, past the door through which Helios enters, and past the Country of Dreams. Thus they came swiftly to the meadows of asphodel where dwell the souls, the images of men whom life has worn out. There they met the souls of the heroes who fell before Troy: on a meadow full of those tall-sprouting asphodels whose colourless blossom waves like a grey-violet veil over innumerable coastal meadows on the Mediterranean.

Concerning the dead, the Odyssey had a further story to tell[806]—a story told in the same style as those of Skylla and Charybdis, of Proteus and the Sirenes. It was Kirke, a daughter of Helios, who sent Odysseus to the House of Hades—or, at any rate, to that place where Hades borders on the stream of Okeanos. Here are the mouths—so Kirke informed Odysseus[807]—of the river Pyriphlegethon, "the river that burns like fire", and of Kokytos "the Lamented", a river that flows from the Styx into Acheron, the river of woe. Here, she said, was a sacred grove of Persephone, a grove of black poplars and sterile willows, on the edge of the realm of sunless darkness. Thus far came the souls from the Beyond to meet Odysseus, around a ditch into which flowed the blood of black rams and sheep that had been sacrificed to Hades and Persephone. The swarming souls took strength by drinking the blood, and they spoke with Odysseus. He also beheld—how he did so, the tale does not explain—those souls who remained behind in the House of Hades: Minos, as judge over the dead, with his golden sceptre; Orion, the eternal hunter; Tityos, with the vultures; Tantalos, King of Lydia, the unworthy guest and table-companion of the gods, who was tortured by thirst and hunger but could reach neither the water that flowed almost at his lips nor the fruits that hung into his very mouth; misguided Sisyphos, who in vain pushed a great stone uphill; and the image of Herakles. Odysseus might also have seen Theseus and Peirithoos, who were being punished for their attempted abduction of Persephone. But he had no time to do so: the whirring voices of the innumerable nation of the dead frightened the hero away; and he feared also that illustrious Persephone might send against him the huge Gorgon's head.

Such was the description given to us of the Underworld: a painting, so to speak, in grey upon grey, images as tormenting as bad dreams. To set against this, however, we also had brightly coloured tales:[808] of the Isles of the Blest, of which I have already spoken, where Kronos maintained his rule and whither heroes were sent, if they were loved by the gods. Here, too, ruled Rhadamanthys, brother of Minos, on the plain Elysion, the Elysian Fields. Or there were tales[809] of the other side of the earth, where the sun shines whilst here it is night. There is the meadow where the deceased make merry with riding and athletic contests, with dicing and lute-playing; the meadow that blooms—so it is said—with red roses and is over-shadowed by frankincense-trees: heavily hang overhead the golden fruit. We probably inherited such accounts as these from the ancient Cretans, since Rhadamanthys was a king of that nation; and from them we perhaps also inherited the word "Elysion", which was only later adapted to our language, in which it can be taken to mean "the plains of arrival". Was it our poets and philosophers who first associated these tales of the Isles of the Blest and the Elysian Fields with the doctrine of the transmigration of souls, and of how lives are several times repeated on both sides of the earth?[810] Or was this association older, originating with the earlier inhabitants of the island of Crete? None of the stories that could be told on the subject give us any information on this point.

CHAPTER XV

Dionysos and his Female Companions

I STILL have to tell the last stories of our gods: tales of Dionysos, Zeus's youngest immortal son, a god whose deification did not, like that of Herakles, occur only later. In a group of the tales concerning him, he was born—as also was Herakles, the son of Alkmene—of a mortal mother. In other stories Dionysos was held to be a son of Persephone, and received the surname of Chthonios, "the subterranean". I must begin by explaining who the father was to whom Persephone bore him.

One of the names given to the child's father is that of Hades.[811] When Persephone had eaten the pomegranateseed she left her husband only reluctantly, or—according to another tale[812]—she never left him at all. She was the honoured and sacrosanct queen of the Realm of the Dead, and did not allow herself to be carried off by Theseus and Peirithoos. Furthermore, the royal couple of the Underworld proved themselves worthy of the dead—or so, at least, uninitiates were told—by remaining childless, like death itself. The very name of Hades conveys only a negative impression, according with men's colourless picture of the Underworld. This represents, however, only one aspect of what was, in fact, a great god. But we know that Persephone's husband was also called Zeus Katachthonios, "subterranean Zeus", and that it was Zeus who seduced his daughter. As Katachthonios, Zeus was the father of the subterranean Dionysos, and in the same quality he was also called Zagreus,[813] "the great hunter". This was also one of the names of his son.[814] I mentioned the identity between the two when I was telling the story of Zeus. I may add that this identity is indicated not merely by the name, which is a particularly common one in Crete.[815] For us Dionysos had very various forms. Even when he did not actually appear as a mask—carried by men or hung up to be worshipped—he had a peculiar, fascinating mask-face. Ancient portrayals show him holding in his hand the *kantharos*, a wine-jar with large handles, and occupying the place where one would expect to see Hades. On a vase by the archaic master Xenokles we see, on one side, Zeus, Poseidon and Hades, each with his emblems of power—the last has his head turned back to front—and, on the other side, the subterranean Dionysos welcoming Persephone, who is obviously being sent to him by Hermes and her mother. Dionysos is striding forward to meet his bride: a bearded, dark bridegroom, with the kantharos in his hand, against a background of grapes. Or is this the scene of parting? If so, one sees that the goddess will return to this spouse.

In most tales, however, Dionysos appears as a tender boy, the son of his mother. She, indeed, immediately disappears and is soon replaced by loving nurses. We can recognise the two aspects that Zeus also displayed: the aspect, on the one hand, of the father and husband, and the aspect, on the other hand, of the son and divine child. In our mythology other beings besides Zeus and Dionysos had this double aspect. But no other god so much appeared to be a second Zeus as Dionysos did: a Zeus of women, admittedly, whereas the Olympian was much more a Zeus of men. The more characteristic animals of these two gods—in the forms of their worship, that is to say, and in certain stories of them, in which even today they are scarcely distinguishable—were the serpent and the bull, both of which appeared on the Mediterranean earlier than the horse. I shall begin my account of Dionysos with a story into which a serpent enters: a story that is already partly known to my audience, since it concerns one of Zeus's love-affairs—perhaps the most secret of all.

HADES, POSEIDON AND ZEUS

I

DIONYSOS, DEMETER AND PERSEPHONE

The tale that Zeus mated with Persephone's mother—and later with Persephone herself, his own daughter—in the form of a serpent, has been preserved only in an Orphic story,[816] and only in a few fragments. The place of these marriages, and of the births that resulted from them, was a cave which the followers of Orpheus imagined as the cave of Phanes and the three goddesses of night.[817] Yet this same cave—as I shall presently explain—was also portrayed independently of the Orphic conception of it, and in that form it was filled with purely Greek figures, none of which need in any way be traced back to eastern tales of deities born in caves. The goddess by whom Zeus begat Persephone[818] was originally his mother Rhea: Demeter appears as a third party interposed between the mother and daughter, both of whom appeared earlier in Greece than she did. She is described as Rhea's *alter ego*,[819] yet she is also identified with Persephone: Zeus begat Dionysos —so it is expressly stated[820]—by Demeter *or* by Persephone.

Here, first, is a late, poetical version of the tale:[821] Demeter came from Crete to Sicily, where, near the spring of Kyane, she discovered a cave. There she hid her daughter Persephone, and set as guardians over her two serpents that at other times were harnessed to her chariot. In the cave the maiden worked in wool—the customary occupation for maidens under the protection of Pallas Athene, in her sacred citadel at Athens. Persephone began weaving a great web,[822] a robe for her

DEMETER, HERMES, PERSEPHONE AND DIONYSOS

father or her mother,[823] which was a picture of the whole
world. While she was engaged in this work Zeus came to
her in the shape of a serpent, and he begat by his daughter
that god who, in the Orphic stories, was to be his successor,
the fifth ruler of the world. This was also revealed to us in a
hymn of the followers of Orpheus[824] in which they told stories
of Zeus's marriage with Persephone. According to them, this
was not a case of a seduction carried out against the mother's
will: it all happened—even Zeus's metamorphosis into a serpent—as Demeter had intended, and at her instigation. This
shows us from what ancient times the original story must date:
from times when it was still the mothers who gave their
daughters to husbands, and not the fathers who had authority
and allowed their daughters to be abducted. The birth of the
son and successor to the throne actually took place in the
maternal cave. A late ivory relief shows the bed in the cave:
the bed in which the horned child—the horns signify that he
is the son of Persephone—had just been born to the goddess.

This same illustration, late but after an ancient original, also
shows the subsequent scene in the cave, with the enthroned
child: this enthronement is an ancient ceremony[825] in the
mysteries of the great mother Rhea and her Korybantes, or
whatever else her male companions were called. In this illustration they are two Kouretes, who dance round the throne
with drawn swords while a kneeling woman holds a mirror
in front of the delighted child. The Orphic story[826] also
named the toys of the new ruler of the world: toys that became
symbols of those rites of initiation which were first undergone

by the divine boy, the first Dionysos: dice, ball, top, golden
apples, bull-roarer and wool. The last two played a part in
the ceremony of initiation, the others had more to do with the
tale itself. This tale can now be told only in the version adopted
by the followers of Orpheus, who introduced the Titans into
the story. There is, however, another version[827] according to
which it was not necessarily the Titans who behaved so cruelly
to the son of Zeus and Persephone, but simply "earth-born
beings", without nearer description. It is known, however,
that the Kouretes were included amongst such beings.[828] It
is also known that of the sons of the Great Mother the two
older ones were always hostile to the third. The number of
the Titans who murdered the first Dionysos is expressly stated
to have been two.[829]

In the Orphic continuation of the story, the Kouretes were
replaced, as I have indicated, by the Titans. It was told[830] that
they surprised the child-god as he was playing with the toys.
Jealous Hera had instigated them to this:[831] it was she who
on a previous occasion had sent the Kouretes against Epaphos,[832] the Dionysos-like son of Zeus and the cow-shaped
Io. The Titans had whitened their faces with chalk.[833] They
came like spirits of the dead[834] from the Underworld, to
which Zeus had banished them. They attacked the playing
boy, tore him into seven pieces[835] and threw these into a
cauldron standing on a tripod.[836] When the flesh was boiled,
they began roasting it over the fire on seven spits.

One would be inclined to regard the meal prepared in this
fashion as a cannibal meal, were it not that the horns worn
by the torn-up, boiled and roasted child suggest that the victim
was in fact a sacrificed kid or small calf—the former animal
being used at certain ceremonies and in certain regions, and
the other animal in other regions. They were treated exactly
as the god was treated in this story. In one tale[837] Zeus himself
appeared at the Titans' meal, drawn thither by the smell of
roasting. With his lightning he hurled the Titans back into
Tartaros and gave the child-god's limbs to Apollon, who took

them to Parnassus and set them beside his own tripod at Delphi. In another tale[838] it seems that when Zeus smote the Titans with his lightning they had already eaten the flesh of Dionysos. They must have been hurled back into the Under-world, since in the Orphic hymn[839] they are invoked as the subterranean ancestors of mankind. But from the steam caused by the flash of lightning, which set them on fire, was formed a sort of ash. The ash turned into that substance from which the followers of Orpheus taught that men were made. This teaching, however, is of much later date than the story of the sufferings of the horned child-god.

The story was also told as follows:[840] The boiled limbs of the first Dionysos, the son of Demeter, went into the earth. The earth-born beings had torn him to pieces and boiled him, but Demeter gathered the limbs together. This may, however, be a story concerning the creation of the vine. We learnt from the followers of Orpheus[841] that Dionysos's last gift was wine, and indeed he himself had by then assumed the name Oinos, "Wine". It was Zeus who brought fulfilment, but it was Dionysos who completed the fulfilment—or, to use a modern expression, "set the crown on the world's creation". But this notion, too, is of later date. In the original tale the boiled limbs of the god were burnt—with the exception of a single limb— and we may presume that the vine arose from the ashes. All tales spoke of this exception of one limb, which was devoured neither by the Titans nor by the fire nor by the earth. A goddess was present at the meal—in later tales,[842] the goddess Pallas Athene—and she hid the limb in a covered basket. Zeus took charge of it. It was said to have been Dionysos's heart. This statement contains a pun: for it was also said[843] that Zeus entrusted the *kradiaios Dionysos* to the goddess Hipta, so that she might carry it on her head. "Hipta" was a name in Asia Minor for the great mother Rhea, and *kradiaios* is a word of double meaning: it can be derived both from *kradia*, "heart", and from *krade*, "fig-tree", in which latter derivation it means an object made of fig-wood. The basket on Hipta's head was

a *liknon*, a winnowing-fan, such as was carried on the head
at festal processions and contained a phallus hidden under a
pile of fruit—Dionysos himself having made the phallus of
fig-wood. It is also reported[844] that the *Liknites*, "he in the
winnowing-fan", was repeatedly "awakened" by the Thyiades,
who were the women who served Dionysos on Mount
Parnassus.

2

DIONYSOS AND SEMELE

In addition to the son of the goddess of the Underworld—the
horned son whom the daughter and subterranean double of
the Great Mother had borne to Zeus—our mythology also told
of a second Dionysos, the son of Semele, who was the daughter
of King Kadmos. *Semele* was the name given by the Phrygians
in Asia Minor, and by their European relatives and neighbours
the Thracians, to Chthonia, "the subterranean". In Asia
Minor the place where Zeus consummated his marriage with
the goddess Semele was said[845] to have been Mount Sipylos.
At Thebes, on the other hand, a burnt ruin was pointed out
in the sacred precinct of Demeter,[846] which was alleged to
have been Kadmos's palace,[847] and visitors were told that this
was where Zeus had consumed Semele with his lightning.
Since the child of the marriage was a son, Zeus took charge
of him. The story is not very different from the previous one.
In the previous story it was the vine that arose from the conflagration, in this story it was the wine-god. Probably the same
thing happened to Dionysos as happened to the Great Mother
of the gods, whose worship, like that of Dionysos, was introduced amongst us more than once. In quite early times we
knew her as Rhea, but later on also under the Phrygian name
of Kybele: for if the term "goddess of many names" can be
applied to any goddess in our mythology, it can certainly be
applied to Rhea. Dionysos also had several names or surnames:
besides being Zagreus, "the Hunter", he was also Bakchos,

PLATE XV

DIONYSOS AT SEA

PLATE XVI

a DIONYSOS WITH HIS ALTER EGO,
THE CHILD IAKCHOS

b DIONYSOS CARRIES OFF ARIADNE, ATHENE
ORDERS AWAY THESEUS

"the Shoot", a word for sprouting branches or vine tendrils. But more often it was his mother who appeared under various names. When she even began to be thought of as a mortal princess, the story-tellers found it difficult to co-ordinate the tales of the son of Persephone—that is to say, of Dionysos as he first came to us, probably from Crete—with the stories of the son of Semele—that is to say, of Dionysos as he was reintroduced to us later.

It was told[848] that when Zeus came to Semele, this was not a divine mating. He had prepared a potion from the heart of Dionysos, and this he gave Semele to drink. The potion made the girl pregnant. When Hera learnt of this, she tried to prevent the birth. She disguised herself as Semele's nurse, and persuaded the unsuspecting girl to make a wish that Zeus should come to her in the same shape as that in which he came to Hera, so that Semele, too, might learn what it is like to be embraced by a god. It is clear that this late tale is a product of the pun I have already mentioned, the pun on "heart" and "fig-wood". The rest of the known versions[849] of the same story agree on only one point, that when Zeus first came to Semele he did not do so in the form of the lightning-bearing god of Heaven. The shape which Semele's secret husband had assumed was a mortal guise. Led astray by her pretended nurse, Semele asked Zeus to grant her just one wish. Zeus promised to do so, and when his beloved wished that he would appear to her as he did to Hera, he visited her with his lightning. Vase-paintings show how she sought to flee from it. It was too late: the lightning struck her, and she descended into the Underworld. Zeus rescued from her body the unripe fruit, the child Dionysos.

The Father sheltered the prematurely born god in his own thigh, either by sewing the child into it[850] or by fastening this paternal womb with golden buckles.[851] It was also asserted[852] that not one of those cities where Dionysos was said to have been born of Semele—for this claim was made for other places besides Thebes—could rightly boast of being Dionysos's birthplace, since his father bore him, when the proper time for his birth had come, far away to the east, on Mount Nysa. Zeus then either sent the child off with Hermes or himself entrusted Dionysos to the divine nurses who were to look after him in a cave. One of those named as nurses of Dionysos is Nysa,[853] the mountain in its quality of a goddess. Other nurses mentioned are Ino, one of Semele's three sisters, of whom I shall shortly have a story to tell, and Thyone, who is Semele herself under another name. An ancient vasepainting shows three nymphs named "Nysai", and it is also known from other sources that the god's nurses were three in number. On the island of Naxos one of the three was called Korone, "the CrowVirgin",[854] like Koronis, that paramour of Apollon whose fate was so much like Semele's.

Later reliefs show four women busied with the suckling Dionysos: this is the number of the daughters of Kadmos—of Semele and her three sisters. One of them is giving suck to the child. His bath is being prepared, or he has already been bathed. A male figure is also present, and is waiting to perform his duties by the child: this is Silenos, who in later,[855] but not very late,[856] tales was Dionysos's tutor. The expression "male figure" is almost an overstatement. As the god's tutor, Silenos became very unlike the Silenoi who were the lovers of the nymphs: he is an aged, effeminate figure with a thick stomach and almost womanly breasts, or he is clad in a long gown—which, by the way, is also the characteristic apparel of the fullgrown Dionysos. It seems as if the only male being in the scene is the nurseling. Although born of Zeus—this fact receives exaggerated emphasis[857]—and, in a way, the continuation of his father alone, he appears only in association with women: at this period of his life, with motherly, breastgiving, tending women. When they had reared him to full stature, he went into the woods—so it was told[858]— wreathed with ivy and laurel, but not yet with vineleaves. He was accompanied by women, the nymphs of the woods: I shall shortly say more of the doings of the god and his female companions during the second period of his life.

The story of Dionysos and Semele did not come to an end when she was struck by Zeus's lightning. Some said[859] that she did not die. She must be thought of as resembling Persephone during the latter's sojourn in the Underworld. Semele had to be brought back from the Underworld by Dionysos. In the region of the deep spring of Lerna (a region where mysteries of Demeter, too, were celebrated) a story[860] was told concerning Dionysos which resembles that of Demeter's journey to Persephone. Dionysos came to the Underworld in search of Semele. He needed a guide and pathfinder, and as a price for this service he had to promise complete female surrender. Only if he did this could he reach his mother and bring her back. He fulfilled his promise with the help of a phallus made of fig-wood, which he erected on this spot. The pathfinder—who must originally have been this cult-object itself—was called Prosymnos or Polyhymnos, "the much sung-of". It was further told[861] that when Dionysos had brought Semele back and had made her immortal, he named her Thyone, "the ecstatically raging". A name of the same meaning, Thyias, was applied to the ecstatic priestesses of Dionysos on Parnassus, who, as I have said, "awakened" the Liknites. Finally, however—so this story ends[862]—Dionysos took the goddess Thyone up to Heaven.

3

FEMALE COMPANIONS AND FEMALE ENEMIES
OF DIONYSOS

When worshipping Dionysos our women kept to themselves. No man might be present whilst they enacted in their own persons the parts of the goddesses associated with the god. Whoever observed them from afar saw them in the various, scarcely distinguishable forms of "the rage": this is perhaps the best translation of our word *mania*, but it must be taken as bearing all its various senses at once—that of raging love as well as that of raging anger. This is why the women about Dionysos were called *mainades*, "Maenads", and the god himself was called *mainomenos*[863] or *mainoles*,[864] meaning "raging" in this extended sense of the word, and not anything like "maniacs"; just as the Dionysiac women were for their part called "Bakchai", female Bacchantes, although they were more properly "Bakchoï", in full identification of the worshipped with the worshippers. There were many portrayals of them, showing them in long robes, with heads rigidly thrown back, wreathed with ivy, carrying the thyrsus—a long staff of narthex with a pine-cone on its end. Thus attired they ran rather than danced, accompanied by flutes, drums and tambourines.

My audience has already made the acquaintance of Dionysos in the first phase of his life: the divine child in the cave, surrounded by womanly care. In this phase he was worshipped as the secret within the winnowing-fan. The divine women about him were not yet "raging" Maenads, but nurses, one of whom was his own mother. I have also given some indication of what Dionysos was like in his second phase: a young god in the forest. The story describing his female companions at this period—the same divine women turned into "raging" Maenads—seemed so strange to later story-tellers that they made them out to have been enemies of Dionysos. It was told[865] that Minyas, King of Boeotian Orchomenos, had three daughters who were extremely industrious. They scolded at the women who left the city and swarmed into the mountains in honour of Dionysos. The god himself appeared to the three sobersides in the form of a maiden and warned them not to neglect the secret rites. The daughters of Minyas did not obey. Thereupon the god turned himself into a bull, then into a lion, and finally into a leopard. Ivy and vines grew over the weaving-chair, serpents nested in the baskets of wool. The three women were afraid, and they drew lots to determine which of them should offer her child as a sacrifice. Then the child was torn to pieces by its own mother and her sisters. Wreathed with ivy, bindweed and laurel, they roamed over the mountains, until they were metamorphosised: one of them into a bat, the second into an owl, the third into an eagle-owl or a crow.

Another story to the same effect[866] was told concerning the daughters of King Proitos of Tiryns, who were either two or three in number: When the daughters of Proitos attained the age of ripening, the rage fell upon them because they had taken no part in the secret rites of Dionysos. According to other tales, it was the wrath of Hera that plunged them into madness, so that they believed themselves to be cows; or else it was the wrath of Aphrodite[867], who filled them with a mad craving for men. It was also said of them that their bodies became covered with white patches: this was only a milder form of the story of their turning into cows. As cows they at last became worthy companions of the bull-god Dionysos. They roamed over the whole Peloponnese and gave themselves to wanton practices in the wildernesses. The seer Melampous, "the black-footed", promised Proitos to cure his daughters if Proitos would give him a third of his kingdom. Proitos refused. The girls became still madder, and also plunged the other women into the rage. They all left their families, killed their own children and set forth into the wilderness. When the evil thus grew, the king was ready to yield a third of his kingdom to Melampous. But now the seer demanded two-thirds of the kingdom, and got it. He drove the raving women to the place where he could purify them. One daughter of Proitos died under the chastisement, the other women were cured.

A third story concerns the sisters of Semele, Dionysos's aunts. Their names were Agaue, Autonoe and Ino. Their number—three, or four including Semele—was the same as that of the god's nurses, and they formed the prototype for the Bacchantic choirs of women[868] who during their secret rites used to erect four times three altars to Dionysos and his mother. Agaue and Autonoe were also mentioned amongst the

Nereides,[869] and Ino, as Leukothea, became a sea-goddess. It will be remembered that, according to a now extinct tale, it was the Nereides who first showed to men the Mysteries of Dionysos and Persephone. Semele's sisters, like herself, had each one son: Ino had Melikertes, of whom I shall speak in a moment; Autonoe had Aktaion, who was torn to pieces by his own hounds and whose bones had to be assembled by his mother; and Agaue, "the sublime", had Pentheus, whom the three women, in their Dionysiac madness, mistook for the quarry of their chase. This tale was elaborated in a tragedy of Euripides, which explained the women's madness by stating that the three sisters were punished for having refused to believe in their nephew's divinity. The punishment was that they were compelled to pay honour to Dionysos in the wilderness like genuine Maenads, and, as I have said, selected Agaue's son as their quarry. Themselves playing the rôle of hounds,[870] and calling out to the god as huntsman[871] and companion in the chase,[872] they tore Pentheus to pieces.

These women, then, under the influence of Zagreus, "the great hunter", pursued an animal that was the son of one of them. The divine child, so recently treated as a suckling, became the hunter within them and their martyred prey. More than one story tells of the persecution Dionysos underwent at this time of his life—either as a handsome boy or as a delicate, half-womanly stripling resembling Adonis or Attis—through having seduced the women into madness. Perhaps the oldest of these tales was that[873] in which Perseus killed him and threw him into the deep spring of Lerna. In another ancient story[874] a murderous king of Thrace, Lykourgos, "the Wolf-Man", hunted the nurses of Dionysos as if they were cows. The terror-stricken little God leapt into the sea, where Thetis caught him in her lap. Lykourgos was punished with madness, and, believing himself to be exterminating the vine, he killed his own son and hacked off his limbs. In the previous story concerning Pentheus, "the man of suffering", Pentheus appeared also as a persecutor of Dionysos; but his name reveals that he was doomed from the beginning to Dionysiac suffering. The tale of the sufferings of the horned Dionysos-child described the manner in which spoils of the chase were boiled and roasted: the story of Ino, which I shall tell presently, contains a somewhat similar description. But we know what resulted from the sufferings of the sacrificed child-god: the creation of wine, which our ancestors regarded as being, like bread, a remedy against animal crudity and savagery. The death of Semele—the prototype of Dionysiac women—must originally have been the punishment for what her immortal son had to suffer, not from the Titans, but from his female companions. Dionysos's reappearance, his epiphany as a bringer of happiness after the dark period of hunting and sacrifice, provided the material for old tales of which there is still some trace. We can, of course, find a remnant of one such tale in the vision that presented itself, in the play by Euripides, to the female Bacchantes as they accompanied their god:[875] the earth flowed with milk, it flowed with wine, it flowed with the nectar of the bees.

4

DIONYSOS, INO AND MELIKERTES

The story of the persecution of Dionysos was told in another form besides that in which he was by himself when he leapt into the sea, or when his dead body was cast into deep water. In this other form he was with his mother Semele, and the two of them suffered together in much the same fashion. This story has been preserved[876] by the people of Brasiai, a small coastal town in Laconia. Semele, they say, secretly carried Dionysos in her womb whilst she was still in her father's palace, and she bore the child at the due time. When Kadmos discovered the dishonour that had fallen upon his house, he shut up mother and child in a chest and had them thrown into the sea. The floating box was cast up on the Laconian coast, where the waves washed it ashore. The local inhabitants found Semele dead in the chest, and solemnly buried her. The child was brought up amongst them. They also had another story peculiar to themselves:[877] Semele's sister Ino came to them on her crazy wanderings and offered to take charge of the little Dionysos as his nurse. The people of Brasiai used to point out the cave where Ino had nursed the divine child. The region was called "the Garden of Dionysos".

Most of the other stories that were told of Ino, Dionysos's maternal aunt and nurse, are connected with the preparations for the voyage of the Argonauts, and therefore belong to heroic saga. In these stories she appears as the wife of King Athamas, and the wicked stepmother of Phrixos and Helle, the King's children. These two were the first people to travel to Colchis, which they did on the back of the ram with the golden fleece, the offspring of Poseidon and Theophane. Ino persuaded the women of Boeotia, so the saga stated,[878] to roast the seed-corn, so that nothing should grow from it. It is possible, however, that originally she did not cause the seed-corn to be roasted, but introduced the practice of roasting corn in general. Moreover, one need not see anything evil in what happened to her own children: this may have been basically only the story of the sacrificed child-god. It was told[879] that when Zeus had released the infant Dionysos from his thigh, he sent the child with Hermes to Ino and Athamas, so that they might bring it up as a girl. But Hera caused the couple to go mad. They had two sons. Athamas hunted the older son, Learchos, as if he were a stag, and slew him. Ino threw the younger son, Melikertes, into a cauldron of seething water, and afterwards hurled herself, together with the dead child, into the depths of the sea. Or else—so it was also told[880]—she threw the slain Learchos into the cauldron, and afterwards hurled herself into the sea with the living Melikertes. Her ward Dionysos was saved by Zeus, who first turned him into a kid and then sent him with Hermes to the nymphs of Nysa, who were later, in reward for their services as nurses, raised up to be the Hyades in the heavens.

THE CHILD IN THE CAULDRON

Ino, after having hurled herself into the sea, took the name Leukothea, "the white goddess".[881] The Odyssey also has a tale concerning her: that she was formerly a daughter of Kadmos, but received the same worship as the sea-goddesses. She lent Odysseus her veil so that, by tying it like a belt around his waist, he was able to escape from the shipwreck and swim to the distant coast. Afterwards he had to throw the veil back into the sea. It was later said[882] that this veil was really that strip of purple cloth which people initiated into the Mysteries of the Kabeiroi received on Samothrace and always wore around their bodies as a protection against the perils of the sea. The child Melikertes became, under the name of Palaimon, a protecting divinity of seamen. In the fate that befell him he came very close both to Dionysos and also to Glaukos, who, as I have said, died in Crete in a jar full of honey, but, according to other tales, became a sea-god. The name "Melikertes" means "the cutter of honey", a term which is connected not only with bee-keeping, but also with the preparation of the intoxicating honey-drink. It was told[883] that a dolphin brought Melikertes—or his corpse[884]—to the Isthmus of Corinth, where the Isthmian Games were founded in his honour. The rider on the dolphin, the divine boy of the sea, is familiar to us from many pictures. He was called both Melikertes and Palaimon, and appeared as a second Dionysos.

But he also bore the name of Taras, the god of the Greek city of Taranto, in southern Italy, and was a second Apollon or Hyakinthos—not to speak of his also being the child-god Eros who rides on the dolphin and holds a cuttlefish.

5

DIONYSOS AT SEA

Although Homer repeatedly calls the sea a place "where there is no wine-harvest", yet in more ancient times there must certainly have been many more tales than now survive of occasions when Dionysos appeared—or, more correctly, re-appeared—on the sea's surface. An old vase-painting shows the god, in his manifestation as a bearded figure, lying alone in a ship whose mast and sails are overshadowed with vines, from which huge grapes hang down: around the ship are dolphins. Another vase-painting shows his ceremonial entry amongst men. He sits, draped, on a wheeled ship which is being drawn upon land by oxen: a symbol of his epiphany from the sea. We had a long tale[885] of how Dionysos once manifested himself at sea in all his divine might.

The god first appeared upon a promontory in the shape of a youth in his first bloom. Beautifully hung the dark locks around his head, purple raiment covered his strong shoulders. At that moment Etruscan pirates were swiftly approaching over the wine-dark sea in their many-oared ship. It was their ill fortune that brought them. When the pirates espied the youth, they nodded one to the other. Swiftly they sprang ashore, at once seized him and joyfully set him in their ship. They supposed that he was a king's son, and they sought to bind him with strong bonds. But no willow-bark cords could hold the youth; the bonds fell from his hands and feet. He sat there with a smile in his dark eyes. The helmsman perceived this and called out to his shipmates: "Unhappy wretches! Who is this strong god whom you have seized and made captive?

This sturdy ship cannot support his weight! He is either Zeus, or Apollon with the silver bow, or Poseidon. He is like unto no mortal man, but to the gods who dwell on Olympus. Let us set him free at once, here on land! Let none lay a hand upon him, or in wrath he will send us adverse winds and storm!" But the captain sternly rebuked the helmsman. "Unhappy wretch! Pay thou heed only to the wind, and hoist the sail with all sheets! Leave what does not concern thee to us others. I hope to take him with us to Egypt, to Cyprus, to the Hyperboreans or yet farther. In the end he will be sure to reveal to us his family and his wealth, since his misfortune has delivered him into our hands."

Thus the captain spoke, for he expected a great ransom for the youth. The sail was hoisted, the wind blew into the middle of it, the sheets grew taut. For the crew this alone was almost a miracle. And now wine began to purl through the swift, black ship, sweet to drink and sweetly smelling: it was a divine fragrance. Astonishment seized the crew. Near the top of the sail a vine suddenly sprouted forth, and the grapes hung down in great number. Ivy twined blooming around the mast, and even began to put forth its agreeable fruit. Wreaths appeared on all the rowlocks. When the oarsmen saw this, they soon enough began calling to the helmsman to put the ship back to land! Meanwhile they saw the youth turn into a lion, there on the ship, a lion that stood threateningly on the deck above them and roared mightily. The god caused a shaggy bear to appear in their midst. The bear stood on its hind legs, and the lion glowered dreadfully down from the deck. The crew fled to the stern and stood trembling by the helmsman, the only one of them who was still in his right mind. The lion sprang and seized the captain. The rest of the crew, in mortal terror, hurled themselves from the ship into the sea, and turned into dolphins. The helmsman was held back by the god, who took compassion on him and comforted him.

To this helmsman the god revealed that he was Dionysos, son of Zeus and Semele. It is a pity that, in the hymn from which I have just been quoting, the name of the helmsman, who must afterwards have spread the report abroad amongst men, is no longer legible. Perhaps he was called Ikarios, like him[886] who was the first to give hospitality to the god in Attica, in the village of Ikaria, and who made known the pleasures of wine and was killed by his countrymen because they believed that the people whom he had made drunk were poisoned. This was another, tragic story of the epiphany of Dionysos. One is entitled to think of the name Ikarios in connection with the story of the pirates, since in one version[887] of this story Dionysos voyaged with the pirates from Ikaria to Naxos. Later story-tellers[888] called the Dionysiac helmsman Akoites, which means "the husband", a form of manifestation of the god himself.

6

DIONYSOS AND ARIADNE

After describing Dionysos's childhood, followed by the periods when he was hunted and persecuted, and then by his re-appearance, the tales went on to tell of his Triumph—a word, by the way, that the Etruscans and Romans had from us. Originally it was *thriambos*, which means a hymn to Dionysos and is also one of the god's surnames. His triumphal procession, which originally consisted of the former nurses and "raging" women converted into transfigured, happy companions, was joined by Satyrs and Silenoi, whose dances and parades were formerly held in honour of a great goddess and of her repre-sentatives, the nymphs. The god's half-female character, which was expressed both in the long robe of the bearded Dionysos and in the almost hermaphroditic body of the young and naked Bakchos, was an attraction to the phallic beings, and so were the Bacchic women. When last heard of,[889] Dionysos and his triumphal procession had conquered India (a late poetical image for the campaign of Alexander the Great), and ever more exotic animals were appearing in his train, which even in earlier times had included great beasts of prey—lions, panthers and leopards—all of them tamed by wine. Amongst the Etruscans the Dionysiac women actually kept tame leopards in their homes. The earliest Maenads wore tame serpents around their arms, and the god appeared to them as a bull. The fawnskins round their shoulders were spoils of their own chase, and the grape-eating he-goats, who can still be seen in the Bacchantic procession, were doomed to bloody sacrifice.

The triumphal god was especially associated in the tales with one particular woman. In a famous story she attained to that very position which all Dionysiac women held in their own minds: that of the wife of Dionysos, his only true companion. She was the only one who was ever spoken of as the god's wife,[890] and her name was Ariadne. In the form in which the story of her became famous,[891] she was the daughter of King Minos and of Pasiphae, daughter of the Sun: a mortal maiden, but with the name of a goddess. "Ariadne", originally "Ariagne", meant the "holy" and "pure": it was a superlative form of Hagne, a surname of the queen of the Underworld. The goddess bearing this name was worshipped on many of our islands. Ariadne the mortal maiden had as her counterpart a sister and rival named Phaidra, "the bright", and indeed also a second, victorious lover of Theseus, her whose name was Aigle, "the shining".[892] This second, bright aspect, however, was directly connected with Ariadne herself: she was also called Aridela,[893] "the visible from afar", a name that she obviously acquired after she had been raised to heaven with Dionysos.

Under the name of Ariadne she was Theseus's accomplice in the slaying of his brother, the bull-headed son of Minos, who is chiefly known as a monster called the Minotaur. To judge by his other name of Asterios, however, he was a "Star" amongst his own people—just as Dionysos, too, was invoked as a star in his quality of boy-child of the Mysteries.[894] In the best-known form of the story, Ariadne's only part in the slaying

was to rescue Theseus and the Athenian children who had
been thrown to the monster. She gave the hero the thread that
enabled him to find his way out of the Labyrinth in which the
Minotaur dwelt. Theseus took Ariadne and her sister Phaidra
aboard his ship, but left Ariadne on the island of Dia, of
which I shall have more to say. The forsaken girl lay deeply
asleep[895] while the ship sailed off with all those whom she
had saved. But she was not left there alone. One story[896]
mentions that her nurse escaped with her and remained on the
island. Theseus never took Ariadne to wife. But this was not
because he was unfaithful to her: for it was further told[897] that
Dionysos appeared to him in a dream and announced that
the girl belonged to the god himself. This seems, according
to most of the tales, to have been actually the case, although
on the other hand it is expressly stated[898] that Ariadne was one
of the great sinners, since she helped to kill her own brother.

According to the best-known tale, Ariadne was asleep when
Theseus left her, and Dionysos appeared on the island in his
stead as rescuer and bridegroom. According to other, much
older tales[899] she was actually dead by then. Artemis had
killed her at the request of Dionysos: a fate that Ariadne shared
with Koronis, the beloved of Apollon. These older tales state
that she was not only disloyal to the bull in the Labyrinth,
but also unfaithful to Dionysos. It was told[900] that the god
had already taken her to wife whilst she was in Crete. At that
time he had given Ariadne the golden, bejewelled wreath
which he himself had received from Aphrodite, and she used
this wreath to light up Theseus's passage through the Labyrinth. The unfaithful girl passed on the gift to the hero, and
originally this was how she helped him, and not with the
thread. Originally the Labyrinth was not a maze, but a spiral
through which one could return after reaching its centre.
Ariadne's shining wreath enabled Theseus to do this, and it
was for this that she was punished. Her grave was said to be
in Cyprus, where it was pointed out to visitors;[901] and on
this same island, where she was worshipped as Aphrodite

Ariadne, it was also said that she had died in travail without giving birth. At her festivals, however, her birth-pangs were mimicked by a young man—a sort of male mother, such as we have already encountered in the story of Semele, Zeus and Dionysos.

The story of Dionysos and Ariadne cannot, in its oldest form, have been very different from that of Dionysos and Semele. The difference arose when heroic saga began to connect the figure of Theseus with the Cretan mistress of the Labyrinth —which was a primitively ancient idea of the Underworld. On our southern islands Ariadne and Aridela were the names of that goddess—under two aspects and with a twofold destiny, a dark one and a bright one—who was known on our mainland as Semele and Thyone, or, in her association with Apollon and Asklepios, as Koronis and Aigle. An ancient vase-painting shows Ariadne as a nurse receiving the child Dionysos into her care. I have already mentioned that one of the nurses of Dionysos was called Thyone, and that this name was applied also to Semele and to a nurse named Korone. But the strongest and most extensive similarity was between the story of Semele and Dionysos, mother and son, and that of Ariadne and Dionysos, wife and husband. It was told[902] that Ariadne finally went to Heaven with the god, in his chariot: a journey that has also been represented in one pictorial record as the ascent to Heaven of Persephone and her husband, and corresponds furthermore to the ascent of Semele with Dionysos. The difference is that it was never told of Semele—or not, at least, in any of the tales known to us—that she ceased to be Dionysos's mother, nurse and companion and became his transfigured wife. This transfiguration was attributed only to Ariadne.

Ariadne's ascent to Heaven occurred after her mating with the god on the island of Dia. This name, Dia, which means "heavenly" or "divine", was applied to several small craggy islands in our sea, all of them lying close to larger islands such as Crete or Naxos. The name "Dia" was even transferred to

the island of Naxos itself, since it was more widely supposed
than any other to have been the nuptial isle of Dionysos. The
little isle off Naxos still has the mighty marble temple doors
showing where the marriage took place. A magnificently
preserved wall-painting in Rome records the tale of how
Dionysos met his divine bride—who was certainly no earthly
maiden, but the risen Persephone or Aphrodite. When he
found her, she was neither asleep nor forsaken. The goddess,
sitting on the island crag with a servant female companion
beside her, welcomed the young god as he approached un-
attended from the sea. She held a bowl out to him, that
Dionysos might fill it and the epiphany of wine might be his
doing. A later tale[903] added that Dionysos commemorated
the goddess, his companion, by setting in the heavens the
famous golden wreath, the Crown of Ariadne.

7

SURNAMES OF DIONYSOS

It must have been the disciples of the singer Orpheus who
assembled the various contemporaneously parallel tales of
Dionysos into a single great tale, in which the god had two
mothers and three births and was therefore called Dimetor,
"the twice mothered", and Trigonos, "the thrice born".
Originally, however, there was only a single story, in which
his mother had two aspects, with a name for each: Persephone
and Aphrodite; Semele and Thyone; Ariadne and Aridela.
It was furthermore told that Aphrodite and Dionysos became
espoused. Various sons of this marriage are mentioned: in some
tales Priapos,[904] in others Hymenaios,[905] in others Hermes
Chthonios,[906] "the subterranean Hermes"; whereas to the
bridal pair Dionysos and Ariadne were attributed[907] such
sons as Oinopion, "the Wine-Man", Euanthes, "the Blos-
somer" and Staphylos, "the Grape".
    The surnames of Dionysos only seldom describe the god as

"the phallic one"; but on the rare occasions when this aspect
of him is openly mentioned, the names plainly have an extensive, although perhaps not complete, common identity: such
names as Orthos, "the erect", and Enorches, "the betesticled".
This latter surname occurs in a particular story: [908] Enorches
was the son of a brother and sister who begat and bore an
egg, from which he sprang like the Molione or the children
of Leda, or the double-sexed Phanes of the followers of
Orpheus. This story was told on Lesbos, in whose vineyards
there was a cult of Hermes—presumably, that is to say, of a
phallus-idol which people did not wish to call Dionysos.
Indeed, to have applied the name of Dionysos to such an object
would have been to take a one-sided view of the god, since
he was also called Pseudanor, "the man without true virility"
—not to speak of all his joke-names such as *gynnis*, "the
womanish", or *arsenothelys*, "the man-womanly". The surname
Dyalos, "the hybrid", must certainly refer to a hermaphroditic
being, and together with other names of the sort must be
derived from hushed-up tales of the god's bisexuality. But
such surnames as Dendreus, Dendrites, Endendros, "the tree-
god" or "he in the tree", or the names connected with vegetable
luxuriance and growth, such as Phleon, Phleus or Phloios,
indicate that what is meant is not a human sexual hybridity,
but the bisexuality that is characteristic of most trees and
constitutes their natural completeness.

Other surnames refer to the opposite extreme of the stories
concerning Dionysos: to the savagery of Zagreus. Omestes and
Omadios mean an eater of raw flesh, whereas Eriphos means
the god as a young kid—a beast which was devoured in his
honour. As Aigobolos he slew goats, as Melanaigis he wore
a black goatskin, as Anthroporraistes he even slew men—all
this in the phase preceding his vegetable manifestations. But
even in his Underworldly period he was associated with plants.
The laurel, which at this time was his property, does not
appear in any of his surnames; for it was still more the property
of Apollon, and the nearness—indeed, perhaps the identity—

of the two brothers in their Underworldly sphere was something that must be kept secret. In this sphere Dionysos was Kissos, "Ivy", or—emphasising another of his aspects in the same sphere—Sykites or Sykeates, "the fig-god". As Omphakites he was the god of unripe grapes; as Lysios and Lyaios he was "the unbinder"; as Nyktelios he was the god of festivals held at night; as Mystes he was "the initiated"; as Bromios he was god of the din of Bacchic processions; as Eues or Euios he was god of the shouts of "Euoi!" Almost all these surnames refer to Dionysos's manifestation as the god of wine.

A special epiphany of the god was expressed in the name Iakchos: it was both a name and a shout of invocation, with which the divine child was hailed at the Eleusinian Mysteries, and which had a more than accidental resemblance to Bakchos, the second name of Dionysos. Iakchos[909] and Bakchos were the same deity, although the former was also supposed to be different from Dionysos. He was the son of Persephone, and both the lover of Demeter, mentioned in the Orphic stories, and the mysterious child, laughing in Baubo's womb. In its tales of Hades and Persephone, and of Dionysos and his female companions, our mythology brings us to the threshold of that which constituted the content of Mysteries and might not be spoken of—and indeed, when it was truly experienced, *could* not be spoken of.

I shall therefore proceed no further. I could go on to tell stories that have less import than those I have told already. But the task I set myself was to expound to the attentive listener, and to the best of my ability, all that is of importance concerning our gods, and also concerning mankind in so far as it enters into our mythology; and this task has now, I suppose, been performed.

SOURCES

KEY TO ABBREVIATIONS

A.: *Aeschylus*
    Ch.: *Choephori*
    Eu.: *Eumenides*
    Pr.: *Prometheus*
    Su.: *Supplices*
AAmbr.: *Anonymus Ambrosianus in Studemundi Analectis I p. 224 squ.*
Ae.: *Aelianus*
    NA: *De Natura Animalium*
    VH: *Varia Historia*
ALib.: *Antoninus Liberalis Mythographus*
Ant.: *Antigonus Carystius Paradoxographus*
Ap.: *Apollodorus Mythographus*
APal.: *Anthologia Palatina*
A.Rh.: *Apollonius Rhodius*
Ar.: *Aristophanes*
    Av.: *Aves*
    N.: *Nubes*
    Pax
    R.: *Ranae*
Arat.: *Aratus*
Ari.: *Aristoteles*
    HA: *Historia Animalium*
    MA: *De Motione Animalium*
Arn.: *Arnobius*
    AN: *Adversus Nationes*
Ath.: *Athenaeus Grammaticus*

Bion *Bucolicus*

Ca.: *Callimachus*
    Ap.: *Hymnus in Apollinem*
    Ce.: *Hymnus in Cererem*
    De.: *Hymnus in Delum*
    Di.: *Hymnus in Dianam*
    Die.: *Diegemata*
    He.: *Hecale*
    Io.: *Hymnus in Jovem*
    LP: *Lavacrum Palladis*
Cat.: *Catullus*
Chr.: *Chrysippus Stoicus*
Ci.: *Cicero*
    ND: *De Natura Deorum*
    TD: *Tusculanae Disputationes*
Cl.: *Clemens Alexandrinus*
    Pr.: *Protrepticus*
    Str.: *Stromateis*
Cla.: *Claudianus*
    RP: *De Raptu Proserpinae*

D.H.: *Dionysii Halicarnassensis Antiquitates Romanae*
D.P.: *Dionysius Periegeta*
D.S.: *Diodorus Siculus*

E.: *Euripides*
    Al.: *Alcestis*
    B.: *Bacchae*
    He.: *Hecuba*
    Hel.: *Helena*
    Her.: *Heraclidae*
    HF: *Hercules Furens*
    Hi.: *Hippolytus*

E.: *Euripides—contd.*
   Ion
   IT: *Iphigenia Taurica*
   Me: *Medea*
   Ph.: *Phoenissae*
   Rh.: *Rhesus*
   Tr.: *Troades*
EGr.: *G. Kaibel, Epigrammata*
    Graeca ex lapidibus collecta
Er.: *Eratosthenes*
   C.: *Catasterismoi*
Et.Gud.: *Etymologicum Gudianum*
Et.M.: *Etymologicum Magnum*
Eu.Od.: *Eustathius ad Odysseam*
Euph.: *Euphorio*
Eus.: *Eusebius Caesariensis*
   Chr.: *Chronica*
   PE: *Praeparatio Evangelica*

Fe.: *Festus Grammaticus*
FGH: *F. Jacoby, Fragmente der*
   griechischen Historiker
fr.: fragmentum

GArat.: *Germanici Aratus*

h.Ap.: *Homeri Hymnus in Apollinem*
h.C.: *Homeri Hymnus in Cererem*
h.Ho.: *Homeri Hymni*
h.M.: *Homeri Hymnus in Mercurium*
h.Ve.: *Homeri Hymnus in Venerem*
Harp.: *Harpocratio Grammaticus*
Hdt.: *Herodotus*
He.: *Hesiodus*
   Sc.: *Scutum Herculis*
Her.: *Herodas Mimographus*
Hi.: *Hippolytus*
   RH: *Refutatio Omnium Here-*
   sium
Him.: *Himerii Orationes*

Hor.: *Horatius*
   AP: *Ars Poetica*
   C.: *Carmina*
Hsch.: *Hesychius Lexicographus*
Hy.: *Hygini Fabulae*
Hy.A.: *Hygini Astronomica*
Hyp.: *Hyperides*

Ib.: *Ibycus*
IG.: *Inscriptiones Graecae*
Il.: *Homeri Ilias*

La.Inst.: *Lactantii Institutiones*
Li.: *Libanius*
   N.: *Narrationes*
   Pr.: *Progymnasmata*
Lic.: *Licymnius Lyricus*
Lu.: *Lucianus*
   Ba.: *Bacchus*
   ITr.: *Jupiter Tragoedus*
   DMar.: *Dialogi Marini*
   Ph.: *Philopseudes*
   Sa.: *De Saltatione*
   SyrD.: *De Syria Dea*
Ly.: *Lycophron*

Ma.S.: *Macrobii Saturnalia*
Me.: *Menander Comicus*
Mi.: *Mimnermus Lyricus*
Mo.: *Moschus Bucolicus*
MVat.: *Mythographus Vaticanus*

N.D.: *Nonni Dionysiaca*
N.N.: *Nonnus commentator Gre-*
   gorii Nazianzeni
N.Pr.: *Nicolai Progysmata*
N.Th.: *Nicandri Theriaca*

Od.: *Homeri Odyssea*

Op.: *Hesiodi Opera et Dies*
Opp.: *Oppiani Halieutica*
Or.: *O. Kern, Orphicorum fragmenta*
Or.A.: *Orphei Argonautica*
Or.H.: *Orphei Hymni*
Ori.C.: *Origenes contra Celsum*
Ov.: *Ovidius*
    Am.: *Amores*
    F.: *Fasti*
    M.: *Metamorphoses*

Pa.: *Pausanias Periegeta*
Par.: *Parthenius Mythographus*
Ph.: *Philostratus*
    VA.: *Vita Apollonii*
Phi: *Philemo Comicus*
Phot.: *Photii Lexicon*
Pi.: *Pindarus*
    I.: *Isthmia;* hyp.: hypothesis
       ad I.
    N.: *Nemea*
    O.: *Olympia*
    P.: *Pythia;* hyp.: hypothesis
       ad P.
Pl.: *Plato*
    Epi.: *Epinomis*
    Ethd.: *Euthydemos*
    Le.: *Leges*
    Mx.: *Menexenus*
    Phdr.: *Phaedrus*
    Pr.: *Protagoras*
    Sy.: *Symposium*
    Ti.: *Timaeus*
Pla.: *Plautus*
    Ru.: *Rudens*
Pli.: *Plinius*
    NH.: *Naturalis Historia*
Plu.: *Plutarchi Moralia*

Plu.Thes.: *Plutarchi Theseus*
PMag.: *H. Preisendanz, Papyri Magici Graeci*
PO.: *Oxyrhychus Papyri*
Prop.: *Propertius*

Q.S.: *Quintus Smyrnaeus*

s.: scholium in (Servius vel Probus in Vergilium)
S.: *Sophocles*
    An.: *Antigone*
    OC: *Oedipus Coloneus*
Sa.: *Sappho*
Scy.: *Scythinus Lyricus*
Sol.: *Solinus*
St.B.: *Stephanus Byzantius Lexicographus*
Ste.: *Stesichorus Lyricus*
Str.: *Strabo Geographus*
Su.: *Suidas Lexicographus*
Syll.: *W. Dittenberger, Sylloge inscriptionum Graecarum*

Terp.: *Terpander Lyricus*
Tert.Val.: *Tertullianus contra Valerianos*
Th.: *Hesiodi Theogonia*
The.: *Theocritus Bucolicus*
Thgn.: *Theognis*

Va.: *Varro*
    LL: *De Lingua Latina*
Ve.: *Vergilius*
    A.: *Aeneis*
    E.: *Eclogae*
    G.: *Georgica*

Zen.: *Zenobius Paroemiographus*

LIST OF SOURCES

The references given below are referred to by the corresponding numbers in the text

1: Il. 14.201
2: Il. 14.246
3: Il. 14.201
4: Il. 14.206
5: Th. 337
6: Th. 367
7: Th. 364
8: Or. 24
9: Il. 14.261
10: Ar.Av. 695
11: Or. 70.2
12: Or. 16.112
13: Or. 15
14: Th. 23
15: Th. 116
16: Th. 176
17: Th. 155
18: Th. 371
19: Th. 404
20: Th. 453
21: Il. 13.365
22: Th. 459
23: Or. 154
24: Pi.O. 2.70
25: Il. 1.399
26: Th. 624
27: Th. 713
28: Th. 687
29: Ap. 1.6.3
30: Th. 821
31: h.Ap. 307
32: Th. 829
33: Plu. 293c
34: N.D. 1.362
35: Th. 186

36: Ap. 1.6.1
37: Ov.Am. 2.1.11
38: Ap. 1.6.1
39: Il. 14.261
40: Or. 99
41: Th. 217
42: Th. 904
43: Or.H. 59.2
44: Or. 33
45: Il. 8.68
46: Ap. 1.6.2
47: A.Eu. 728
48: Hy. 171
49: He.Sc. 259
50: Th. 211
51: Il. 16.334
52: Th. 233
53: Ve.A. 6.439
54: Ap. 1.3.1
55: Th. 361
56: Th. 382
57: A.Pr. 1
58: s.A.Rh. 3.467
59: Th. 404
60: Th. 412
61: A.Rh. 4.829
62: s.Od. 12.124
63: Th. 931
64: PMag. 4.1434
2530
2550
65: Od. 12.73
66: Od. 12.246
67: Od. 12.101
68: s.Ve.A. 3.420

69: Ly. 45
70: E.Med. 1342
71: s.Od. 12.124
72: D.S. 20.41
73: s.Ar.Pax 758
74: Hor.A.P. 340
75: Tert.Val. 3
76: Ar.Pax 758
77: Ar.fr. 500/1
78: Ar.R. 288
79: PMag. 4.2334
80: Th. 346
81: Or. 16
82: Or. 114
83: Th. 237
84: Od. 4.354
85: Th. 233
86: Th. 270
87: A.Pr. 792
88: A.Eu. 150
89: Pa. 8.34.3
90: A.Eu. 416
91: S.OC. 40
92: s.Ly. 406
93: s.S.OC. 42
94: Euph.fr. 52
95: Or.H. 69.8
70.2
96: A.Eu. 50
97: E.IT. 293
98: A.Ch. 924
99: A.Ch. 290
100: Th. 274
101: Th. 275
102: Th. 277

210: s.A.Rh. 1.916

211: D.S. 3.55.3

212: D.S. 3.55.2

213: Str. 10.3.19

214: D.S. 3.55.1

215: s.Ve.A. 4.377

216: Pi.O. 7.61

217: D.S. 3.56.1

218: Arn.AN. 5.5
    Pa. 7.17.10

219: h.Ve. 1.24

220: Ov.F. 6.319

221: Th. 481

222: Ca.Io. 10

223: Pa. 8.36

224: Ca.Io. 32

225: Ath. 375f

226: Ath. 491a

227: Hy. 139

228: Ca.Io. 47

229: A.Rh. 3.132

230: Ap. 1.1.6

231: La.Inst. 1.22

232: ALib. 19

233: Ca.Io. 48
    D.S. 5.70.3

234: Er.C. 13

235: Er.C. 27

236: s.Ve.A. 1.394

237: S.fr. 320

238: Il. 14

239: Il. 14.295

240: E.Hi. 748

241: Er.C. 3

242: Chr.fr. 1072

243: s.Il. 1.609

244: s.The. 15.64

245: s.Il. 1.609

246: Eus.PE. 3.1.3

247: Il. 8.477

248: Pa. 2.38.2

249: Pa. 8.41.4

250: A.Rh. 1.503

251: Ori.C. 1.6.42

252: s.S.OC. 42

253: Pa. 9.38.1

254: N.Pr. 2.12

255: Ci.ND. 3.44

256: s.Il. 14.276

257: s.Ly. 680

258: Pi.O. 14.3

259: Th. 909

260: Pi.P. 9.90

261: Pi.P. 9.89

262: Pa. 9.35.1

263: Pa. 9.35.2

264: APal. 15.25.14

265: Pa. 9.35.5

266: Hor.C. 1.4.5

267: Pi.fr. 10

268: Er.C. 13

269: Il. 20.4
    Od. 2.46

270: Il. 11.134

271: Il. 5.749

272: Il. 15.88

273: Pal 2.13.3

274: Th. 55

275: Op. 197

276: Arat. 127

277: Th. 55

278: Pa. 9.39.8

279: Th. 24

280: Th. 66

281: Th. 1

282: Th. 77

283: Plu. 743d

284: Pa. 9.29.2

285: D.S. 4.7

286: Hor.C. 3.4.1

287: Pa. 9.29.3

288: ALib. 9

289: Th. 79

290: Th. 223

291: Op. 200

292: Pa. 9.35.6

293: Pa. 9.36.6

294: Pli.NH. 36.17

295: Pa. 1.33.3

296: s.Ly. 88

297: Ath. 334b

298: Sa.fr. 105

299: Ap. 3.10.7

300: Hy.A. 2.8

301: Ap. 3.10.7

302: h.Ho. 17

303: Hor.AP. 147

304: Pi. 10.55

305: Th. 357

306: Ap. 3.1.1

307: Hy. 178

308: s.Il. 12.292
    Mo. 2

309: PO. 11.1358

310: Lu.DMar. 15.4

311: Er.C. 33
    Hy.A. 2.33

312: ALib. 36

313: Ap. 1.9.26
    A.Rh. 4.1639
    Or.A. 1358

314: s.Il. 12.292
    Ap. 3.1.2

315: Ap. 3.1.3

316: MVat. 1.47

317: Li.N. 23

318: Ap. 3.3

318: Hy. 136
  s.Ly. 811
319: Ath. 296b
  s.Ly. 754
  Ov.M. 13.917
320: St.B.
321: s.Il. 2.494
322: Pa. 9.12.1
323: Ap. 2.1.3
324: A.Pr. 640
325: Hdt. 2.153
326: Su.
327: Th. 911
328: s.Pl.Go. 497c
329: Th. 970
  Ov.Am. 3.10.25
330: Od. 5.128
331: Or. 58.59
  Ov.M. 6.114
332: Or. 60
333: Or. 86
334: Or. 148
335: Or. 137
336: Or. 145
337: Or. 164
338: Or. 167
339: Or. 21a
340: Th. 896
341: Th. 886
342: Th. 358
343: Ap. 1.2.1
344: Ap. 1.3.6
345: Th. 887
346: Th. 924
347: Chr.fr. 908
348: Pi.O. 7.35
349: E.Ion 455
350: s.Pi.O. 7.66
351: h.Ho. 28.5

352: Th. 376
353: Ci.ND. 3.59
  s.Ly. 355
  Cl.Pr. 21
  Arn.AN. 4.14
354: s.Il. 8.39
355: Et.M.
356: Ap. 3.12.3
357: Pa. 9.33.5
  St.B.
358: D.H. 1.33;
          61.2
359: Th. 384
360: Pa. 5.3.2
  E.Her. 771
361: Hy. 166
362: Ant. 12
363: Hy. 166
364: Ap. 3.14.6
365: Ap. 3.14.6
366: Hy.A. 2.13
367: N.D. 41.64
  Ca.He. 1.2
368: Cl.Pr. 2.28
  Ci.ND. 3.55; 58
369: Hyp.fr. 70
  Ma.S. 1.17.55
370: Ap. 3.14.1
371: s.Ve.G. 1.12
372: Eus.PE. 10.9.22
373: s.Ar.Pl. 773
  Ath. 555c
374: S.fr. 643
375: Ap. 3.14.2
376: Hsch.
377: Ov.M. 2.708
378: Ap. 3.14.3
379: IG. 14.1389
380: Ap. 3.14.6

381: Ph.VA. 7.24
382: Pa. 1.18.2
383: Hy.A. 2.13
  Ov.M. 2.561
  E.Ion 23
384: Ant. 12
  Ca.He. 1.2; 3
385: Ap. 1.5.3
  Ov.M. 539
  s.Ve.A. 4.462
386: Ap. 2.5.12
387: Pl.Le. 796b
388: Harp.
389: Arn.AN. 3.31
390: h.M. 100
391: Hsch.
392: Pi.O. 7.34
393: Th. 919
394: h.Ap. 3
395: Th. 406
396: Od. 6.106
397: Th. 403
398: Hy. 140
399: Her. 2.98
  D.S. 2.47.2
400: Syll. 590
401: Hy. 140
402: Ari.HA. 580a
403: Ae.NA. 4.4
404: ALib. 35
  Ov.M. 6.317
405: Th. 409
406: s.Ve.A. 3.73
407: Pi.fr. 42.7
  Ca.Del. 37
410: Ar.Av. 870
  s.Pi.P.hyp.
411: Pi.fr. 79
412: Ca.Di. 22

413: Str. 14.1.20
414: h.Ap. 25
415: Thgn. 7
416: Ca.De. 249
417: Ae.NA. 4.29
418: s.A.Rh. 1.760
 Ap. 1.3.4
419: Pi.P. 4.90
420: A.Rh. 760
421: Hy. 55
422: Od. 11.576
423: Hy. 55
424: Hy. 140
425: MVat. 1.36
426: Ath. 701c
 h.Ap. 300
 E.IT. 1246
427: h.Ap. 300
 s.A.Rh. 2.706
428: h.Ap. 305
429: s.A.Rh. 2.706
430: E.IT. 1249
 A.Rh. 2.707
 Ca.Ap. 100
431: h.Ap. 363
432: h.Ap. 383
433: Pa. 10.6.9.
434: Him. 14.10
435: s.Ve.A. 4.377
436: s.Ve.A. 6.618
437: Hy. 32
 Ca.Ap. 248
438: s.E.Al. 1
439: Plu. 293b
 418b
 Ae.VH. 3.1
440: Ap. 3.10.4
441: Ap. 1.3.3.
442: A.Eu. 728

443: Ca.Ap. 49
444: Ap. 1.3.3.
445: s.E.Rh. 347
446: Ap. 1.3.3.
447: Pa. 3.19.4
448: Zen. 1.54
449: Ov.M. 10.162
450: Ov.M. 1.452
451: h.Ap. 208
452: Li.N. 19
453: Ov.M. 1.452
454: Pa. 8.20
 Par. 15
455: ALib. 32
456: s.Ve.A. 4.377
457: Pi.P. 9.5
458: Ca.Di. 206
459: A.Rh. 2.509
460: D.S. 4.81.2
 Plu. 757d
 PsAri.MA. 100
461: Il. 5.401
 899
462: Prop. 2.2.11
463: He.fr. 147
464: Ci.ND. 3.56
465: He.fr. 148
466: Pi.P. 3.5
467: IG. 4.1.128
468: Pa. 2.26.3
469: Hy. 49
470: Ca.Di. 14
471: ALib. 17.5
472: Ca.LP. 110
 Ov.M. 3.143
 Hy. 180
 Ap. 3.4.4.
 Pa. 9.2.3.
473: Ap. 3.8.2.

474: Hy.A. 2.1
475: St.B.'Arkas'
476: Ov.M. 2.409
 F. 2.155
477: E.He. 375
478: Er.C. 1
479: s.E.Rh. 36
480: Sol. 9.8
481: Ca.Di. 189
 Pa. 2.30.3
482: ALib. 40.3
483: h.Ap. 182
484: Scy.fr. 1
485: Il. 5.890
486: Il. 5.761
 834
487: Il. 21.406
488: Il. 5.859
489: Il. 1.599
490: h.Ap. 309
491: Ov.F. 5.299
492: Fe. 97
493: Th. 928
494: Ib.fr. 2
495: Od. 11.305
496: Ap. 1.7.4
497: Hy. 28
498: s.Il. 5.385
499: s.Pi.P. 4.156
500: Il. 285
501: s.Ve.A. 10.763
502: s.Il. 14.296
503: s.Ve.A. 8.454
504: Il. 18.395
505: Il. 1.590
506: Il. 15.18
507: s.Il. 14.296
 s.Ve.A. 10.763
508: Hsch.

609: Hy. 154
Il. 11.735
610: Pa. 9.35.5.
611: Od. 10.136
612: Il. 11.735
613: Ci.ND. 2.20
614: Hy.A. 2.42
615: Pl.Epi. 987c
616: Hy.A. 2.42
617: Th. 986
618: Hy. 52A
619: E.fr. 771
620: Hy.A. 2.16
621: Hy. 52A
622: Hy. 54
Ov.M. 1.751
623: Arat. 358
624: N.D. 11.131
12.217
625: Sol. 11.9
626: Hy. 205
627: h.Ho. 32.1
628: h.Ho. 32.14
629: Q.S. 10.337
630: A.Rh. 4.57
631: Ci.TD. 1.92
632: Lic.fr. 3
633: Pa. 1.5.4
634: s.A.Rh. 4.57
Ap. 1.7.5
635: Th. 372
636: Pa. 1.3.1
637: Ly. 941
638: s.Ly. 941
639: E.Tr. 856
640: Il. 11.1
641: Th. 987
642: Hy.A. 2.42
643: Th. 381

644: s.D.P. 509
645: Ap. 3.14.3
646: h.Ve. 218
647: s.Il. 11.1
s.Ly. 18
648: Th. 984
649: Ap. 1.4.4
650: Od. 15.250
651: Et.M. 144.25
652: E.Hi. 454
653: Od. 11.310
654: Pi.fr. 239
655: Hy.A. 2.21
s.Arat. 254
656: Il. 18.487
657: s.Il. 18.486
658: Er.C. 32
659: s.Il. 18.487
660: s.Od. 5.121
661: s.Ve.A. 1.535
662: Ap. 1.4.3.
663: s.N.Th. 15
664: Er.C. 32
Hy.A. 2.34
665: Par. 20
Ap. 1.4.3
666: Hy. 132
667: ALib. 5.4
668: Ap .1.4.3
669: s.Ve.A. 10.763
670: Hy.A. 2.34
671: Er.C. 32
672: Ap. 1.4.4.
673: Er.C. 32
674: Arat. 638
675: Hor.C. 3.4.70
676: Od. 5.121
677: Ap. 1.4.5
678: Hy.A. 2.34

679: Od. 11.572
680: Th. 278
681: Th. 376
682: Arat. 99
683: Th. 869
684: Il. 16.150
685: Pa. 5.19.1
686: Il. 20.224
687: Hdt. 7.189
Pl.Phdr. 229
A.Rh. 1.214
688: Od. 10.1
689: Th. 207
690: Od. 1.34
691: Il. 8.479
692: Th. 507
693: Ap. 1.2.3
694: s.Op. 48
695: Th. 510
696: Th. 517
697: Od. 1.52
698: Op. 108
699: Th. 183
700: Op. 145
701: Th. 563
702: s.Th. 563
703: Hi.RH. 5.6.3
704: Pl.Mx. 237d
705: Pl.Mx. 238a
706: He.fr. 76
707: Str. 10.3.21
708: Eus.PE. 3.1.3
709: Th. 546
710: s.Il. 5.205
711: E.Ion 455
712: s.A.Rh. 2.1249
713: Hsch.
714: Pa. 9.25.6
715: Pl.Pr. 320c

716: s.GArat. 437
717: Hy.A. 2.42
718: Ap. 1.7.1
719: Phi.fr. 89
720: Pa. 10.4.3
721: Lu.Ph. 3
722: Me.fr. 535
723: Th. 535
724: Op. 50
725: Hy.A. 2.15
726: s.Ve.E. 6.42
727: Th. 567
728: Op. 53
729: s.Ar.Av. 970
730: Il. 5.312
731: A.Pr. 4
732: Th. 521
733: Th. 523
734: s.A.Pr. 4
 Hy.A. 2.15
735: A.Pr. 774
736: Th. 539
737: A.Pr. 210
738: A.Pr. 1027
739: Ap. 2.5.11
740: Ath. 672f
741: Cat. 64.295
742: Hy.A. 2.15
743: s.Il. 24.602
744: s.E.Ph. 159
745: Cl.Str. 1.21
746: Pa. 2.15.5
747: Pa. 2.19.5
 s.S.E. 4
748: Hy. 274.8
749: Hy. 143
750: Pl.Ti. 22a
751: Ap. 2.1.1
752: Eus.PE. 55

752: Chr. 278
753: Sa.fr. 119
754: S.An. 834
755: Ov.M. 6.148
756: Il. 24.603
757: Hy. 9; 10
758: S.An. 828
759: Th. 244
760: Pi.I. 8.30
761: A.Pr. 907
762: Hy.A. 2.15
 A.Rh. 4.790
763: Il. 24.58
764: Pi.I. 8.39
765: Ap. 3.13.5
766: Pi.N. 4.60
767: s.Pi.N. 3.60
768: S.fr. 161
769: s.Ly. 178
770: s.Il. 16.140
771: s.Il. 1.5
772: N.D. 3.204
773: Op. 109
774: Ap. 1.7.2
775: Ov. 1.350
776: s.A.Rh. 3.1086
777: Pi.O. 9.41
778: Or. 47
779: Pa. 4.1.8
780: Il. 9.4.57
781: A.Su. 231
782: A.Su. 156
783: Pa. 2.2.8
784: h.C. 2
785: Or. 49.47
786: Ov.M. 5.385
787: Pa. 1.14.2
788: Or. 52
789: Pa. 1.14.3

790: Or. 50
791: Or. 52
792: Cl.Pr 21.2
793: Or.H. 41.5
794: Or.A. 1194
795: Ov.F. 4.497
796: s.Pi.O. 6.95
797: Or.H. 43.7
798: E.He. 1349
799: Il. 19.259
 Op. 327
 Ar.R. 147
 Pa. 10.28.4
800: Pa. 10.28.7
801: Pa. 10.29.1
802: Pa. 10.28.2
803: Ve.A. 6.409
804: Or. 32
805: Od. 24.1
806: Od. 11.1
807: Od. 10.508
808: Od. 4.563
 Pi.O. 2.70
809: Pi.fr. 114
810: Pi.O. 2.61
 fr. 127
811: A.fr. 228
812: Ve.G. 1.39
813: A.Su. 156 *cum*
 Et.Gud.
814: Ca.fr. 171
815: E.fr. 472
816: Or. 58
817: Or. 98; 105
818: Or. 58
819: Or. 145
820: D.S. 3.64.1
821: N.D. 6.121
822: D.S. 5.3.4.

823: Cla.RP. 1.246
824: Or.H. 39.7
825: Pl.Ethd. 277d
826: Or. 34
827: D.S. 3.62.7
828: D.S. 5.65.1
829: N.D. 48.29
830: Or. 34
831: Or. 214
832: Ap. 2.1.3.
  D.S. 3.74.1
833: N.D. 6.169
834: Euph. 88
835: Or. 210
836: Or. 35
837: Or. 34; 35
838: Or. 220
839: Or.H. 37.2
840: D.S. 3.62.6
841: Or. 216
842: Or. 214
843: Or. 199
844: Plu. 365a
845: s.Il. 24.615
846: E.B. 6
847: Pa. 9.16.5
848: Hy. 167
849: Hy. 179
  Ov.M. 3.260
  N.D. 7.312
850: Ap. 3.4.2
851: E.B. 97
852: h.Ho. 1
853: Terp.fr. 8

854: D.S. 5.52.2
855: Or.H. 54
856: E.C. 4
857: h.Ho. 1.6
858: h.Ho. 26
859: Pa. 2.31.2
860: s.Ly. 212
861: D.S. 4.25.4
862: Ap. 3.5.3
863: Il. 6.131
864: Cl.Pr. 11
865: ALib. 10
  Ov.M. 4.1; 389
  Ae.VH. 3.42
866: Ap. 2.2.2
  Ae.VH. 3.42
867: He.fr. 29
868: The. 26
869: Th. 247; 258
870: E.B. 731
871: E.B. 1189
872: E.B. 1146
873: s.Il. 14.319
874: Il. 6.130
  Ap. 3.5.1
  Hy. 132
875: E.B. 141
876: Pa. 3.24.3
877: Pa. 3.24.4
878: Ap. 1.9.1
879: Ap. 3.4.3.
880: s.Pi.I.hyp.
881: Od. 5.332
882: s.A.Rh. 1.917

883: Pa. 1.44.8
884: s.Pi.I.hyp.
885: h.Ho. 7
886: Ap. 3.14.7
887: Ap. 3.5.3
888: Ov.M. 3.582
889: Lu.Ba. 1
890: Th. 948
  E.Hi. 339
891: Plu.Thes. 19
  D.S. 4.61
  Ov.M. 152
892: Plu.Thes. 20
893: Hsch.
894: Ar.R. 342
  S.An. 1146
895: Hy. 43
896: Plu.Thes. 20
897: D.S. 5.51.4
898: Hy. 255
899: Od. 11.321
900: Hy.A. 2.5
901: Plu.Thes. 20
902: Prop. 3.510
  Ov.F. 3.510
903: Arat. 72
904: Pa. 9.31.2
905: s.Ve.A. 4.127
906: Or.H. 57.3
907: s.A.Rh. 3.996
908: s.Ly. 212
909: s.Ar.R. 324

INDEX

I

MYTHOLOGICAL NAMES
(Relevant Greek forms are given in brackets)

2

GEOGRAPHICAL NAMES

3

GREEK TERMS

(Surnames of the Gods begin with capital letters)